REALITY GAMES

REALITY

GAMES

BY

SAVILLE SAX

and SANDRA HOLLANDER

The Macmillan Company NEW YORK, NEW YORK
Collier-Macmillan Limited LONDON

The Macmillan Company
866 Third Avenue, New York, N.Y. 10022
Collier-Macmillan Canada Ltd., Toronto, Ontario

Library of Congress Catalog Card Number: 79-139467

First Printing

Printed in the United States of America

ACKNOWLEDGMENTS

We thank Merrill Harmin for his work in conceptualizing the values area on which the values section of this book is based; for his help and support in the writing of this book; and for his having set up the Nextep program* at Southern Illinois University, which provided the stimulation, freedom, and space to develop the game strategies. More specifically Dr. Harmin helped in sharpening the Public Interview Game, the Action Game, the Free Choice Game, and the Production Focus Game.

We thank the first games group including Gerald Montgomery, Dudley Schoales, Robert Chrisman, Art Draper, Margie Walker, Wanda Penny, and Martin Liebowitz. It was the power and the magic of our experience of the first games that provided the energy to develop and elaborate the first germinal conceptions.

We thank Joshua Sax who read the manuscript for logical consistency.

We thank Leland Howe of Temple University for participating in and stimulating early elaborations of the games. The General Community Meeting, Keying-in, Group Whip, Inner Dialogue, and Production Focus games were produced with his collaboration. Doctor Howe has produced a number of other elaborations which he will publish separately.

Molly Person participated in the writing of and testing of the Production Forms Game. Bruce Shattuck worked on a revision of the Rank Order Game.

We thank Karen Connell, Associate at the Center for Educational Development, University of Illinois College of Medicine, for her early support in the games development, and for her help and participation in applying the games to medical education.

We thank Albert Schatz, Professor of Curriculum and Instruction at Temple University, who pressured and encouraged us to devote the energy necessary to putting the games ideas and strategies into book form.

* Nextep is a program for experienced teachers designed to train educational leaders and to develop innovative educational methods.

Finally, we thank the thousands of people who have participated in games workshops and reported their experiences to us.

Saville Sax
Sandra Hollander

Edwardsville, Illinois
1970

CONTENTS

PART TWO

SPONTANEITY AND SELF-EXPANSION

PART THREE

COMMUNITY GAMES:

SEEDS OF A NEW ECOLOGY

FOREWORD

My wife Vivian, my seventeen-year-old daughter Linda, and I were fortunate in having learned the Reality Games from Saville Sax and Sandra Hollander themselves. We have played the games ourselves and seen others play them with students, friends, acquaintances, members of their families, etc. We can therefore attest to the value of these games and their broad applicability from our own personal experience and observation.

Vivian found that the games transformed junior high school students who had picked on one another destructively into people who recognized that they all had problems, in some cases similar ones, which they could deal with more effectively if they learned how to handle them constructively. In small groups of six to eight, students learned how to talk freely and honestly about deep personal feelings that they had previously concealed. Classroom discipline problems often were resolved when discussed with honesty and understanding of the feelings of those concerned. After a while, students themselves asked to play the games because they recognized their usefulness. We believe that the games have the potential to revolutionize the way we teach our youth.

My experience as a professor in a college of education leads me to believe that the games can motivate profound changes in the way we prepare teachers. Many so-called education courses are considered, and with good cause, to be a waste of time. One reason why "methods of teaching" courses in particular are so notorious in this respect is that they usually attempt to *train* people to be teachers. However, the simple truth of the matter is that good teaching is not something that a person can be *trained* to do. Soldiers, dogs, seals, and bears can be trained to obey and perform. But people cannot be trained to be good teachers. To the extent that teacher-training programs succeed in training, they inevitably produce poor teachers.

When I introduced the games in "methods of teaching" courses, in lieu of the usual nonsense, the results were amazing. Students were told that they did not have to come to class at all if they chose not to, and that they would not be penalized if they did not attend. They came regularly because they considered their time well spent that way. Not infrequently, those who were teaching or student teaching at the time carried over into their own classes some of the attitudes and understanding they gained while playing the games.

However, these games have a broader purpose than the resolution of problems in our schools. While we have been polluting our external environment in ways that affect large numbers of people, we have also been wreaking havoc with our internal environment on an individual basis. We have been literally polluting our bodies by dousing them with alcohol, cigarette smoke, thalidomide, cyclamates, contraceptive pills, carcinogenic food additives, pesticides, tranquilizers, addictive and non-addictive drugs. What others have not done to us, we have done to ourselves.

In addition, and perhaps more important than these problems, there is the emotional and psychological pollution from which we all suffer in one way or another. The constant threat of a nuclear holocaust, the Vietnam war which has grown into the Indochina war, the increasing tempo of our daily lives, noise, urban congestion, the population explosion, racial problems—all produce tensions from which none of us escape. As the world becomes increasingly technological, people find themselves more and more automated. Machines, originally controlled by men, have evolved into monsters that control our lives. Few people find constructive, creative, satisfying work. They are alienated from one another and from themselves. They have lost their social identity and, what is worse, their self-identity.

If we are ever to resolve these problems, we must first of all communicate our real feelings to one another. The games in this book are a means by which we can learn to do this effectively. They help us to understand others as well as ourselves. They are a truly human way of bringing people together. They are therefore an antidote to the pressures that separate and isolate people. These games can help restore us to the beautiful and wholesome people we can be, just as antipollution measures can restore this planet to its beautiful, natural self.

By enabling people to get to know and understand each other, the games promote a new kind of social cohesiveness. This is not a cohesiveness where the individual is submerged in the group, but one based on mutual understanding and respect. Cohesiveness makes it possible for the group to engage in rational, organized, and effective action. So the games provide a way to apply wisdom, determination, and social organization to problems we must resolve if we are to survive.

While we strive to repair and heal this planet of the ravages of pollution, we must simultaneously deal with our own problems of emotional and psychological pollution. Solving environmental pollution problems goes hand in hand with developing better personal relationships among ourselves as people. In this respect, Saville Sax and Sandra Hollander's *Reality Games* may be a factor in determining our survival as a species.

ALBERT SCHATZ, PH.D.
Temple University
Philadelphia

REALITY GAMES

Introduction

FUNCTIONS OF THE REALITY GAMES: TO EXPAND ONESELF—
TO BECOME SKILLFUL—TO CREATE A BETTER SOCIETY

The Expansiveness of Play

Play is a way of learning and perfecting body and mind, in contrast to *Work*. Work demands the perfecting of specialized habits, at the cost of loss of flexibility and range. Animals and children learn through play; and man—the animal with the greatest intelligence—is the most playful. Through play, the flexibility and range lost in work are recovered, and totality is reestablished.

GAMES, A SPECIAL FORM OF PLAY

Have you ever wanted to start anew, with everyone equal?

Have you ever been impatient at the slowness with which things are resolved?

Has it ever happened that so much was going on that unity was lost?

A game of cards resolves these difficulties. Everyone starts equal. Issues are quickly resolved, and complexities are reduced to simple rules.

What job involves accurate coordination of the whole body, quickness of movement, precision, strength, and continuous challenge? There are few such jobs—so that work atrophies the capacity for total physical and mental involvement. But a game of tennis involves just that kind of coordination, thus maintaining and expanding one's capacities.

In the games set forth here, the areas of communication and feeling that have been restricted and divided by life's demands are regained, and one experiences a sense of expansion and revitalization. These are the Reality games, and we will learn and practice them in the course of this book.

WHAT CAN THE REALITY GAMES DO FOR YOU?

The games can help you to relax the restrictions and strictures, the rules, the Do's and Don't's, the Say's and Don't-Say's, the stamped limits of what people think you are, the deeply grooved channels of relationship, and the tired patterns of habit.

They can help you to stretch your mind and feelings in all directions, enable you to be close, honest, playful, and direct in relationships. They can help you to utilize the energies of your full self, of all your perceptions and feelings. They can help you to resolve differences and misunderstandings and unite with others, yet remain yourself. By becoming freer in exploring yourself and in understanding others, you can find unknown portions of yourself emerging to make you stronger and more creative.

Each game is a pathway into a new country, a new realm of experience. There are games that open a world of acceptance in which our thoughts can reach their full sweep without collision or cramping. There are games that open doors into worlds where ideas fit together, like the colored glass in stained-glass windows. There are games of order and beauty built from the clash of conflict; games in which the shadow of our potentiality is given flesh and lives.

Each game is a new model of interaction, a short utopia, that opens, blooms, and dies.

The rules and procedures of the games are maps of these new realms. Cautions tell of rocks, storms, and currents that must be overcome. Needed skills in map reading and navigation are developed as one plays the games, and the countries you will discover are not in this book, but in yourselves.

THEORY IN BRIEF

What the Games Are

The games are a method for stimulating insight, wisdom, personal growth. They belong to the domain of doing and being. They are a way of arriving at truth through the sharing of experience, but they are neutral concerning the specific content of the truths arrived at. In their neutrality the games differ from other psychological methods which delineate in advance the psychological truths to be discovered. DO THE GAMES WORK?

Most people who have tried the games report that they have worked. Each game implies or states that certain results can be expected from playing it. When you play a game, you are in effect conducting an experiment testing whether or not the results claimed for the game take place. We would like to hear from you concerning how well or how poorly particular games have worked for you. Include data concerning the number of times you played a game, and your reasons for playing it.

On What Assumptions Are the Games Based?

1. A group can decide by means of a contract openly entered into by the members, what the form of their interaction will be.

2. Certain forms of interaction greatly increase the efficiency of individuals and groups.

3. Since the forms of interaction that we enter into determine in many ways the kinds of persons we are, we can have more control over what we are if we consciously spell out contracts for our interactions with others.

What Are Some of the Background Influences Entering Into the Construction of the Games?

The games have been influenced by many intellectual and social currents.

They have been influenced by the T-group and encounter group movements, by Freud, Rogers, Rank, Jung, Berne, Hess, Lao Tse, Zen Buddhism, Toynbee, Korzybski, Marx, existentialism, Russell, Synanon, to mention a few offhand.

To What General Problems Do the Games Address Themselves?

The games address themselves primarily to the problem of splitting and fracturing. Within the individual, knowledge, feelings, skills, values, needs, roles and actions are separated off from one another, making for a sense of disunity and self-alienation. In the social sphere, the fracturing of knowledge into separate and isolated domains with no serious attempt to re-unify this knowledge leads to a widespread incapacity to master problems of general scope. This splitting results in a proliferation and intensification of crisis in every domain—government, education, industry, international relations.

In What Way Is the Games Approach Related to These Problems?

In the individual, the games give rise to a fusion of knowledge, feeling, skill, and action. The splitting of objective and subjective which is at the heart of the western faustian thrust for domination over man and nature is healed in the games approach. In the domain of knowledge, the games work to resocialize the separate disciplines and increase the domain of common shared experience and understanding.

Games, Roles, and Skills

In professional life, the roles and objectives of the teacher, speaker, doctor, actor, therapist, and writer are clearly defined. For example, much time and effort are taken to help a person to become a good teacher. But no one teaches a person how to be a good student. It takes a doctor years to learn his professional role, but no one is ever taught how to be a good patient. The same holds true of other professional roles. The result is that the efforts of teacher, doctor, writer are often brought to naught because the reciprocal roles of student, patient, and reader are undefined.

In ordinary life situations, none of the roles is defined: We aren't taught how to handle conflict constructively, how to listen helpfully and empathically, how to explore ourselves, how to make decisions, etc. The objectives of social life are mixed, confused, and ill-defined: People talk and no one listens; people give advice when it isn't needed and fail to give it when it is. People are afraid to confront differences because they can't handle the conflicts that might arise.

Games differ from these professional and social situations in that everyone's roles and objectives are clearly defined. For example, a therapy game would differ from ordinary therapy in that the role of the patient would be as clearly defined for the patient as that of the doctor and the objectives of the game would be clearly stated and understood by all. In a teaching game, the role of the learner and his objectives would be as well defined as that of the teacher. Once the rules and objectives are stated, thus defining the roles and goals, just playing the game helps one perfect one's skills.

Just as we can learn chess if we know the rules and we practice, so, too, can we learn skills through the playing of the Reality games. Some of the skills we can learn are listed below.

1. To explore our own thought processes and feelings in greater depth.
2. To be more sensitive, perceptive, and empathic.
3. To reflect another person's thoughts and feelings.
4. To draw out another person, and help him to clarify his thoughts and feelings.
5. To clarify our values.
6. To help others clarify their values.
7. To better integrate feeling, knowledge, and skill.

8. To confront and resolve conflicts in such a way as to strengthen and deepen rather than weaken relationships.

9. To create a cohesive, supportive group which is capable of working together to accomplish both common and individual objectives.

10. To teach and learn more effectively.

Seeds for A New Social Ecology

Games are extremely powerful means of molding behavior. Consider a game of poker. Suppose you wanted to be open, honest, and generous while playing. What do you think would happen if you revealed your hand honestly and offered to share your winnings out of generosity? I tried it once as an experiment. First they laughed. When I persisted, they got mad and wouldn't let me play. The fact is, you cannot be open and honest and generous and play poker at the same time.

Society can be compared to a very complicated poker game. It has its rules and its rewards and punishments, which make the players act in a certain kind of way—not for an hour or two as in a poker game, but for all their lives. Money, power, status, position, the responses of others, their interest, indifference, approval or disapproval are the rewards and punishments in the total game. Law, order, morality constitute the stated rules, while practice constitutes the actual rules of the total game. Just as the poker game makes the players closed and greedy, at least in their behavior, so the rules of the life game make people into certain types, for all their lives.

Having been shaped by the rules, the responses of others, the rewards and punishments, we become part of the game and shape others. The game takes on a life and power independent of the players.

A good, pure American boy takes part in a mass murder in Vietnam. This action grew out of the rules and objectives of the game to which Americans committed themselves. Who made up this game? Who created it? Who wants to play it? No one.

Suppose you have to practice dishonesty day and night to get along and are sick of it. You have to practice it so much, it's hard to tell truth from falsehood. Perhaps you'd like to know who you are. You'd like to get close to people, to be generous and outgoing, yet, every time you try, people treat you as they treated me when I tried to be honest and generous in a poker game. Suppose you want to be all of these things without being crucified, but you can't be because of the games that are being played all around you. That's a tough problem. But the very power of these games, which can keep you from being honest and loving, can also be turned around. The game of soldier can make you a killer once you decide to play. So other games, turned to a different purpose, can make you truly yourself.

When we choose to play tennis, chess, or poker, we enter a mini-society that shapes us temporarily in a variety of directions of our own choosing. Thus, during the course of the chess game, we are thinkers and planners. In poker, as we have mentioned, an honest, open, and generous person can turn into a greedy, closed, and acquisitive one. While tennis may turn a sedentary, sedate person into an athletic and quick-moving one.

Why not use the transforming power of these mini-societies we call games, to become the kinds of persons we want to be, at least for the course of the game? Instead of making mini-societies or games, such as poker, that reflect in purified form the competitiveness, dishonesty, and greed of the larger society, why not make games that create in miniature the utopias in which we would like to live? Why not create games that make us more honest and real, closer to others? Why not play games that help make us the kinds of persons we really want to be, the kinds of persons we perceive ourselves to be at the center?

In order to change human behavior radically, a game must contain the following elements:

1. A set of rules.
2. A clear statement of objectives.
3. The agreement of all the players to abide by the rules and objectives.
4. A procedure for critiquing or looking back at the process of each game.

Once we have a clear statement of objectives, a set of rules to support the achievement of the objectives, and agreement of a group on the rules and objectives, we have a game or mini-society. Such agreement isn't difficult to get on a time-limited basis in a small group. This society becomes alive and begins to evolve as a result of the insight and understanding of its members when critiquing becomes an integral part of the process of doing.

When these four elements work together the results are fantastic. Men and women and even children can begin to create the social order, instead of being its helpless victims as in the past. Since man is the product of the social order, this means that he can begin to shape himself, by shaping the social order of which he is a part.

Man can begin this reshaping process best when families, classes, people working together on projects, and political groups play the games to deepen communication, to resolve conflict, to give support. The playing of these games permits the group to reach a more satisfying, enjoyable, human, creative, and productive level of being. Thus the games, with the new ways of social relating that they foster, are the seeds of a new society.

HOW TO USE THE BOOK

This is a book for doing, not a book for reading. One can understand and learn the games only by practicing and experiencing them, not by merely reading about them. We have therefore organized the book to facilitate the learning of the games.

Part One of this book deals with the basic communication skills that will be used throughout the book. These are of two kinds: focus skills and T-Group skills, explicated in Chapters 1 and 2, respectively.

In the chapter on focusing we learn several models of ideal communication. These models make for deeper, more relevant, and more effective communication.

In the chapter on T-Groups, we try to become more aware of how we communicate through being increasingly open and honest with one another. Thus we learn to change our patterns in a variety of constructive and creative ways.

All other games in the book, with the exception of the Values games, depend upon the mastery of these basic games and the communication skills acquired through such mastery. It is advisable to spend considerable time in mastering these early games before moving on to the more complicated games that follow.

This book is written for diverse situations—for use with family and with friends, individually and in groups; for many types of organizations and institutions; for the layman and the professional. Having mastered the basic skills, one can select from the remainder of the book according to one's personal needs and interests, and according to the diverse situations in which one finds oneself.

Selecting a Game

If you want to get involved, the opening-up games are best for you. Use the Focus Game, the Ongoing T-Group Game, or other basic games.

If your feelings are very strong, if you find yourself wanting to make vast changes immediately, if you find yourself possessed of many new insights, what you need most is integration of the newly emerging feeling, insight, and capacity to act with skill, knowledge, and a sense of reality. See Chapter 6 for Values games and the Feelings, Knowledge, and Skills Game; and Chapter 1 for the Position Statement and Understanding Response.

When you have learned the games but want a second opening, see Part Two of the book for Spontaneity and Self-Expansion. Some of these games are happy, light, and pure fun. The Transcendental games in this section can be very intense and extremely involving.

For professional or organizational use of the games, see Part Three of the book.

If you want to deepen your skill in game play, look at the Advanced Critiquing section early and use more and more of the critiquing skills with all the games you play. The continual use of critiquing is the best way to develop your skill in game play.

EXPLANATION, AND A CAUTIONARY NOTE

The opening-up games reveal that we have much more energy and ability than we previously thought we had. The old boundaries that restricted and enslaved us to an unrealistically limited notion of ourselves fall away. There is often a feeling that we are omnipotent, and as a result, we may attempt foolish and unrealistic things which lead to disappointments. The truth is that although we are not as limited as we thought, we cannot do everything at once; what is needed is an integration of our new capacities with skill, knowledge, and a sense of reality.

As a result of insight given us in the free communication of the games, we often become aware of the fact that many of our relationships are constricting or neurotic. This awareness comes with such strength and conviction that often we determine to change everything at once. This is obviously impossible without a great deal of pain and disorganization, if one goes about it by way of ultimatum and assertion. One must understand that not only oneself, but the other members of the relationship, need to grow. Use of the Conflict Resolution games may enable one to integrate one's own insight into what a relationship should be with the insights of other people. See also Coping games, Free Safe Program, Limit Setting.

Getting Started

Try the games with your family (Focus Game, Reflection Game).

Try the games with a group of friends.

Introduce the games at a party.

Introduce a game to meet some professional problem.

In order to develop skills, some experience with an ongoing, stable games group is helpful. Get a group of eight to thirteen people together.

Once the group has been established, membership should be closed and the members should commit themselves to come regularly.

At the beginning of meetings, the Paired Interaction or Focus games may be used, followed by the Ongoing T-Group Game. This constitutes the stable fare of the group process.

Other games are introduced as the need arises in the group, either because of some problem or simply for variety.

When the group is well established and skills well developed, members may wish to use their game skills professionally. They may serve as leaders to get other game groups started.

A stable games group can spread the games concept by holding workshops in which various games are introduced to large numbers of people. They can hold workshops in schools, businesses, social or political organizations to humanize and improve the social interactions.

PART
ONE

BASIC GAMES
FOR LEARNING
OF SKILLS

CHAPTER 1

The Positive Focus Game
and Related Games

The Positive Focus Game provides a means for exploration of one's thoughts and feelings in depth, with a group of three to six persons. Playing this game well involves a number of complicated skills.

1. One must learn how to create an accepting, safe atmosphere both by becoming more aware of one's positive feelings toward others, and by learning how to communicate them honestly and warmly.

2. One must learn how to suspend one's own needs and beliefs temporarily and to give one's full attention and interest to another person.

3. One must learn to use this self suspension to concentrate on the others so as to be sensitive to their feelings, ideas, and assumptions, and thus to encourage them to communicate freely, openly, and honestly.

4. It is not sufficient to give warm supportive space to others, one must also take space for oneself. This means one must learn how to become aware of one's own inner feelings, needs, and thoughts, and learn how to communicate them directly, openly, and honestly.

These skills are learned through applying the following rules:

1. The rule of focus.
2. The rule of positive feedback.
3. The rule of drawing out.
4. The Position Statement.
5. The Understanding Response.

These five rules and the skills and perceptions they involve reinforce each other. This makes it appear desirable to try to learn the whole complex of skills at one time. But practicing the skills one at a time seems necessary for mastery of any one skill in depth. Alternating between the Positive Focus Game and some of its subgames seems the best strategy for learning. For gradual and systematic mastery of Focus Game skills, see Focus Game Series. Here the rules are introduced and practiced one at a time.

The Compliment Game, the Drawing-out Game, and the Reflection Game stress one or another of the skills that are integrated in the Positive Focus Game. In the Compliment Game we learn to become more aware of our positive feelings and more able to express them warmly. This is necessary to create an atmosphere of trust. In the Reflection Game we learn to listen more sensitively and perceptively to what a person says, and to convey our sense of understanding. In the Drawing-out Game we learn how we may actively help a person explore his own interests in his own terms. In the position statement we learn to draw our own thoughts and feelings together in a unified whole. In the Understanding Response Game, we convey an understanding of a person in depth.

Each of these games is a complete game in itself. It is not merely an adjunct to the Positive Focus Game. There are circumstances in which one or another of the games is preferable to the Positive Focus Game. But they are related to the Positive Focus Game in that any one of them might appropriately be practiced during a Positive Focus session. Thus, playing the Positive Focus Game may facilitate learning of the subgames.

Learning subgames and the Positive Focus Game is best seen as an interactive process. Hence, this set of games is best learned by frequently switching from one to another.

THE COMPLIMENT GAME

The frozen snow of winter
Drenched in the warm sun turns gold,
And melts into reviving spring.

Objectives

The Compliment Game helps to create trust and good feeling in a group.

It can help one to become more comfortable, more skillful, and more sensitive, honest, and direct in both giving and receiving positive feelings.

Uses

Since the Compliment Game is one of the most simple, easy to learn, and nonthreatening of the games, it is good as a first game to try out.

It is good as a get-acquainted game at a party, a conference, or a workshop. It will create trust and facilitate the opening up of communications.

It can be used as a way of increasing one's ability to relate intimately, warmly, and sensitively to others.

It is a way of creating or increasing the commitment of individuals to each other and to the group of which they are members.

It is adaptable for improving communication at home, at school, or in social groups.

Introducing the Compliment Game to a Group: Voting Questions

If you are going to introduce the Compliment Game to a group, a good way to start is to ask all or most of the following Voting Questions. Start like this. Either read the following or say it in your own words.

"I am going to ask you some Voting Questions.

"Voting Questions differ from ordinary voting in that they are designed to reveal feelings, not to decide an issue. They help a person explore his feelings about certain issues as well as reveal what others think about it. The issues explored by the following questions relate to the purpose of the Compliment Game and its rules.

"If the answer to a question is strongly true of you, raise your hand very high. [Leader demonstrates.] If less true, raise your hand less. If only a little true, raise your hand a little. If very untrue, lower your hand down as far as it will reach."

The following questions get at some reasons for giving positive feedback.

"How many are more committed, work harder, and are more giving when you are appreciated rather than criticized?

"How many find that you learn better when your strengths rather than weaknesses are stressed?

"How many find that others frequently emphasize weaknesses, faults, and inadequacies, while taking the good for granted?

"How many of you frequently overlook the good points of your friends, your parents, your children, and focus primarily on their faults?

"How many wonder about this contradiction between belief and behavior?"

The following questions get at feelings about receiving compliments.

"How many have ever felt uneasy about being complimented?

"How many have ever wondered if a compliment you received was sincerely and genuinely meant?

"How many have ever been suspicious of the motive behind a compliment, have wondered whether it hid jealousy or hostility?

"How many enjoy being complimented and praised?

"How many would like to enjoy it more?"

The following questions get at some of the feelings about giving compliments.

"How many are sometimes afraid that expressing your positive feelings might be misinterpreted?

"How many feel that you are too inhibited in expressing your positive feelings?

"How many express positive feelings through kidding or teasing?

"How many have ever covered positive feelings by pretending or actually feeling dislike?

"How many would like to be able to get more genuinely close to people?

"How many would like to be more direct, more honest, and more open and free in expressing your positive feelings?

"In the following game we are going to practice giving and receiving compliments to each other, after which we will discuss how we felt both on the giving and the receiving end."

(In playing, it is best for every player to have a copy of the game. If a facilitator is introducing the game, he need not read the following paragraph, but should skip to the procedures.)

We are often apt to be bland or negative. Receiving and giving positive feelings is one of the hardest things to do, yet it is one of the most important things to be able to do.

In this game we practice giving and receiving compliments.

Procedures for Compliment Focus

Break up into groups of threes or fours. This is the optimum size for groups using focus techniques. When everybody has gotten into groups, continue.

The procedures are simple:

1. One person volunteers to tell the group something he is proud of.

2. Immediately afterward the other members of the group give their positive impressions of the volunteer or focus. This may be based either on previous knowledge or on what he has just said.

3. After each round, the focus discusses how he felt in receiving compliments, while the other group members discuss how they felt in giving them.

4. When everyone has had a turn telling the focus his positive feelings, steps 1 and 2 and 3 are repeated until everyone has had a turn being focus.

5. When everyone has had a turn, the critique sheet can be used for further exploration of giving and receiving compliments.

Suggestion and Evaluation Sheet for Compliments

The use of this sheet is optional. It is probably better to use the sheet *after* the first or second time the game is played. While you are getting used to the game, evaluations may merely make you self-conscious rather than self-aware.

When you are comfortable with the game, this sheet will help you become more honest, more helpful, and more empathic in giving compliments.

1. The facilitator was sincere in giving compliments.

VERY TRUE_____NOT TRUE

        [mark where the facilitator falls on this continuum]

2. The compliments should be honest and true. For example, to tell someone, "I'm sure you'll succeed because you have so much enthusiasm," is not true. The facilitator cannot be sure that another person will succeed. Such a statement might be harmful in keeping the focus from being self-critical. Saying, "You've got a lot of enthusiasm, which should be a great help in undertaking what you want to do," is accurate and encouraging, and doesn't set up unrealistic expectations.

The facilitator was honest, perceptive, and accurate in his compliments.

VERY TRUE_____NOT TRUE

3. Compliments should be freeing, not restricting. Talk about the person and what he does, not about products, conclusions, or things.

To say, "You have a good color awareness in clothes," is better than saying, "That is a pretty dress." The first statement encourages the focus to choose more freely; the second statement ties her to her present dress. Similarly, to say, "That is a great idea," ties one to the idea, while the statement, "You really think things out," encourages one to think more deeply about many things.

The facilitator was liberating rather than restrictive in his compliments.

VERY TRUE_____NOT TRUE

4. The facilitator was warm in giving compliments. This was reflected in his voice tone, posture, and gesture.

VERY TRUE_____NOT TRUE

5. The facilitator was empathic, and sensitive to the needs, feelings, and interests of the person.

VERY TRUE_____NOT TRUE

6. The facilitator was specific in his compliments. He gave reasons for his compliments and proved them on the basis of fact.

VERY TRUE_____NOT TRUE

7. The facilitator's compliments tended to be bland, trite, and meaningless.

VERY TRUE_____NOT TRUE

Supplementary Exercise: Situations in Which Compliments Are Appropriate in Life

In the Compliment Game, we practice giving compliments so that we may become more comfortable, more sensitive, and more precise, and hence more truly ourselves in giving and receiving compliments. We are also made more aware of the discomfort and embarrassment that compliments can create.

Having become sensitive to this in a game situation, how and when should we use compliments in a life situation?

DIRECTIONS

Break into small groups. Each person takes a turn stating when he most needs compliments, and what kind of compliments are most helpful. The other members of the group draw out each person through the use of reflection and clarifying questions. (See Drawing-out Game and Reflection Game.)

After you have finished, look at the authors' suggestions below:

1. A realistic statement of a person's capacities, resources, and good qualities at a time when he is discouraged or faced with a difficult situation is very helpful and constructive. At such a time it is particularly important to be precise, clear, and concrete, since a person may find it hard to believe compliments when he is feeling low, and it is important to prove them by use of facts and logic.

2. When one is evaluating someone, one's positive statements should be as numerous, clear, and detailed as one's criticisms. For example, if one is teaching handwriting, it would be at least as important to point out the best-formed letters, and the most neatly written passages, as to point out lapses and errors.

3. The highest form of compliment is an act of divination. It is the perception of a talent, a strength, a feeling in the person before he is aware of it. The compliment makes the person aware of this hidden portion of the self in such a way that it is brought to flower. This form of compliment is appropriate at any time.

4. Express your positive feelings at times of tension such as meetings and partings. At times of meeting, compliments ease the tension of resuming a relationship after an interruption or a lapse. At times of parting, they ease the pain of separation. In easing moments of tension, the compliment is most useful if it is honest, empathic, and precise.

5. Compliments are helpful in disagreements and discussion. If they are honest and apt, they ease the tension of confrontation and make a productive outcome more likely. Compliments that show respect and appreciation for the honesty and good will of one's opponent make it possible for the opponent to look at the possibility of being wrong without feeling bad about himself.

Poor: "You are all wrong because your premise is wrong."

Good: "Your position is clearly, movingly, and logically stated. Unfortunately, I cannot agree with your premises, because . . ."

Because respect has been shown to the speaker's skill in the second example, he is more likely not to hold on to his position out of pride, and he is less likely to develop a personal animosity.

THE DRAWING-OUT GAME: WIDENING COMMUNICATION FOR PAIRS

Voting Questions

(for explanation of Voting Questions, see Compliment Game, page 5):

Have you ever met someone with whom you communicated on a deep level after a very short time?

Was the communication based mostly on common interests, common experiences, common viewpoints?

Did it ever happen that the common ground tended to disappear and the relationship cooled?

This game is designed to enable two people to broaden their relationship to include differing interests, differing points of view, and differing experiences.

Procedures

1. Two people get together to play the game.

2. One volunteers to be focus. The focus will talk about something he is interested in—a problem, an experience, a feeling, or a decision.

3. The other person will take the part of the facilitator. He will draw out the focus by asking questions, by indicating that he understands through clarifying or reflecting what is being said.

4. After a set period of time, or when the focus feels that he is finished, the process is critiqued. Critiquing includes a discussion of how both the facilitator and the focus felt; and what each thought was helpful or not helpful in furthering communication.

5. If the participants wish to increase their skill in the use of this game, they can use the suggestion sheets and evaluation sheets for both focus and facilitator, in the critiquing process.

Suggestions for the Focus

Often when we talk about something, we merely reel off old ideas, old feelings, old perceptions. When we do this, there is a kind of mechanical deadness in our discourse. Our old perceptions, old ideas, and old feelings no longer fit us. If we are truthful, we would like to escape from the prison of our old selves and talk about what we really feel and think now. Hence the following suggestions.

1. Talk about what you really feel *now* concerning the topic.

2. When you say something, listen to what you say, and if it doesn't fit how you now feel, change it.

3. Talk about how you really think, and what you really believe, *now*. If what you think or believe contradicts old thoughts or beliefs, change the old way of thinking.

4. Considering and facing up to the questions and observations of your facilitator will help you do steps 1, 2, and 3.

Evaluation Sheet for Focus

If the evaluation sheets are used, both the focus and facilitator should fill out both evaluation sheets separately. Afterward they are to compare results and discuss. Answers can be written on a separate piece of paper.

DIRECTIONS

Mark where on the continuum the focus person fell.

1. The focus person gave his own true perceptions, thoughts, and feelings.

VERY TRUE_____NOT TRUE

2. The focus person was willing to explore and go into his feelings even when this was difficult.

VERY TRUE_____NOT TRUE

3. The focus person was willing to look at and explore the facts in the situation.

VERY TRUE_____NOT TRUE

4. The focus person was willing to confront contradiction in feeling.

VERY TRUE_____NOT TRUE

In values.

VERY TRUE_____NOT TRUE

In behavior.

VERY TRUE_____NOT TRUE

In thought.

VERY TRUE_____NOT TRUE

5. The focus person expressed his feelings and his thoughts as integrated, rather than isolated.

VERY TRUE_____NOT TRUE

After the focus and facilitator have finished filling out both sheets, they critique the process.

First, they discuss in general how it went.

Second, they compare how they marked their sheets, and discuss their answers.

Suggestions for the Facilitator

1. Some questions that help draw out.

How do you feel about that?

Do you have any other feelings on the subject that you have not expressed, such as fear, love, hate, affection, or guilt?

Have you considered any other alternatives?

Are those all the necessary facts?

How do you feel right now?

2. Some suggestions about drawing out.

Listen carefully till you are able to discover the central idea of the focus. Then ask questions that will help the focus expand on it.

Ask about the last thing the focus was talking about.

3. Notice the *nonverbal clues* that the focus gives.

Be sensitive to the feeling conveyed by the tone of voice, by gesture, by posture, by hesitancies in speech, etc.

Respond to these nonverbal clues by calling attention to them, by calling attention to discrepancies between verbal and nonverbal clues, by meeting the needs that the nonverbal clues may signify.

4. Clarify and reflect thoughts and feelings.

Rephrase what the focus said in such a way that you show that you understand and respect what he is saying and feeling.

5. Give suggestions of what and how only when asked for them. When you do this, be sure you do not argue or take the focus away.

6. Make note of what the focus leaves out and ask him about this.

If the focus talks only of feelings, ask him about facts and ideas.

If the focus talks only about facts and ideas, ask about feelings.

If the focus talks only about one feeling, ask about other feelings.

If the focus talks only about the whole, ask about the parts.

If the focus talks about one part of the problem and then another, but never sees the problem as a whole, ask questions that help him relate the parts to each other.

7. Ask questions that help the focus relate the various things he has said to each other.

Evaluation Sheet for Facilitator

If evaluation sheets are used, both focus and facilitator should fill them out separately. Afterward they are to compare the results and discuss.

Mark where on the continuum the facilitator fell.

1. The facilitator helped the focus talk freely.

VERY TRUE_____NOT TRUE

2. The facilitator helped the focus explore his topic the way he wanted to.

VERY TRUE_____NOT TRUE

3. The facilitator was sensitive to the feelings that the focus expressed verbally.

VERY TRUE_____NOT TRUE

That he expressed nonverbally.

VERY TRUE_____NOT TRUE

4. The facilitator got the point of what the focus was trying to say.

VERY TRUE_____NOT TRUE

5. The facilitator helped the focus come to new understandings and insights.

VERY TRUE_____NOT TRUE

6. The facilitator was understanding, accepting, and respectful of what the focus was saying.

VERY TRUE_____NOT TRUE

After the focus and facilitator have finished filling out both sheets, they critique the process. First, they discuss in general how it went. Second, they compare how they marked their sheets, and discuss their answers.

THE REFLECTION GAME: LISTENING AND UNDERSTANDING IN PAIRS

He heard beyond the walls of his security
And the chrysalis burst.

Objectives

It sometimes happens that two people get enmeshed in a situation in which neither can hear what the other says without changing its meaning or interpreting it as something else. In such a situation, a generous gesture may appear as a deadly insult, and an offer of peace as a declaration of war.

In the Reflection Game the listener must show that he heard and understood exactly what the speaker said, to the speaker's satisfaction. The process of really listening rather than interpreting, answering, or insulting often permits communication to get back into a constructive channel once more.

Sometimes a person needs someone to listen to him. But he has too much going on in his mind to receive more advice or suggestions. He merely wants to clarify his thinking by talking with somebody who is friendly and interested.

The rules of this game are such that a person can get a sympathetic ear without being burdened or confused with more advice or suggestions.

Voting Questions

(For an explanation of Voting Questions, see Compliment Game, page 5.)

Have you ever had something on your mind that you wanted to think out with somebody, but about which you didn't want advice? Or additional ideas? Or criticism? Or reassurance? Or agreement? Or denial?

Have you ever wanted someone to just listen and understand?

Have you ever felt that advice or suggestions were additional pressure, when you had all the pressure you could cope with already?

If your answer is "yes" to several of these questions, this game is for you.

How to Play

1. If you have something on your mind that you want to talk about without pressure, advice, or criticism, approach a friend whom you know to be understanding and ask if he will play the game as facilitator, with you taking the role of focus. If he agrees, have him read the rules and set a time for playing the game.

2. The focus talks about his problem while trying to explore all his feelings, all his thoughts, and all the facts concerning it.

3. The facilitator shows that he understands and respects and appreciates not only the words of the focus, but his feelings, his situation, and his point of view—by reflecting back to the focus his understanding and respect for what the focus communicates both verbally and nonverbally.

The Reflection Game is sometimes preferable to the Game for Widening Communication in that it is nonthreatening.

Suggestions for the Focus

Same as in Drawing-out Game (page 10) with these additions: (1) When you talk about other persons, talk about how they make you feel or consider how they must be thinking and feeling. (2) Do not pigeonhole, categorize, or stereotype others by labeling.

Evaluation Sheet for Focus

Same as in Drawing-out Game, with this addition: In talking about others, the focus either:

a. Stated what feelings they stimulated in him, without projecting, interpreting, or labeling.

VERY TRUE_____NOT TRUE

Or *b.* Attempted to understand how others were feeling inside.

VERY TRUE_____NOT TRUE

After the focus and facilitator have finished filling out both sheets, they critique the process. First, they discuss in general how it went. Second, they compare how they marked their sheets and discuss their answers.

Suggestions for Facilitator

1. Try to put yourself in the focus's place. Try to think, feel, and see from his point of view.

2. Be sensitive to voice, tone, facial expression, gesture, and posture as well as the words that the focus says.

3. Show that you understand and respect the words, feelings, and point of view of the focus.

4. Convey your understanding, respect, and interest not only with words, but by your whole being.

Evaluation Sheet for Facilitator

1. The facilitator showed he understood and respected the thoughts, feelings, and point of view of the focus.

NOT AT ALL_____VERY MUCH

2. Sometimes the words of the facilitator showed understanding, but the tone showed

a. lack of interest	_____	*c.* a cold uninvolvement	_____
b. a critical, judgmental attitude	_____	*d.* an overly solicitous concern	_____

(Check one or more.)

3. The facilitator interpreted or changed what the focus said.

NOT AT ALL_____VERY MUCH

4. The facilitator understood things from his own point of view only, and was unable to penetrate the focus's point of view.

NOT AT ALL_____VERY MUCH

5. The tone of the facilitator was accepting.

NOT AT ALL_____VERY MUCH

Was warm.

NOT AT ALL_____VERY MUCH

6. The facilitator expressed through his tone of voice and words the feelings as well as the thoughts of the focus.

NOT AT ALL_____VERY MUCH

(See also Reflection Game for Conflict, Chapter 3.)

THE POSITIVE FOCUS GAME

The following version of the Positive Focus Game is intended for (1) the first trial of the game, and (2) introduction of the game to large groups. A version for mastery comes later in this chapter, the "Focus Game Series," pages 20–24.

Before We Play the Positive Focus Game

For an explanation of voting questions, see Compliment Game, page 5.

Have you ever been in a group in which no one was listening and everyone was talking?

Have you ever been in a conversation in which you were talking about one thing and found that the other person was talking about something entirely different?

Have you ever been in a group in which you wanted to say something, but couldn't get in a word edgewise?

Have you ever been in a group in which everyone was talking, but nobody was saying anything of interest? People were just making conversation?

Have you ever wanted to say something, but were afraid that nobody would listen or be interested?

Have you ever had something on your chest, but were fearful of talking about it, afraid that others would misunderstand, laugh, moralize, or use it against you in some way?

Have you ever worried when you said something because you didn't know what the other person would think about it?

Have you ever been afraid that the other person thought less of you because you opened up?

Introducing the Positive Focus Game

This game is designed to solve some of the communication problems shown by the raised hands. It does this by the use of two simple rules: (1) the rule of focus, and (2) the rule of positive feedback.

1. The rule of focus

The rule of focus determines who shall speak and what will be talked about. One of the reasons that conversations often get nowhere is that there is no decision as to who should be talking or what they should be talking about. The result may be confusion. A raising of voices and a breakdown in communication will often occur. This sometimes becomes destructive, with each person trying to get the floor by cutting his competitors down so that they will fear him. Sometimes it ends with no one talking about anything that is important, or one person becoming the center.

Only on rare occasions do we have a solution in which everyone gets a turn to talk about what he is interested in with the full attention of the group. The rule of focus helps reduce the conflict in conversation and increase the satisfaction that all participants derive by making this ideal the norm.

One person has the focus at a time. This person talks about what he wants to talk about or gives his feelings on an agreed-upon topic. The others make him feel safe and comfortable in talking by listening attentively, by asking questions that help him continue, by clarifying or mirroring some of the things he says. While sometimes expressing a common feeling to give reassurance, they try not to steal the focus and become the center of attention themselves. After a person has completed his focus, it passes to another member of the group until everyone has had a turn.

2. The rule of positive feedback

The rule of positive feedback is designed to make it safe for a person to talk openly, and to feel good about his experience. When a person has opened up, he needs to know, not guess, how he has come across. Silence can often leave room for doubt and fear to grow, turning a positive experience into a negative one. Tell the focus person how you felt. Stress the positive. Be sure that you are honest. Mild negative statements are also permissible, but they should be constructively and reasonably stated without being insisted upon or argued about.

"How many are ready to start the game now?"

(If a majority raise their hands, start as follows. If not, you may want to play a demonstration game before the group. After the demonstration game, continue with the introduction.)

Procedure

1. In this game you can talk about anything you wish. Some suggested topics:

a. Write down two or three things that others can do to make you feel good about yourself.

b. Think of your ideal self. What are some of the things which might help you or hinder you in achieving the ideal? (Make some notes.)

c. Think of something that is important to you. It could be something that you are proud of, something that you are anticipating doing, some problem that you have. (Make some notes.)

2. Break up into groups of four or five people.

3. One person volunteers to be facilitator. In the first round, he should be the most experienced player. If he has not played before, it will be best if he is at least very familiar with the rules. (See rules for the facilitator at the end of this section.)

4. One person volunteers to be focus. The facilitator may help out in the process preceding the choice of focus. The focus talks about anything he wishes to talk about. He may use the notes he made as an aid to getting started. As focus, be honest, open, and direct. Try to be in touch with and talk about your present ideas and feelings. (For additional suggestions, see guide for the focus in the Drawing-out Game, page 10.)

5. The other group members draw out the focus person. In drawing out, ask about feelings, needs, and thoughts. Clarify assumptions. Be sensitive to cues in tone of voice and posture. Check out your understanding of what the focus said by paraphrasing. For example, "Did I hear you say . . . ?" or, "If I understand you right, you said . . . ?" (For additional suggestions, see facilitator guides in Drawing-out Game and Reflecting Game.)

6. After drawing out, each person takes a turn giving positive, neutral, or slightly negative feedback. The most powerful positive feedback consists of a feeling of being understood and accepted. Show your understanding of the focus, his feelings, his needs and objectives, his thinking and his point of view as you see it. (See Understanding Response Game, page 28.)

7. When positive feedback has been given, critique the process. Talk about how you felt as focus or when asking questions. You may have held back negative or painful feelings during the focus process. This is a time to bring them up, and to try to understand them. This is important, for feelings that you have forcibly held back for too long a period, will spoil the experience for you or for others.

8. Move on to the next focus. If there is a problem in getting volunteers, go around counterclockwise. The old focus becomes the new facilitator at this point.

Rules for the Facilitator

It has been found that the use of a facilitator helps keep the focus game from degenerating to a simple conversation.

Choice of facilitator:

During the first playing of the game, the facilitator is the most experienced player or organizer. During subsequent playings, the focus person of one round becomes the facilitator of the next round.

Rules:

1. The facilitator helps to enforce the rules of the game. If a group member starts to take the focus away, he may gently remind him who is focus.

2. The facilitator may participate in the drawing-out process. He may encourage others to take part in the drawing-out, as well as set limits on a group member who monopolizes the questioning.

3. If the game is being played with some time limits, the facilitator may remind the group of them. In doing this he should be sensitive to the involvement of the focus and his need for a comfortable ending of the focus.

4. He will enforce the rule of positive feedback. This includes seeing to it that feedback is in fact given, and in preventing or limiting destructive, irresponsible attacking.

5. He will facilitate the critiquing process of the round with emphasis on getting to the feelings that the players held back during the focus process.

6. He will make sure that the facilitator role is passed to the focus person of the prior round. In special cases of teaching the game, he may retain his role for more than one round.

Large-group Final Critique

When most groups have finished, announce that everyone will meet in a large group in ten minutes. Ask the groups that have not yet finished to try to finish up by that time.

When they get together, ask some voting questions to get at the variety of feelings in the group. Some suggested questions follow:

How many enjoyed the process?

How many followed the rule of focus all the time?

How many followed it generally, but slipped off on occasion?

How many were nervous during part of the game?

How many became more relaxed afterward?

How many were surprised at how much people opened up?

How many had trouble listening and found their minds wandering at some point?

Yes, this often happens and is one of the difficulties in playing the game.

How many found things that they wanted to say, and found it hard to hold back?

How many had some negative feelings that they had trouble with because they felt inhibited about expressing them?

How many found that their negative feelings diminished without talking about them?

How many didn't find this to be true?

How many brought out their negative feelings during the critiquing process?

It is very important that this be done. If we have negative feelings and hold them in, they can build and eventually either explode or cause us to withdraw. In the Focus Game, we keep back our negative feelings for a time. This helps the opening up of communication. During the critiquing process, we have a chance to express these negative feelings. Since there is a wait, we have a chance to think about them and express them more constructively. But it is important that they be brought out and not given a chance to fester.

We are now going to break into new groups to discuss the process. There should be one member from each of the focus groups in every new group. These new groups may have between four and eight members. In the new groups, you are to discuss the process of playing the focus game in your original groups. Discuss what happened: How you felt; what was good about the interaction and what was poor concerning it. Discuss also the possibility of using the game in your home setting.

(After these groups have finished their discussion, a large meeting can again be called. During this meeting, ask:

"Does anybody have a question to ask the whole group, or something they want to say to the whole group?"

If nobody comes up with anything, you might ask a few voting questions to get it going. When discussion seems to falter or people show signs of restiveness, end the meeting.)

Focus Game Series for Gradual and Systematic Learning of Focus Game Skills

GAME 1

Procedures

A group of three to five players convenes to play. If it is a large group, break into smaller groups.

Each person introduces himself and says something about himself. Talk about things of personal interest or general interest: family, friends, love, politics, religion, work, etc.

A facilitator is chosen. He will have the job of seeing that all members have a chance to speak. He will encourage the shy or quiet members and perhaps limit the more aggressive members. He will enforce time limits if some are agreed upon.

When the game series is being learned, the most experienced player will be the facilitator. When the game has been learned, either the facilitator role is dispensed with, or the focus of one round is the facilitator in the next round.

Rule 1
Rule of Positive Feedback

On the basis of what the person said or your previous knowledge, give the person your positive feelings and impressions. Some neutral and mildly negative statements may be introduced within a positive context.

Discussion

Positive feelings are often difficult to express. We may be in the habit of taking them for granted and focusing on differences.

Critiquing

After each person has had a turn speaking and receiving positive feelings, critique the process using the following criteria.

1. The compliments were felt to be genuine.
2. The compliments were specific and justified.
3. The person giving them was sincere.
4. How did it feel to give compliments?
5. How did it feel to receive compliments?

Play Compliment Game for additional skills in giving and receiving compliments.

GAME 2

The procedures differ in that the players may talk about any subject or about a particular subject agreed on. The same rules are used with this addition:

Rule 2
Rule of Focus

People take turns being the center of interest. This central person is called the focus. He speaks and the others listen.

Suggestions for Listeners

Show that you are listening by posture, by looking at the focus, by asking questions that help him clarify or elaborate on what he is saying.

Do not take away the focus by relating your own experiences. The focus's time belongs to him. Your turn will come later.

Do not impose your ideas on the focus. This is often done with questions that are really statements. Avoid questions starting with "Don't you think . . . ?"

Procedures After Each Focus

After each person has had a turn speaking, the other members of the group may give their thoughts on the subject.

This is then followed by giving positive feedback to the focus.

Use the following guide for critiquing.

1. Did anyone take the focus away? If so, who did it and how was it done?

2. Was everyone listening attentively to the focus? When and why did interest lapse?

3. What questions helped the focus continue?

4. What questions were seen as blocks?

GAME 3

Same procedures and rules as games 1 and 2 with the following additions or modifications:

Rule 3
Rule of Reflection

Show the focus that you are listening and understanding by reflecting back to him what you understand him to be saying or feeling. A reflection may start with, "I understand you to say" or "I hear you saying. . . ."

1. A reflection may be a paraphrase of what is said.

2. A reflection may stress the feeling or thoughts.

3. A reflection may be a condensation or summary of a great many things that were said.

4. A reflection may emphasize certain things rather than others.

5. A reflection should be warm in tone and accepting.

6. Avoid satirizing or mocking reflections.

After each focus, critique the reflections using the following guide:

1. Which reflections were accurate? Which were not?

2. What kind of reflections were most helpful?

3. Did the focus feel sarcasm or ridicule in any of the reflections?

4. Did the focus feel warmth and concern from the reflectors?
5. How did those doing the reflection feel?

See the Reflection Game (page 13) for practice in greater depth.

GAME 4

Procedures and rules the same as games 1 to 3 with these modifications and additions:

Rule 4
Rule of Drawing-Out

Ask questions that help draw out the focus.
Kinds of Drawing-out Questions

1. Ask questions that help the focus elaborate, clarify his thoughts and feelings.
2. Ask questions that help the focus explore in a total way by asking about what is missing.
3. If he talks about the past, ask about present relevance.
   If he talks only about ideas, ask about feelings.
   If he talks about emotions, ask for facts and situation.
   If he talks about details, ask about relationships.
   If he talks in general ideas, ask about examples.
After each focus, critique the process using the following guide:

1. What questions help the focus elaborate and clarify thoughts and feelings?
2. What questions helped the focus get a better balanced view?
See Drawing-out Game for greater exploration of drawing out in depth.

GAME 5

Same rules and proceedings as previous games, with the following additions and modifications:

Rule 5
Rule of Understanding Response

When the focus comes to a natural stopping point, an understanding response may be given.

1. This should communicate to the focus that his feelings, emotions, needs, objectives, and wishes are understood and respected.

2. It should communicate an understanding of the point of view of the focus, of how he sees the world, of his assumptions and perceptions.

3. It should communicate an understanding of the thinking of the focus, of his opinions and conclusions.

After each focus, critique the session with respect to this question:

What understanding responses actually communicated a real understanding of the focus? his feelings? his needs, objectives, wishes? his point of view? his thinking?

See Understanding Response and Position Statement game for greater mastery of understanding responses.

GAME 6

The same as the previous games with this modification of procedures: After each focus is completed, there should be:

1. A general discussion of the issues—time limited by agreement.
2. Positive feedback to focus.
3. A critique of the session around the general feelings and concerns of the participants.

ABBREVIATED RULES OF THE FOCUS GAME

For speedy introduction—and guide to discussion. Suitable as a hand-out at workshops to facilitate discussion.

Procedure

Break into small groups of three to five members. One person volunteers to be focus. He will give his answer to the question or problem presented. The other members of the group will draw him out with questions. After this is finished, another person becomes focus.

Rules for Focus

1. Be honest, clear, and direct.
2. State your thoughts and feelings.
3. If you don't want to answer a question, you may pass.

Rules for Group

1. Do not take away the focus from the focus person.
2. Check out your understanding of what the focus said by para-

phrasing. You might start with, "I hear you saying. . . . Is that right?" "Are you saying. . . ?" "I understand your position to be. . . ."

3. Draw out the focus about what he was saying. Ask about feelings, thoughts, point of view. (See Drawing-Out Game.)

4. Show that you understand the totality of what the focus is saying by an understanding response which communicates an awareness of his feelings, objectives, needs, thoughts, and point of view. (See Understanding Response Game.)

5. Do not change the focus until the focus is formally over. If the focus tends to slip away from the focus person, try to bring it back.

USES AND MODIFICATIONS OF THE FOCUS GAME

1. *For Self-exploration.* An involving question is asked. Each player takes a turn answering.

Rules of focus, drawing out, reflection, understanding response, and critiquing apply unchanged.

The values program in Chapter 6, and "Dealing with Various Modes of Behavior," Chapter 5, in this book, illustrate this use of focus.

2. *For Sharing.* One member shares an experience, report, or product with the group. The group draws out. All basic rules remain unchanged.

3. *For Quality Control.* One person brings a product, composition, or plan to the group.

a. The group draws out.

b. The focus draws out the group for help and suggestions.

Modification of basic rules for Quality Control:

a. Rule of focus—focus shifts. The focus person first is drawn out and then he draws out the other group members.

b. Reflection, drawing out, the understanding response, and positive feedback are given both to focus and to group members.

4. *For Student Teaching Student.* Rules identical to that of "Quality Control."

The teacher first presents and is drawn out by the group. He then draws out the group members.

5. *For Consensus or Group Learning.* A problem is given concerning which the group needs to reach consensus. In school, the problem may be several math problems or history problems, etc. The group must come to a common answer.

Here, focus, reflection, drawing out, understanding responses, and positive feedback are given by everybody in the process of finding an answer. The focus shifts informally, and is generally brief in duration.

6. In nongame situations, the focus technique can be used to give a little more space to each person for developing his point of view.

Problems and Difficulties in the Positive Focus and Compliment Games

By giving the players warmth, attention, and positive feelings, the Positive Focus and Compliment games raise the expectations of the players. They may expect that they should get the same warmth and attention in a nongame situation. When this expectation is disappointed, it makes them mad.

Another source of anger arises from the need to inhibit the expression of anger and negative feelings during the course of the game. The result is that strong negative feelings push for expression. If these feelings are not to come out disruptively or destructively, safe channels need to be found for their expression.

The Drawing-Out Game and Focus Game permit much of this negative feeling to be expressed in a nonconflict situation. The Challenge Game and Reflection Game for Conflict, as well as the Ongoing T-Group Game, provide relatively safe ways in which conflict can be resolved.

A further note on some difficulties: The Positive Focus and Compliment games give a person a sense of oneness with the group and community. This sense of unity tends to obscure the fact that there are many unresolved and perhaps unresolvable differences between members; that the unity is a genuine feeling, but it is only one aspect of reality. Our separate identities, responsibilities, needs, and interests are also real. Recognition of this can prevent disappointment based on unrealistic expectations.

THE POSITION STATEMENT

Much unnecessary confusion, distrust, suspicion, waste of time, misunderstanding, conflict, indifference, and boredom is caused by people talking around an issue, avoiding it, intellectualizing it, or emotionalizing it, implying but never saying clearly and simply what they feel, what they think, what they want, and how they see things.

Objectives

In this game you will learn to state your position clearly, directly, and completely so that:

You will know yourself better, and others will know you better.

Your life will be more together.

It will be harder for others to manipulate you, and you will manipulate others less.

Your relationships will be more honest and clear, hence more secure, more stable, and more loving.

Less of your life will be given over to conflict and confusion; hence you will have time for more productive, more fulfilling, and more joyful experience.

The Position Statement Defined

A position statement should make clear that you are talking about your position, and not some absolute truth. This can be done by starting with one of the following phrases: "My position is. . . . From my point of view. . . . The way I see it . . . ," etc.

The position statement should include all of your feelings and all of your thinking on the issue. The complete statement of feelings includes:

a. Emotions such as hope, fear, love, hate, frustration, anger, etc.
b. Needs and related wishes, objectives, or plans.

The complete statement of your thinking should include:

a. The here-and-now thoughts about the problem, the facts, how they relate to each other, how they relate to a wider whole, etc.
b. The point of view, which includes your assumptions, past experiences, prejudices, and beliefs that you use in interpreting the problem at hand.

Procedures

1. Get into groups of between three and five people.
2. Think of some topic on which you would like to make a position statement. Family, friends, work, religion, politics, some recent event provide excellent subject matter for a position statement.
3. After having selected a subject, go over it in your mind. Try to include your feelings and your thinking.
4. In thinking of your feelings, include emotions, needs, and objectives.
5. In going over your thinking, give the facts of the problem and your thoughts about it. Also give your assumptions, prejudices, beliefs, and past experiences that influence your thought.
6. After about five or ten minutes of thinking, each person takes a turn stating his position. The other members of the group compare the statement with the definition to see whether or not it had all of the elements of a position statement.

7. Where some elements are missing, the person states his position, filling in the missing elements, until he succeeds in stating a complete position.

8. The person then discusses how he felt in thinking through his position, and whether the process was useful and helpful or not.

The Meaning of Some Difficulties in Making Complete Position Statements

Difficulty in getting hold of one's emotions or current thinking concerning an issue may suggest that you are deceiving yourself or avoiding confrontation of the issue.

Difficulty in stating your objectives, needs, wishes, or opinions suggests that you may be distrustful or fearful of the others involved, and as a result may be unconsciously or consciously manipulating them. Example: Talking about it's being nice outside may be a relatively ineffective attempt to manipulate others into taking a walk. Directly stating that you want to go for a walk because it is nice outside and you enjoy walking is nonmanipulative because your objectives and point of view have been stated.

THE UNDERSTANDING RESPONSE

Objectives

The purpose of the "understanding response" is to communicate in an empathic, respectful, and accepting manner an understanding of another person's position so that:

a. The person will know that he has been heard and understood.

b. The person will not feel alone, but will have a sense of someone's being there with him.

c. The person will have a clearer picture of what he himself thinks, feels, and desires.

d. The person will have something substantial and clear to think about.

The understanding response tends to reduce anxiety and promote integration. It is thus extremely valuable in any situation involving high anxiety and tension.

Professionally it is useful to teachers, counselors, psychologists, and psychiatrists in situations of high tension or conflict.

Where Used

An understanding response is appropriate whenever difficult, personal issues are being discussed. It is particularly appropriate in the following circumstances:

1. When a person has talked a long time about something concerning him, the understanding response 's used to focus and bring together what has been said.

2. When involved in a discussion or conflict, give an understanding response to your opponent before stating your own position or your reaction to what he said. Knowing that one is understood helps smooth the way to conflict resolution.

The Understanding Response Defined

The understanding response should make clear that it is your understanding of the other person's position, and not some final truth. This can be done by beginning with one of the following: "As I understand what you are saying. . . . What I hear is. . . . It seems to me that you are saying. . . ."

The understanding response should be friendly, empathic, and respectful in tone.

An understanding response should communicate to the sender that you understood:

a. All of his feelings, not just the central tone.

b. All of his relevant reasoning.

The complete statement of feelings includes:

a. Emotions such as love, fear, frustration, ecstasy, etc.

b. Needs and related wishes, objectives or plans.

The complete statement of the person's thinking should include:

a. The facts, how they relate to each other, how they relate to a wider whole.

b. Point of view: the assumptions, prejudices, beliefs, and past experiences which the focus uses to understand the problem.

Learning the Understanding Response Game

Play a focus, drawing-out, or reflection game.

At the end of a round or at a stopping point, give the focus person an understanding response.

Use the following critique sheet on the Understanding Response as a guide in discussing the Understanding Responses made.

Critique Sheet

1. The statement began with one of the following or an equivalent: "As I understand your position. . . . What I hear . . . etc."

yes   1 . . . 2 . . . 3 . . . 4 . . . 5   no

2. The statement was friendly, empathic, and respectful in tone.

yes   1 . . . 2 . . . 3 . . . 4 . . . 5   no

3. The statement communicated an understanding of the focus's feelings.

yes   1 . . . 2 . . . 3 . . . 4 . . . 5   no

4. The statement communicated an understanding of his thoughts.

yes   1 . . . 2 . . . 3 . . . 4 . . . 5   no

5. The statement communicated an empathic understanding of the needs, objectives, plans of the focus.

yes   1 . . . 2 . . . 3 . . . 4 . . . 5   no

Questions That Help Clarify a Person's Position

I. CLARIFYING FEELINGS

EMOTION-CLARIFYING STATEMENTS

Do you have any other feelings?

Ask about specific emotions: Do you feel sad? Do you feel happy? Do you feel inadequate, frustrated, mad?

Sometimes when emotions are buried, one can get to them by putting one's questions in indirect form: If you felt sad, what about the problem would make you feel that way? If you felt happy, what would . . . etc?

RESPONSES TO CLARIFY NEEDS AND OBJECTIVES

What did you wish would happen?

Where do your needs fit into the picture?

What do you want out of it?

What would you like to see happen?

Check out specific needs that seem to be implied verbally or non-verbally:

Is it possible that you just want to be noticed?
Could you be trying to save your pride?
Do you really want to be liked?
Did you stop because you were afraid of failure?

II. CLARIFYING THINKING

CLARIFYING HERE AND NOW THINKING

Have you considered all the relevant facts?
How do you see these facts relating to each other?
How do you see the problem as a whole?
You have been talking in generalities, let's get to some of the details.
How does the situation relate to what you want or feel?
Have you looked at alternatives?
Have you considered consequences?

CLARIFYING POINT OF VIEW OR BACKGROUND

How did you come to that conclusion?
What led you to expect that?
What makes you (angry, sad, happy)?
What evidence do you have for that?
What happened to make you feel that way?
What past experience influenced you to feel that way?
(Check out the assumption implied by the person's words or actions concerning personal issues.)
Do you think that the best way to handle an unpleasant situation is to withdraw? (Use when the person's words or actions indicate such a belief.)
Do you believe that the only way you can maintain your self-respect is to avenge insult? (Use when this is clearly implied by what the person says and does.)
Concerning objective issues:
(Check out the general belief implied by particulars.)
Do you believe that marriage is best when the man has the final responsibility in making all decisions? (If this is implied by a series of statements.)
How did you come to believe this? (Ask about the basis of belief.)
Does your assumption fit the facts? (Consider alternate assumptions.)
Can you think of any other assumptions that would fit the facts better?
Can you think of other assumptions that could lead to more constructive consequences?

THE ANALYTIC RESPONSE

Examining the Position Statement for
Consistency and Completeness

The Analytic Response tests a position statement for consistency and completeness. It enhances the soundness and effectiveness of a position and of the action based on it.

It is best used with the agreement of focus and facilitator.

Procedure

Break up the position statement into its parts. List the relevant facts, emotions, thoughts, needs, objectives, and plans.

Check each list for internal consistency.

See if the lists are consistent with each other.

See if anything has been left out.

QUESTIONS THAT HELP CHECK FOR CONSISTENCY

Are all of these parts consistent with each other?

Are all of the thoughts compatible?

Are the assumptions compatible?

Are the needs compatible?

Are there some irrelevant needs expressed that might be hurtful or destructive, for example: the need for revenge, the need to escape responsibility, the need to show off, the need to be proved right, the need to blame others?

Are the objectives and needs consistent with each other?

Are the feelings consistent with the needs and objectives expressed?

Are the assumptions consistent with the facts?

Can the needs and objectives actually be met by the plans? (If the position defined has some self-defeating elements, explore to see if there is some hidden need to fail.)

Is there a need to fail in order to keep fantasy rewards?

Is there some satisfaction gained by self-pity or guilt?

Is there a fear of the consequences of success?

Is there a desire to fail in order to hurt or blame others?

CHECK FOR COMPLETENESS

Have any facts been left out?

Have all the feelings, needs, and objectives been expressed?

Are there some reservations that have not been expressed?

Resynthesizing Position Statement

After the position has been analyzed, restate the position in a more consistent, more complete, more self-actualizing way.

Consistency may require that you do not express or act out some of the destructive or self-defeating needs. The needs you hold back may later be transformed or expressed in more constructive ways.

THE FOCUS GAME FOR EXPLORING THOUGHTS AND FEELINGS: NEUTRAL FEEDBACK

This game is best played concerning issues that do not demand immediate action or decision. The purpose of the game is to encourage free and open expression. Positive agreement and approval tend to fix our behavior by rewarding it. It is hard to change when you are told you are perfect or very good. Similarly, disagreement often makes people defensive and less likely to explore new behavior or thinking. An interested, neutral response is best for enabling a person to explore and think something through. The interest of the group rewards the thinking process, while the neutrality doesn't tie the person up. This process of exploration leads to creativity. In this game the players practice responding with interested neutrality.

Procedures

1. A group of between four and six players get together for the purpose of playing the game.

2. One volunteers to be focus. One or more additional players volunteer to be process observers. The other group members will help with the drawing-out.

3. The focus talks about something he's working out that interests him, but doesn't require a quick decision.

4. The group members respond by showing a neutral, nonjudgmental interest.

5. Their responses may include asking questions, exploring relevant feelings, related skills, or possibilities for application. They may respond by restating or clarifying the thinking or feeling of the focus. Taking over by adding to or giving alternatives concerning the subject of discussion should be avoided in this game.

6. After the subject has been explored to the satisfaction of the focus, the process observers describe what they saw going on.

7. The participants discuss these observations as well as their own feelings concerning the process.

CONTROL OF FEEDBACK AND COMMUNICATION PATTERNS: A FOCUS GAME FOR MEETING CHANGING NEEDS

Our communication needs and moods shift from time to time and from situation to situation. Sometimes we want and need encouragement and praise without hearing criticism, even if it's true.

We already know that all is not well, and what we want and need is encouragement. On the other hand, there are times when it is important that something be perfect, and we want criticism so that any weakness can be pointed out and corrected. At such times praise sounds like false reassurance. Sometimes we want advice and information. We may want and need somebody's objective appraisal of our actions. Many people would be very willing to respond to our communication needs, if they knew what they were. Without knowing, they can only guess, and they often guess wrong.

Objective

This game is designed to permit one's changing communication needs to be met as precisely as possible.

Rules and Procedures

The game may be played as a paired interaction game or a focus game, with this additional rule:

THE RULE OF FEEDBACK CONTROL. At the start of the game, the focus person states the kind of feedback he wants. He may want positive feedback. He may want criticism or advice. He may want to leave the group free to respond as they choose.

He also specifies the kind of communication pattern he wants. He may want to ask questions, instead of being drawn out. He may want to be asked questions of kinds that he specifies. Feedback may be on anything the focus says or presents. And the focus may present what he chooses— a picture, something he wrote, a dance, a song—anything.

IMPLICATIONS

This form of focus game is the freest and potentially the most creative. The focus person has the power to structure the interaction process as he chooses during his focus. Each way of structuring is a new game, and may be as valuable as any of the standard games presented in the book.

TAPE OF AN EARLY FOCUS GAME

Following is a sample of one of the earliest Positive Focus Games ever played. Our skills at the game were still undeveloped, and our conception still not completely clear. But there was a feeling of euphoria and discovery about the game, which grew as focus followed focus. It was an intense experience. We were all very excited.

I do not know if our excitement comes across to the reader; but it is a good game, and it shows that an intense, integrated experience can be had with only beginning game skills.

Participants are Saville Sax, Gerald Montgomery, Bob Chrisman, Art Draper, Dudley Schoales, Wanda Penny, Marty Liebowitz, and Phil Shelton.

The First Focus Game

Saville: Bob invited me down to the Job Corps Center to tell them what we are going to do. They were kind of interested in our methodology. They had a number of teachers and volunteers there. Some of them are interested in learning our methods. So we may have some responsibility in training them. Well, I thought about this, and I tried to work up a unit using games for training teachers and tutors in our methodology. This session will be the second meeting. At the first meeting the trainees simply play the game in which they tell about themselves and about what is important to them, while others ask questions and then give positive feedback. This session is designed to get at some specific things that teachers can do with students and how they feel about it, so as to motivate actual changes in teacher behavior.

The procedure is this. First ask an involving question. One that involves thinking, feeling, attitudes, and values. Each person answers this question in his mind. One is chosen as focus. He answers the question orally with the others drawing him out and helping him answer these questions in depth. They then give him positive feedback. After one person has finished, the focus moves to the next person.

Saville [Addressing the immediate group]: We're probably too large a group. If we played the game properly, we would probably have to break into two groups. This group is too large for everyone to have a turn. I have some of the tentative questions. Let me give you the first question. Think of some teachers that you liked and learned from— some that you did not like and did not learn from. After you have thought about it, I want a volunteer to talk about his answer.

Bob: Describe them and so on?

Saville: Think about them; describe them and talk about them. [This was a rather poor exposition of the game.]

Art: Is it permissible for others to ask us questions?

Saville: Yes.

Monty: I think the teachers I learned from most were perhaps those who had a dynamic personality, sense of humor, and were a little bit easygoing—and they were people I like, first of all. And then perhaps, secondary—they seem to have an understanding of their subject so they could put it on my level as well as—well, put it on my level, I guess.

Saville: You said they had dynamic personalities.

Monty: Well, I think more of the idea of charisma rather than dynamic, but they were people I liked and they attracted me.

Wanda: Well, one teacher that I liked most was herself first and her individual personality, and the teacher second. You got all this flavor of hers, and then the teaching was sort of secondary, but I learned most from her because of this.

Saville: Excuse me for a second—let's focus on Monty for a while. [Note: Bringing the group back to the focus is perhaps the only leadership role exercised in this particular session.] Let's help Monty discover some of the feelings he had about these teachers. We can draw on some of our own experiences, but relate them to Monty rather than generally.

Wanda: I'm sorry—I didn't realize I was taking the focus.

Art: Were you thinking of a specific teacher?

Monty: Yes, there's a specific teacher, and if I were to add to what I have said already, he was so willing to give of himself anytime I wanted help. He would go down, for example (he was a college professor), with me and we would have coffee together and would talk. And he was willing to give his time and himself to help me understand what he was trying to teach and what he was talking about.

Dudley: Do you think you could become anything like him?

Monty: I've tried to become somewhat like him. I think I'm a long way from being like him. I think maybe I've strayed quite a bit from him in the last year or so. In this group I think I'm regaining some of his—

Bob: Would you see him as a model?

Monty: Yea, right.

Bob: How many children did he have?

Monty: He had two. By the way, he happened—I hate to say this because it will sort of build up a stereotype of this sort of individual perhaps, but he happened to be a minister. But he was different from any minister I have ever met. You know, he loved people; really loved people and he wasn't a closed-minded type of a minister. He had a doctorate in philosophy—terrific man.

Art: Do you think you got a better sense of God from that type of minister than from another type of minister?

Monty: Yes, I think so, although I never felt he tried to teach. In fact, he was very willing for me to be an atheist. He was this type of individual. But from him, I got a deeper meaning for my religion.

Art: How did he act toward you when he had to criticize you? Or make negative comments toward you?

Monty: That's a good question. He did it in a way I considered to be a very positive way. In a way that I didn't have to feel defensive. It didn't hurt me to make mistakes.

Art: Did he seem to separate dealing with you intellectually and dealing with you as a human being?

Monty: No, they weren't separated; they were one. I think this is one of the things I liked about him.

Art: In other words, when he was dealing with you intellectually, if he were criticizing something you had done, he was also at the same time, simultaneously, dealing with you as a human being.

Monty: Yes.

Bob: What are some of the ways that you are a different person because of having known him? [Comment: Note how Bob's and Art's questions draw out by asking questions that are central to the self.]

Monty: I think I'm a more understanding person. He also had a quality of throwing out things which stimulated. A lot of times things I didn't agree with. I tried to develop this quality—a little bit of throwing out intriguing questions. Sometimes it's a little bit shaky and often gets students a little bit upset. He was a guy you talked about when you got together in your bull sessions. He was also shot down by some people who were quite conservative in this; they really became upset with him because they were really, I think they were really, closed-minded about these things.

Saville: How did he respond to the criticism of him?

Monty: Very magnanimously. I think this would upset people more.

Wanda: Did he teach you "to err is human and to forgive is divine"?

Monty: I suppose. I don't particularly like the cliché.

Bob: I don't either. I don't particularly like that cliché. Because it sets up a dichotomy between being divine and being human. And that which is called error (which I don't consider error), it assumes that error is not good and it also assumes that if you overcome your error, then you're God. It's loaded therefore with values that I do not accept. The only thing is that if someone says "forgive," it means that he has— first—that he feels that he has sinned or violated something.

Wanda: Could you say, "to err is human and to forget divine?"

Bob: To *accept* is divine.

Saville: This is a very good point, but let's focus on Monty. This is more structured than the free use of the game. It's perhaps the form where a lot of content can be used in the game. I'd like to focus on Monty again. [Again the facilitator brings the focus back to the focus person. Note that the facilitator gave the group a chance to get back to the focus person on its own before he intervened. The brief digression to deal with Wanda's remark bent the rules. Flexibility in permitting an occasional lapse makes for a richer, fuller, more involved game.]

Dudley: Is there anything about your relationship with him that is somewhat puzzling to you? [Note this excellent drawing-out question. See how it involves the self—feelings and thoughts.]

Monty: Yes, I felt very close to this man, and he has even invited me to come and see him a couple of times, but I never have, but I kind of admire him too much, you know. I didn't feel like this when I had him in class. This is the paradox. Maybe I set him up on too high a pedestal.

Art: Did you josh with him? Behave in a friendly and familiar manner?

Monty: Pretty much so, I think. Maybe there's just a little bit of a feeling of inferiority as compared to him.

Saville: You're saying that the one element that disturbs you is that you may have sometimes felt a little inferior to him.

Monty: Yes, I think so.

Wanda: Well, if you could feel that you had developed some of his qualities, you would probably be ready to meet with him.

Monty: Yes, since the beginning of this year, I have wanted to relate some of my experiences here to him, and I have more of a desire to go see him.

Wanda: Being here has made you feel more positive about yourself?

Monty: Yes, like I have a little bit to offer in return.

Wanda: I know how you feel. With my art teacher I felt this way, after I started teaching art. I wasn't ready to talk with her yet. I hadn't reached pinnacles that I wanted to share with her. And now I could.

Dudley: I was wondering if there was any authority differentiation or role differentiation. Did you always feel you were the student and he was the teacher? Or did you feel that he was pushing that kind of definition away? Did that ever enter into the relationship? [Wanda shares an experience with Monty. Yet the focus is not taken away as Dudley brings the focus back to Monty with his question.]

Monty: I think this may be a part of it. He tried to abdicate that role.

Dudley: He consciously tried to—

Monty: Yea. He would call me by my first name. He reminded me a lot of Merrill.* Only, he was a little more forward, a little more dynamic, I guess, in one sense of the word. There's a lot of similarities.

* Merrill Harmin, Director of Nextep Fellowship Program at Southern Illinois University, where this dialogue took place.

Saville: I think that for me, at any rate, I would take the selection of somebody who has ideal teaching qualities as the best indication, as a very good indication, that Monty is developing these same ideal teaching qualities. [I started giving positive feedback because I thought the focus on Monty had gone long enough.]

Dudley: Can I ask a question? Can you tell me about your worst teacher? [Dudley attempts to continue the focus. This makes me anxious, so I handle the next few minutes of play poorly.]

Saville: I asked for too much in the beginning. What I should have done is ask for a teacher you liked and then go around the group. Asking for one you disliked in addition makes for too long a focus. The game really focuses so intensely and deeply that you can only discuss a bit at a time. My lesson plan is therefore too long. So I'm shifting it so that everyone can have a turn.

Wanda: I'm enjoying hearing about the good things he liked and I don't really want to hear about the bad things.

Saville: Yes, well, I think it would just be too much for each person to talk about his "bad" as well as his good teachers, and I think everybody else wants to talk about the good things. I just shifted there and began giving positive feedback and it sort of rounded Monty's turn. I think it would be important in using this game to estimate how far to go before changing focus. My feeling is that we ought to take a long time with each person. Saying one's say fully is something very few people get to do in real life. They are allowed a couple of sentences and then cut off. I think this is one of the good things we can gain in this game.

Monty: Think of the side effect this has on people who are forced to listen. Kind of a by-product.

Saville: Yes, I think it forces everybody deeper by not diffusing the conversation. Should we continue to refocus on giving positive feedback to Monty?

Wanda: I think someone else should probably do so.

Saville: Well, I gave him mine. [Long pause with no one talking.] It's also possible that one person could express the positive feelings of everybody; it's positive just going through the process of listening and being interested and asking questions. [I was talking too much; it would have been better just to wait.]

Monty: I kind of feel that way right now. I think, in some of the questions, I've felt a positive feedback.

Saville: If we apply this to these students [a reference to the Job Corps, mentioned at the beginning], we are going to have to estimate if asking questions is enough positive feedback. It is a subjective thing. [My anxiety is preventing others from giving Monty positive feedback.]

Dudley: I find it very difficult to add to what you have said. I don't have any other feelings in dealing with Monty right now.

Saville: This might be a way if somebody in the group expresses something positive and if you wanted to kind of generalize it you could say, "I feel the same way." In this way you get a little bit of a consensus.

Dudley: You know, there is a positive feeling in listening to you, which is that there is a difficult relationship with a person, and that Monty feels very intensely about it, and understands it very deeply, and I thought he had a very beautiful thing.

Saville: And I am very glad that you said that because I didn't perceive it. Are you still interested in continuing?

Bob: One of the things I thought very positive, which impressed me very much, was your awareness of how you were educated, and it might mean that for any teacher to be effective he must understand how he is educated, and by whom, and the strengths and weaknesses of that education, and if you are able to do that with your selected best teacher, then you are both a well-educated man and good teacher.

Wanda: I would like to encourage you, Monty, to get in touch with this man. I think this is the time to do it, and that you might be rewarded at this time by doing so, feeling now the way you do.

Bob: I would like you to do that now, but for a more selfish reason. Not to tell you what to do, but because the man interests me and I would like to meet him. He was unlike any minister I've met because he loved people.

Monty: He is one of the most positive persons that you would want to meet.

Wanda: I would like to meet your friend.

Saville: I feel the same way. You know, I feel it is like the kind of joy of getting more together. I meant that ambiguously. More of this, because he is a part of you and more because he is another person.

Bob: Well, he has been added to my store of human images, and I think another good thing to point out is that in one sense, like an artist or a good parent, a good teacher lives forever because part of him is carried on.

Saville: That's a nice thought. I think it's true. Is there anybody else that would like to be the focus?

All of you, if you come to a point where you think that you should move on, don't depend upon me to do it. Anyone of you could say that. You don't have to depend upon me as a leader to go to another focus. There may be times that I may not be here, and this group ought to be able to continue. [Bob volunteers and takes the next focus.]

Bob: This man was my English instructor at the University of California. I was a junior, I was eighteen years old, and I was there for my first semester; and I had decided to take seriously the prospect of writing poetry. His name was Benjamin Layman. He went to Harvard from

1912 to 1916. T. S. Eliot was one of his classmates. Santayana, Irving Babbitt, and William James were some of his teachers. After I enrolled in his class, he picked me before I picked him. But I dug him immediately. He walked into our classroom and he was about 5'6", I guess, stocky build, in his late sixty's with a kind of magnificent fringe all around, a nice tan, very conscious in his dress. He used gray, and I saw him walk in, but uncertainly, and I got a kind of "so what" feeling. And then he spoke with a vibrant, resonant voice and defined himself to the class, the purpose, and got us moving in about two minutes. The first thing he did to me, as an individual student, was ask us to define a novel, and present it in a conference, which I did.

Saville: Define a novel that was written.

Bob: What is a novel? And so I wrote a definition in fifteen minutes over coffee, just before the conference, and gave it to him. He went through it with precision, with precise nuances of words and structure and the idea as an organic unit that I had never encountered before. Then he looked at me and said, "How long did it take you to write this?" And I said, Fifteen minutes." Then he pushed the paper aside and said, "This doesn't cut any hay." So in that ten minutes he got over my thresholds, which most teachers never got over. He busted me right there. He then proceeded by holding a carrot in front of me constantly to make me read Conrad's *Victory* three times—rewrite a paper four times—and on and on with everything I wrote.

He was also a mentor in all of the important areas: sex, sexual identification, racial identification, and art. He shared some of his experiences with me in this. Genetically he is only partly Jewish, but as a statement of identification of himself he said, unequivocally, "I am a Jew."

Saville: How did this help you?

Bob: It helped me to identify myself as a black man, without equivocation. . . .

He had been married two different times. The first didn't turn out too well. He had been married to Judith Anderson a while—that didn't turn out too well. It was his second marriage. He knew the whole field of people that were magic to me. Robinson Jeffers was, of course, one of his students. Wallace Stevens, so there's the whole concept of urbanity that was given to me, which I had not encountered before. He told me, for example, this quote from Henry James, "An aristocrat is a man who is in a better position to enjoy the other fellow than he is himself." This sort of thing. He is an excellent critic and teacher of poetry. He would take a poem of mine. I showed him eight straight poems before I got a word of praise. He pointed out to me how words did not match—did not fit images—were not solid images, were weak, or the picture was not clear. Till finally on the eighth poem he said positive things and I felt great. But, of course, by the eighth poem I had done something that was good. That opened up for me a whole new style or technique which I pursued throughout the year.

The relationship began to fade in several ways. He retired about a year and a half after the intense teaching relationship. I had outgrown that particular style and had begun to work with, I guess, my number two teacher, a lady named Josephine Miles, who taught me different things about poetry which didn't contradict what he did, but simply expanded upon the foundation he had given me.

He married the Goodyear heiress at the age of 68. He was quite well off! [Chuckles.] He lived down in the valley about seventy miles from San Francisco. I've planned and wanted to visit him, but haven't done so, and I want to because the man is over seventy now and has angina; I would feel very badly if I did not see him before he died. As I grow older, I begin to see in more and greater depth the variety of things he taught me and I would like to tell him that, and give him some poetry. He was visiting Miss Miles about three or four years ago and she had been published in the anthology *Best Poems of 1962* and I had been published in the same anthology. She was his student at the University of California. There are about ten others in that book who had been his students. . . .

Art: I've been afraid. I've been afraid of several things—several emphases we've gotten about teachers. This tough-minded, discriminating, learned, masterful, cantankerous kind of teacher was getting defined out of the teaching. I think there is a way of demonstrating caring for a student besides being constantly kind and constantly supporting. This demands much more of me as a teacher, to get inside the kid's mind and really root around in there, than it does simply to pass him off with a pat on the back and "try again."

Saville: A pat on the back is sort of meaningless—it gains a great deal more respect to deal with the content, to deal with where he is, than to say "that's good." Something superficial could turn one off. Seen as "maybe he doesn't care enough to really think about it."

Art: The important thing in behavior is caring.

Saville: Yes, but he cared and he gave the essence of his being.

Bob: Let me talk on that a minute. The sessions we had going over a poem were tremendous in intensity for both of us because he was carving out the nuance of each word and I had to remember and see; and then at first I came up with more negatives than positives, and it was a strain to keep at it. He gave a lecture on *Julius Caesar*; the opening sentence was "Julius Caesar has been compared to Roman statuary; it seems to have been carved out of marble," which was a brilliant image for the tight structure of that play and for the color tone, which remains gray, and for these very classical characters. He kept that image sustained throughout the entire lecture—magnificent lecture with color touches here and there. I've heard him talk about the play as being concerned with gray against sunlight and sky— great vast distances and people who have the power to move these distances with fleets, give away kingdoms as trivial—this grandeur. Also, two people in their sexual prime who have the time for all these luxuries. He could, at a seminar, hear a student read a forty-minute paper and say, "In paragraph two you used this term which you did not develop." I think my sense of form I learned from him. Miss Miles learned her sense of form from him; I learned her chance mutation of it.

Wanda: You certainly use his precise nuance—this poem we got yester-day that I was so excited about—some of the beauty of what you said, I had to put down while we were talking. Do you mind my reading some of it back? "In a vibrant, resonant voice my teacher defined the lesson with amazingly precise nuance of the word . . . he captured the interest of my classmates and held their usually wandering, restless minds. . . . He crossed the threshold of my conversational brightness and pushed toward its limits."

You speak in paragraphs, did you know that?

[Tape not clear at this point. . . .]

Bob: He was a magnificent man. The last lecture he gave, before he retired, in his course on the Bible as literature, he focused on the farewell speech of Moses in its great nineteenth-century grandeur. He was the Moses of the University of California. He came there in 1922. He built the entire English Department—he was really the chairman of all time even if he wasn't elected chairman. A man of passionate loyalties and passionate hatreds—he polarized people—terrified some —others loved him—some followed him faultlessly and some—he was a very sweet man.

Saville: WE WILL HAVE TO BRING HIM HERE! [Notice how Bob continues on his own momentum:]

Bob: I don't know all of his students. One of his students, for example, is Thomas Parkinson, who was a member of the English faculty at Cal and was quite active. Another was Leonard Woolf. He could give you as much as you could take.

Art: You said earlier that he found you before you found him. I wonder what this attitude is?

Bob: I'll answer that in just a minute.

[Wanda has to make a contribution.]

Wanda: Ah, let me try to answer that. I think this is true of Bob gen-erally. I think people become conscious of Bob and want to know him. And maybe it was the same way with the teacher who heard you. He found something there that he wanted to know better. I've heard

people say, "Bob, I like you, but you don't seem to like me." Or something like that.

Bob: I don't think he would have that anxiety.

Wanda: I don't really think it is an anxiety. Or it may not be the anxiety
of wanting to know you better, but it is like material to be developed.

Saville: I think so.

Wanda: Maybe not.

Marty: I think Bob's teacher is interested in people, particularly interesting people, and found Bob to be one of those people.

Bob: Yes, but he wasn't just interested in interesting people. He was
interested in minds, because there were several other excellent students
who were not interesting people but who had extraordinary minds. I
got a "B" out of that course by the way. Which was only by his
standards. I did an "A" amount of work. [Bob didn't need any help in
getting back the focus.]

[Break in tape. Some discussion about everybody's feeling overly
excited and elated.]

Wanda: It might have been a way of pushing you.

[Bob finally responds to the drawing-out question rather than to
his own inner momentum.]

Bob: Yes, I think that was it. He must have cased me pretty well. If I
got an "A" from him, I would have felt that I had gotten it all.
Another reason he was interested in me was that at that time there
were few Negro students going to the University of California. He had
set up trusts for bright Negro students to help them in various ways.
[Marty turns off the tape. He says he's very high and needs a break.]

Art: I feel this a little differently than Marty—I don't know if anyone
else shares this with me, but I have a feeling that I cannot follow this.
[Art feels he can not take a turn at focus after Bob, because we had
reached the limit of our capacity for excitement.]

Art [to Bob]: Do you feel like you're finished?

Bob: I could go on for hours.

[Bob is really turned on. Sometimes the Focus Game breaks through
our limits of emotional involvement and keeps going till five in the
morning, then starts again.]

Art: I sensed that.

Bob: He's really a teacher of the stature—the style and grandeur of
George L. Kittridge of Harvard. We will not see that type of man
again. He was a magnificent scholar, an encyclopedia of knowledge.
And in every frame of reference he was a scholar in the best sense
because he did not publish much. But he absorbed it into his being.
He said, for example, that his best essays and lectures had been given
spontaneously.

Art: I've had a little difficulty finding for myself what really happened in attempting to define what kinds of things I've learned and what ways I've grown.

Saville: I'd like to say two things. We've gotten a tremendous amount from Monty and a tremendous amount from Bob about their experiences. This is an existential kind of thing.

The second thing is sort of simple. How to get this method worked up so that others can have an opportunity to be themselves. Because if others can become genuine through an opportunity to really express themselves and know where they are, they might become real teachers.

You know, it is kind of fantastically simple. I just asked one question, that was all—and it got this started.

Wanda: It is fantastically simple. Did you notice every one of the sessions we have had in your method, we get involved first of all, in feelings, and deep feelings. And this does something. Everybody has a seriousness, thoughtfulness, involvement, that happens as a result of it—like Monty's first comment was about somebody he felt very strongly about. And this made what he had to say much more meaningful. And the same is true with you [to Bob].

Bob: What Monty and I really seemed to get at—our only concern, primarily, is the person, the human being. Now, if that's the case, then it means that a lot of emphasis on skill as such and techniques as such might be irrelevant. From his passion, the passion of truth, Layman developed tremendous organization for form. So maybe what we're saying is that what we remember about our ideal teachers is focused on the person, and that maybe this is where teacher training begins.

Saville: I think his major skill, which cannot be translated, is that he is showing you something that you didn't see about yourself and he brought it to life. To me this is the definition of a teacher. He sees something that isn't there yet, and that enables him to—

Wanda: You made me aware of the skills with which he captured the attention of the class. And some of the skills you mentioned are skills that you yourself have developed as a result of your knowing him.

Bob: Well, he could capture that class because he knew who he was.

Art: I agree with you very much. A teacher is a person first and his skill and knowledge take second place. They cannot be eliminated because that person in your life would have been nothing more to you than a very interesting and enjoyable acquaintance had he not had certain skills, certain knowledge.

Bob: Which comes first?

Art: The person comes first.

Bob: Right. So I think this is where we focus.

Phil: One thing about this, in teacher training. I don't know what kind of teacher training Bob's teacher had, but I doubt if it was very different than we had.

Bob: He didn't have any.

Phil: OK, even if you had none. Then how important is training in that way. Maybe the kind of training he had was in knowledge. And maybe the kind of training he had was the person he was, that he studied under, and what he studied, his skills, what he saw, and what he embodied in his character.

Bob: What bothers me though, Phil, is that if we emphasize skills too much, then we assume that we can put together potage teachers. Whereas this skill, you know, like this head, this arm, this leg, and so on is part of me, so it is bound to work. I am afraid of that extension of the idea.

Phil: We are really agreeing, but our terms are different perhaps. My point is that, yes, we are bringing into the teacher education program certain persons. We allow those persons, first of all, to explore and discover themselves. Then we attempt to let them find the skills that they feel are going to be useful to them. We cannot avoid the knowledge and the skills.

Bob: But my comment is that if a person has a self, then the other stuff will come almost automatically. There are some things he would have to learn, but not nearly as much as we would think.

Wanda: You say, self-image.

Bob: No, self.

Wanda: An awareness of self.

Bob: No, *self*.

Saville: This self and self-image would become one at a certain point. When it gets to this level, it becomes awfully difficult to define exactly. One can only really feel it. It is the person, his capacities, his skills, and his knowledge. But it is his passion which brings it into focus and makes it one. And the willingness, maybe, to relate to the other person through *his* passion and *his* skills and *his* drive and *his* being that makes him a real teacher and a real person.

Teacher education looks only partly to aid the person who is asserting himself from the center; instead, it works towards stopping him, fixing his position. It needs to go to the center.

THE FIRST USE OF THE GAMES IN THE CLASSROOM

In the first few months of experimentation, we used the Focus Game to explore our own identities and the ways each of us wanted to relate to others in the group. Since the context was that of a teacher education program, we also explored our feelings and experiences on various ques-

tions connected with education, such as: What is a good teacher? . . .
A bad teacher?*

We found that the Focus Game worked very well for personal exploration. Most of us were able to open up to each other much more readily
and deeply than we ever had before with any group. Competitive feelings were reduced, and we experienced a deep solidarity.

At this point, I** felt that I would like to find out how the games
would work with subject matter, in order to determine if they could be
used for studying content in the classroom. At the time, I was the only
member of the group teaching regular classes. I was an instructor at a
state university, teaching introductory classes in poetry and drama so I
decided to develop an adaptation of the games for my own classes and
try it out.

* * * * *

Many of the English teachers I knew, myself included, often felt discouraged because the students weren't very involved, particularly in
required introductory courses like the ones I was teaching. We often felt
futile, and we sometimes blamed the students, believing they were either
stupid or insensitive for failing to appreciate the profundity and beauty
of the literature that we were presenting to them. We felt ourselves
equally stupid, or misguided, for persisting in such an unprofitable and
frequently unpleasant effort.

But the disturbance went even deeper. Many in the English Department, though sensitive and understanding of the literature to which we
were devoting ourselves, nevertheless felt, or perhaps had long since
forgotten to care, that the inspiration of great literature had not transformed or filled our own lives with beauty and idealism as we might once
have thought it could. Some of us felt that our early joy in literature had
been blunted by overzealous academic demands for the application of
the traditional scholarly disciplines to our "study."

The games offered the possibility of tapping the vital roots of the
meaning of literature. They provided an excellent structure for subjective
exploration; and, with this, the chance for a closer integration of our
learning with our individual personalities.† The games offered the possibility of moving a lot closer to the creative and transforming power that
we sense in literature, but which baffles us when we try to take hold of it.

* * * * *

So I brought the games to my classroom.
The basic rules of the Positive Focus Game for Literature‡ were

---

* See tape of early game, above.
** This section by Sandra Hollander.
† Since this time I have developed a number of other techniques for achieving
this purpose in most subject matter areas, and in learning generally. This work is
now being completed in book form under the title *The Book of Self-Expansion*.
‡ See page 116 for this game.

rather simply explained to the students. They were also given a written set of rules with a statement explaining the purpose of what we were doing. We would use the basic rules of Positive Focus to provide a structure of safety, trust, and mutual interest.

The focus person would decide the aspect of the poem or play that he wished to explore. He could choose to concentrate primarily on an "objective" analysis of the literature; on his own reactions to it; or, as often happened, on an interactive examination of work and self. Each student would be free to take or not to take the position of focus; to explore, or if he wished, to pass over questions put by group members in drawing him out; to relinquish the focus whenever he wished.

The chief function of the group in drawing out the focus was to try to stay within the lines of interest set down by the focus person; to give him their concentrated attention and try to understand him in depth as best they were able; to summarize the statements of the focus as a means of conveying their understanding to him, or to ask questions when they did not understand; to give positive feedback, when they could do so honestly, on what they had gained from the focus person in insight and sharing; and to express appreciation of his openness, acumen, courage, etc.

A useful refinement of the game was added later. This was a discussion of the game process at the end of each round. We sometimes had a person in the group play process observer, and he would break in if we had wandered away from the focus or violated some other rule of the game. Or, we might just go around the group, starting with the focus, and give everyone a chance to say how he had felt during the game, whether he had had any problems, and how the game might have been improved.

I found that the game was not difficult to learn, and that students could sometimes play a good game right from the start, just as we had in the first experimental games group. A "good" game was sometimes one in which a lot was brought out: The focus was satisfied that he had explored his subject fully, had expressed himself, and had been understood and appreciated; the group members had participated, had learned and shared, and had definitely enjoyed themselves. Or a "good" opening game might be one in which we became aware of some of the difficulties of playing the game, like listening to one person for a protracted time, and having to hold back when we thought the focus might be misunderstanding the poem.

I strongly felt that at the beginning the opening up of the student was more important than complete understanding of a poem. Students are so used to being under continual attack of criticism that they need some loosening up and self-confidence more than anything else if the learning is to have real value to them as individuals. Skill of interpretation emerged through practice, and through continued probing in the Focus and Challenge games.

I did introduce the Challenge Game after about five weeks, when the students had gained skill in the basic game. The Challenge Game was brought in for its value in sharpening skills in interpretation, and for its general value in giving practice in the discipline of making the effort to try to get inside the position of one's opponent.

I introduced the Discussion Game at a later point in the term, and some of the drama students preferred this to the Focus Game because it gave the opportunity for getting a variety of views very rapidly. The poetry students generally preferred Positive Focus and Challenge. This may be due to the nature of the subject, which works best with in-depth focus. It is clear that a variable series of games with specialized adaptations of basic games is best for various subject matters.

❀ ❀ ❀ ❀ ❀

A Closer Look at Some Early Games in the Classroom

The course opened with a demonstration game. Four or five was the best size for a group since everyone would have some chance to talk, yet no one would have the great burden of having to feed questions constantly in the drawing-out process. We began with a group of volunteers, who were a bit shy at first. They played the first game in front of the class, with myself as one of the group to help demonstrate how the game worked. (In subsequent class sessions, we would split into four or five such groups which operated simultaneously, and thus there was a great opportunity for participation and involvement for all the students.)

The student who volunteered to be the first focus was a rather courageous, even daring young person. As I recall, there was a quality of earnestness, sometimes combined with wit, or perhaps a certain wryness, brought out by the circumstance of being in the spotlight in this very personal undertaking.

In general, the focus would begin by giving an "objective" account of the play or poem. He would then proceed to explore in greater depth the complexity of relationships within the work. Usually personal involvement and reaction came to the foreground at this point, and the student was drawn out along this line, if he wanted to pursue it.

If the focus chose to concentrate mainly on the cognitive level, he might use some of the traditional methods of analysis along with other methods. The learning was greatly enhanced by the safety and the constructive emphasis of the focus game. If he focused on the subjective, he would find his own level of personal feeling and reflection in order to experience and explore the relation of self to literature. This proved to be an opportunity for full involvement, with powerful interaction of the emotional and the ideational, which is rare in the classroom.

The discussion sometimes moved rapidly to deep levels. The deepening process was helped through group support and solidarity. If, despite this support, the movement in depth proved uncomfortable, the focus had control: He could stop the process at any time, or "pass" on a particular question. Also, group members shared responsibility for making the experience a good one for the focus. The trust and interest created by the basic structure of the Positive Focus Game, plus the built-in controls, are what make the game work, and its workings are powerful.

Of the many sessions I experienced over a year's time, I can recall very good games in which concentration was primarily on cognitive learning. A student might pursue "objective" clarification of a poem: its basic idea, the meanings of specific words, images, metaphors, symbols, etc. But the most moving sessions were those with some depth of sub- jectivity; and with interaction, sometimes by alternation, of the idea and the feeling levels.

This latter type of session brought out the outstanding personal quali- ties of some students, the shy students as well as the outspoken ones. The poem selected by the student was often one with strong negative or positive identification. Bassey, a young Nigerian, chose a poem which conveyed his own aloneness, and his feeling that this isolation would endure, that men turn away from each other. A high point in my own experience was a session late in the course when Bassey was once again the focus, and he said, at the end of the game, "Today I feel that I am almost myself."

Jeanne chose several poems by Blake. She found in "The Lamb" a recreation of her own childhood's innocence and belief. In her discussion of "The Little Black Boy," she brought out her puzzlement at the irra- tionality of color strife, and her pride that she had been raised in a family free of prejudice.

These explorations of the student's involvement with literature per- mitted and supported the development of stronger self-identity through the stimulus of the subject matter and the group interaction. The use of the games in the classroom had achieved what teachers have often desired but seldom realized: assimilation of a subject on a deep level, the ready possibility of incorporating elements of the learning for self-expansion, and more generally, the nurturing of personal growth through the study of art.

CHAPTER 2

Sharing Perceptions in the Here and Now

In this series of games you will develop skill in sharing perceptions and using feedback to promote growth, self-awareness, and sensitivity to others.

There are four games in this series.

1. The Ongoing T-Group Game. Here we practice talking about present issues of concern in an open and honest way. The openness and honesty of exchange will make you more aware of yourself and others, and will provide an impetus for change.

2. The Sensitivity Game of Total Response. In this game one practices expressing all one's feelings and thoughts about the focus. As focus, one practices receiving all of the feelings and thoughts one has stirred up in the others.

3. The Blocks to Communication Game. This makes you aware of the destructive or blocking games that people play in life. This awareness provides an impetus toward honesty, self-knowledge, and growth.

4. Finally, there are the Critiquing games. These can be used at any meeting or gathering. They provide a way in which any group or social situation can be used to increase awareness and growth.

ONGOING T-GROUP GAMES

In introducing the game to a group for the first time, it is best that the following portion be read aloud.

Voting Questions

(For an explanation of Voting Questions, see Compliment Game, page 5.)

Have you ever been in a conversation and felt you wanted to get away?

Have you ever been in a conversation and had strong feelings that you couldn't bring yourself to express?

Have you ever avoided people because they did things that bothered or offended you?

Did these people always know why you disliked them?

Have you ever been cut dead without knowing why?

Have you ever been in conversations in which people talked only about what was relevant to themselves?

This series of games is designed to help you cope with some of the problems brought out by the above questions. It is designed to help people become more direct in expressing their present needs and interests directly. It is designed to help us become more sensitive to how we come across to others, and more direct in letting others know in a constructive way how they come across to us."

To Play the Game Series

A group of between five and thirteen people come together to play the game. They are committed to becoming more aware of how they relate to each other, and to becoming more direct, more honest, and more constructive in their interactions. All games may be played with or without a facilitator—see facilitator sheet at the end.

Rules for Game 1

1. Two facilitators volunteer or are selected. These should be the most experienced players. The facilitator role may be rotated during the course of the game after each critiquing session. (See facilitator guide sheet at the end.)

2. Rule of Here and Now. As far as possible, members are to express their present feelings. It is permissible to bring up things out of the past, but these should be related to the here and now.

3. Rule of Positive Feelings. Express your own positive, neutral, or mildly negative feelings toward others in the group.

4. Rule of Drawing Out. Draw out members of the group concerning how they feel and think.

5. Rule of Sharing. Say how you feel and think about the issues brought up.

6. Rule of Critique. Periodically the action is stopped for critiquing. A critique is a consideration of the process that has just gone on. What happened? How did it happen? What did people feel about it? A critique can be called at the suggestion of a facilitator or a group member.

After a critique session is a good time to change facilitators.

Game 1 should be played for several sessions before starting on Game 2.

Rules for Game 2

The rules are the same as for Game 1 with the following additions:

7. Rule of Shifting Focus.

a. Do not change or take away the focus from the person who is most deeply involved.

b. Try to complete one focus before shifting to another.

c. When the focus becomes repetitive, or simply too long, raise the issue of changing it.

d. Feedback should be offered the person or persons primarily involved in a focus before moving on.

e. If you feel very uncomfortable about continuing the focus because of its intensity, delicacy, or for some other reason, state so openly under the rule of discomfort that follows.

8. Rule of Discomfort. If you feel uncomfortable or feel that it is improper for the group to go on with its present focus, say why you think so. Your feelings of discomfort have first priority and become the focus of the group. Only after this issue has been resolved may the group go back to its former focus if it so wishes.

Rules for Game 3

Continue with the rules of Games 1 and 2 and add the following rule:

9a. Rule of Feedback. A group member may ask one or more members of the group to express all of their feelings concerning himself. Under these conditions, strong negative feelings may be expressed.

9b. When a topic or focus or session has been completed, each person should briefly state how he felt during the process. An attempt should be made to understand what went on and why.

Rules for Game 4

Game 4 is played following all previous rules in Games 1 through 3 with this addition:

10. Rule of Confrontation. When two people are involved in a dialogue or confrontation, a third may not get in the middle unless the dialogue is really over or has degenerated in fruitless repetition. At such times a third party can facilitate the discussion by drawing out both persons and accepting their feelings.

Rules for Game 5

Rules for all previous games apply with this addition:

11. Rule of Negative Feedback. One may express the negative feelings another group member arouses in us without name-calling or projection.

Some examples:
Permissible: When you ask a question, "I get the feeling you're looking for a fight."
Not permissible: "You're an argumentative person, always trying to get in a fight."
Permissible: "I felt very angry when you ———. I feel like I want to kill you."
Not permissible: "You're a no good son of a bitch."
Permissible: "I feel that I'm being pushed around."
Not permissible: "Why are you always trying to push people around?"

Rules for Game 6

12. Rule of Therapy or Problem Solving. It is permissible for a group member to bring up and explore past events that are still felt and influential in the present and to bring up present problems outside of the group.

Where this rule conflicts with previous rules, it takes precedence. When this is done, the following rules apply:

a. Responses should be nonjudgmental.
b. In drawing out the person, one should not interrupt the direction of his thought or feeling.
c. Group members may respond by asking clarifying questions and reflecting feelings.
d. Rule of Alternatives. When the feelings on a subject have been explored, group members may suggest alternative solutions to a problem, but may not attempt to argue or impose these solutions.

Rules for Game 7. Final Rules

13. Rule of Interpretation. One may present explanations or interpretations of another person's behavior or feelings or motives in the here and now along with the evidence backing it. These interpretations should be stated as opinion, not fact.

Permissible: "I see you as appeasing Martha, as if you were really scared of her. Your high tone of voice and your smiling at her after she attacked you lead me to think so." (Permissible, because it is a here-and-now interpretation and evidence is given.)

Not permissible: "It seems as though you had a dominant mother." (There-and-then interpretation—no evidence.)

14. The Rule of Variety. When a new member is introduced, or when failure to apply the rules makes for unsatisfactory interaction, the group should start over at Game 1. The group may also wish to play other reality games for variety.

15. Rule of Growth. An additional rule. Periodically, at least once a year, several open sessions are held in which the game is introduced to new people. During these sessions, the original group is split up with several of the old members meeting in groups with new people. The people introduced to the game are invited to set up ongoing groups of their own.

Role of the Facilitator

In all games, the objective may be more quickly reached if two people are chosen as facilitators at the beginning of each round. The facilitators do not have a monopoly of the role of facilitation. Anyone can facilitate.

But if everyone else in the group is too much involved with his own feelings and perceptions to be aware of some of the things going on, then it becomes the facilitators' responsibility to protect the group process.

1. Each facilitator sits opposite the other in the group so that between them they can see all group members. If someone violates a rule and no one calls him on it, it is the facilitator's responsibility to intervene.

2. The facilitator helps all the members become involved. If the conversation is dominated by one or two individuals, the facilitator helps draw the others out. He facilitates the movement from one focus to another.

3. The facilitator tries to keep interaction on a meaningful level. In this connection he keeps people from escaping from the meaningful either through intellectualizing or through display of feeling which they are unwilling to support or explore.

4. The facilitator notes people who may have been hurt or may be feeling things strongly and helps open an opportunity for them to express themselves. (Often the facilitator uses nonverbal cues in identifying people who have strong feelings that are not being expressed.)

5. The facilitator sees to it that the Rule of Negative Feedback does not become an excuse for everyone to zero in on one person. When this happens, the facilitator invokes the Rule of Confrontation to the one individual under attack and one other group member. Alternatively, the

facilitator may draw out the feelings of the person under attack and accept them. He may also do this with one or more of the attackers. His acceptance of both sides of the conflict helps it become a growth-producing exchange.

6. At intervals where there is either a natural break or when tension gets out of hand, the facilitators may call for a critiquing of the round. During this time, the group discusses feelings they had while the round was in progress. They discuss which responses helped the communication process and which hindered it. They consider how effective the facilitators were in furthering the group process. They discuss the group process. They determine the next set of facilitators.

7. Sometimes it is hard for a group to get started, or to begin a new round. Besides outwaiting the silence, the facilitator may ask some voting questions, followed by a mini-focus (a few, brief drawing-out questions). This often permits a more sensitive use of the time. Some suggested questions for getting the group going are:

1. Who did something exciting during the past week?
2. Did anybody try anything during the week that they never tried in the same way before?
3. Who did something during the week that he is proud of?
4. Is there anybody who feels anxious?
5. Is there anybody who feels depressed?
6. Does anybody have something from last week's session on his mind?

SENSITIVITY GAME OF TOTAL RESPONSE

The facilitator or person introducing the game reads the following voting questions (remember, you indicate the extent to which the answer is true of you by how high or how low you hold your hand):

Have you ever talked to somebody without knowing what impression you made?

Are you clear about how the things you say strike others?

Would you like to know more clearly the impact you have on others?

These three questions indicate a need to have more precise knowledge of how one affects others. This need is often unsatisfied for reasons of tact, safety, or convention. In this game you will have a chance to learn more about how you come across to others.

The following questions get to the second purpose of the game, honesty.

Do you often conceal a large number of your reactions to others?

Do you often feel uncomfortable or bored because you conceal too much of yourself?

Would you like to practice revealing more of your reactions to others? The game will give you practice in revealing more of yourself than you may have been in the habit of doing.

Game 1. Total Response: Nonverbal Form

1. Two or three people get together to play. If more are present, the larger group breaks up into smaller groups of two's or three's.

2. One person volunteers to be focus. The focus may not speak. He sits silently and tries out various expressions, gestures, and motions.

3. The rest of the group take turns in giving all of the associations and feelings stirred up in them by the gestures, expressions, and motions of the focus.

4. After five minutes, the focus passes to the next volunteer until everybody has had a turn.

5. Any player may call a halt if the process becomes too uncomfortable for him.

6. After everybody has had a turn, the group talks about what they learned from the game.

Game 2. Total Response: Simple Verbal Form

In Game 2 the focus says something, instead of remaining silent. All the other rules are the same.

Game 3. Total Response: Dialogue Form

In Game 3 the focus says something. Then, after the other players respond with all their feelings, thoughts, and associations, the focus says something more. This is repeated so that a dialogue starts and is continued for a previously agreed-upon length of time. Fifteen minutes may be a good time limit the first time Game 3 is played. All the other rules are the same.

GAMES FOR DISCOVERING AND REMOVING BLOCKS TO COMMUNICATION

In this game we will learn to recognize how and why communication is often blocked, and what we can do about it.

Procedures

1. A group gets together to play the game.
2. The group breaks into subgroups of between five and ten members.

3. A focus person is chosen.

4. The focus person chooses and acts out one of the ways of blocking communication that are listed below.

5. The group tries to discover the way or ways he is blocking communication and to find ways of countering it.

6. After a round the focus person and the group members discuss what they thought and felt while the interaction was going on.

7. The above steps are repeated again with a new focus.

Blocks to Communication

1. MAINTAINING STATUS BY RESTRICTING INFORMATION

The focus person implies that he knows something, but isn't telling all he knows. He uses jargon, or refers to events or people that others aren't familiar with to give them a sense of being out of it. He dogmatically asserts his conclusions without giving either his reasons or his feelings.

2. MAINTAINING STATUS BY MISUSING CONFIDENTIALITY

The focus person talks to the group members separately, telling them things that will divide them and make them trust only him. He stresses the confidentiality of what is being said.

3. MAINTAIN STATUS AND POWER BY BEING A MEDIATOR

The focus person tries to keep all communication channeled through himself. He prevents other individuals from relating directly by always getting in between. This prevents other people from forming a relationship of their own and insures the power of the mediator.

4. MAINTAINING STATUS AND POWER BY LYING ABOUT YOURSELF AND COVERING UP ALL THAT IS UNCOMPLIMENTARY

Here the focus person paints an idealized picture of himself, covering up all faults and weaknesses

5. PUT-DOWN

The focus person attacks and diminishes everything that others say in order to put them down and build himself up.

6. SELF PUT-DOWN

The focus person tears himself down to build others up in order to get their good will. Acting helpless, dependent, or stupid are all part of this strategy.

7. NOT TALKING OUT OF FEAR

The focus person is bland, avoiding any statement that might be criticized or laughed at out of fear.

8. BLOCKS COMMUNICATION FOR FEAR OF EXPRESSING NEGATIVE FEELINGS

The focus person acts overly nice. Some negative feelings should get through despite himself. But these should be stated so nicely and help-fully and so indirectly that it will be impossible to recognize them or deal with them.

9. BLOCKS COMMUNICATION BY EXPRESSING NOTHING BUT EMOTION AND CALLING ALL THINKING INTELLECTUALIZING

The focus person acts and speaks very emotionally. He stops any attempt to deal with him in terms of facts or reality.

10. BLOCKS TO COMMUNICATION BY INTELLECTUALIZING

The focus person attempts to block communication by intellectualizing, theorizing, excluding feelings and concrete facts from the discussion as far as possible.

11. CHANGING THE SUBJECT

The focus person prevents the discussion from getting anywhere by changing the subject.

12. IGNORING

The focus person blocks communication by ignoring certain persons or themes.

13. COMPETING

The focus person blocks communication by topping anything anybody says.

14. CHANGING FOCUS

The focus person blocks communication by changing the focus from person to person or topic to topic.

15. JARGON

The focus person blocks communication by using a jargon that others can't understand.

16. FREE CHOICE

The focus person chooses to role-play, another way of blocking communication that is not listed here. If this is done, he should inform the members of the group that he is choosing to represent a form of blocking communication not on the list. They can try to identify the form of blocking, and to find ways of countering it.

ADVANCED CRITIQUING

Voting Questions

Have you ever done something extremely well, then found you didn't know how you did it?

Did it ever happen that you couldn't repeat what you had done?

Do you ever find yourself making the same mistake over and over again?

How many days of your life can you remember?

Does it ever happen that you live through a day, and when you look back at it, it's as if nothing happened?

Most people have a great deal of experience which they never look at. The result is that sometimes nothing is learned from the experience. The experiences we learn from are rare compared to those that pass us by and leave no lasting mark.

In general, we learn from experiences when we look back at them and evaluate them. When we think about what we did, how we felt about it; when we recall our expectations and perceptions and contrast them with the actual reality as it developed, we learn and grow as people.

Critiquing is a method of systematically looking back and seeing what was done, how it was done, how and why we thought and felt about it as we did. Through critiquing, experience is captured and made to serve as an aid to growth and learning. We become more aware of others, of ourselves, of the world. Through the intensification of awareness that critiquing creates, we become more skillful, more effective, more flexible, stronger, and more real.

In this unit you will experience a large number of critiquing methods that can be used to look back at and become more knowledgeable about almost any group activity.

The critiquing includes a number of complex processes. This outline is included to give you an overview.

Introduction

After a game or a round is over, a process of critiquing is helpful. Critiquing helps us unify our experience, learn from it, and grow in it. Many of the games have special critiquing sheets that go along with them and are designed to teach some of the game skills as well as the game rules. Here we will go into greater detail about the use of these sheets, the use of game rules, and general nonstructured critiquing as well as other critiquing techniques.

These critiques are arranged in order of difficulty. One should achieve some mastery of each critique before moving on to the next. It is understood that as the player advances from simpler to more advanced critiques, he can and should continue to utilize the simpler critiques while doing the more advanced ones.

One, or better, two, experienced players should be present for advanced critiquing to work most effectively and safely.

There are three additional safeguards that should be used with all the games, but particularly with advanced critiquing.

1. You yourself are the best judge of what you can handle. Do not attempt to handle feelings, issues, or anything else unless you feel reasonably sure you can handle them. Consider the people, circumstances, and time limits.

2. Do not force somebody else to go into something that he does not want to discuss.

3. If any member of the group is very uncomfortable, his discomfort should be discussed before getting into a touchy area.

I. THE RULES AND SKILLS CRITIQUE

OBJECTIVES

1. To learn to apply the rules of the games and gain skill in game play.
2. To gain a deeper insight into oneself, one's ways of relating, one's feelings, one's assumptions, and one's perceptions.

WHERE USED

The Rules and Skills Critique may be used at the end of a game or in any situation where skills and rules apply.

All of the games have rules. In addition, many of the games have special sheets that are designed to help one learn the necessary game skills and rules. Often, awareness of when and where a rule is broken or where our skills were lacking is enough to learn the appropriate skill or rule better. However, in the following two situations, pointing out a broken rule or an inadequacy of skill is not enough to lead to a change.

1. When a person persistently breaks a rule, even when the rule-breaking has persistently been pointed out to him.
2. When one feels an inner justification for not learning a rule or a skill. It may be that the rule makes one feel silly, dishonest, unnatural, or uncomfortable. It may also be that the rule interferes with manipulative, controlling, or neurotic ways of interaction that a player does not want to give up even temporarily. More than likely, the person breaks a rule or refuses to try to learn a skill automatically without considering his inner reasons or motivation. He may justify the breaking of a rule by calling it stupid, silly, dishonest, etc.

If after becoming aware of the fact that we are violating a rule or refusing to learn a skill, we explore in depth our feelings and motivations concerning this, we may become more sensitive to our patterns of communication, and we may open up new ranges and new depths in our ways of relating.

PROCEDURES FOR RULES AND SKILLS CRITIQUE

1. After a game, each person takes a turn being focus.
2. Ways in which he has violated a rule or ignored certain game skills are identified by himself and the group. If the violation of the rule or the ignoring of a skill are repeated, the following additional steps may be taken:
3. Questions are asked exploring some of his motivation in violating a rule or failing to apply a skill. Examples follow:

What did you feel?

What did you think?

What would be the worst consequence of not violating the rule?

What would be the best consequence?

4. The situation in which the rule was violated or the skill ignored are then role-played, with the person trying to do better a second time.

5. His feelings and thoughts in attempting to do better are then explored with the group.

The repeated use of this critique will prepare the players for more advanced critiques to follow.

LEADS TO FURTHER INSIGHTS

The persistent violation of a rule or the inability to apply a skill, points to feelings, fears, wishes, expectancies, perceptions, and assumptions which we may never have critically examined, and of which we may not at first be fully aware.

II. THE PROCESS CRITIQUE

OBJECTIVES

1. To become more aware of and sensitive to group process.

2. To become more aware of the different ways that individuals may relate themselves to each other and to the group as a whole.

3. Most importantly, to become more aware of how you yourself behave in a group.

These three objectives are reached by focusing on what happened, and why.

WHERE USED

The process critique is very general. It can be used not only at the end of a Reality Game, but at the end of any group process, meeting, or activity.

The process critique, in its generality, includes in embryo all other critiques that follow.

FORMS OF THE PROCESS CRITIQUE

1. THE PROCESS WHIP (Good for a quick critique)

Objective: The point of this critique is to become aware of how each of the participants saw the process (and perhaps felt about it); the purpose is not to resolve differences in perception.

PROCEDURES

1. Each person takes a turn relating what he saw happening.

2. People speak in order, moving in a clockwise direction. While it is permissible to pass when one's turn comes, it is not permissible to interrupt or to start a discussion.

3. The whip may consist of one round or several rounds, with people speaking in turn. General discussion is to be avoided.

2. THE PROCESS FOCUS

Objective: The purpose of this critique is to explore in depth how each of the participants felt about the process.

PROCEDURES

1. Each person takes a turn stating what he saw happening. Others draw him out in order to explore in depth his perception of the process. As we shall see later, this exploration may get into the feelings, expectancies, wishes, and assumptions of the focus person.

2. Here again, the focus is on the exploration of each person's perceptions in turn. Discussion or confrontation are to be avoided at this point.

3. THE PROCESS DISCUSSION

Objective: The process discussion critique is designed to confront differences in perception and feeling concerning the process, so that we may be able to face the possibility of distortions, irrational or archaic elements in our perceptions.

Caution: If it is to have any depth, a process discussion should take place only after the process focus critique. One cannot constructively confront differences in perception unless one knows what perceptions are being confronted.

WHEN USED

The process discussion is best used after a process focus has taken place. On occasion, a brief discussion may be fruitful after a process whip.

RULES FOR PROCESS DISCUSSION

1. Rule of Shifting Focus. Do not change or take away the focus from the person primarily involved without good cause. Remember that involvement is constantly changing.

2. Rule of Discomfort. If you feel very uncomfortable about the group going on with or starting on some topic or focus, say so. Your feelings of discomfort have first priority and become the focus of the group.

3. Rule of Confrontation. When two people are primarily involved in a confrontation that is significant, a third person may not get into the middle unless the dialogue has degenerated and become fruitless or destructive. When he does intervene, he draws out and accepts the feelings of both parties.

4. Rule of Negative Feedback. One may express the negative feelings another member of the group arouses in one without name-calling. Say how the other person makes you feel, don't say what he is.

5. Rule of Reference. Try to make your statements refer back to what has already been said. Do not start a new topic unless you have checked to see if the old topic is exhausted.

III. THE CRITIQUE OF FEELINGS

OBJECTIVES

The Feelings Critique is designed to help us:

1. Become more aware of and more sensitive to others' feelings as well as our own.

2. Become more direct in the expression of our feelings without losing their complexity or subtlety.

3. Understand and unify our feelings in depth, so that we are not controlled by first one partial feeling and then another.

WHERE USED

The Critique of Feelings may be used as a summing-up after the Skills or the Process Critique.

The simpler Feelings Critiques may be used instead of the Skills or Process Critique when time pressure or fatigue makes a longer critique difficult.

The Feelings Critique may be used at the beginning of, during, or at the end of, any group activity or meeting.

A Feelings Critique may be used whenever a group gets bogged down, seems uncommitted, confused, or diffused.

It is very useful in any situation where a number of participants have not expressed themselves or said where they stand.

INTRODUCTION TO THE GAME

Feelings are one of the broadest integrations of mental processes. Feelings integrate needs, plans, and wishes with perceptions and actions.

Plans, wishes, perceptions, and anticipations of which we are unaware or only dimly aware contribute to feelings as do the more rational, conscious thought processes. Feelings are thus central in the unity of our being. We cannot ignore them and remain whole.

The Critique of Feelings helps us become more aware of our feelings as well as the feelings of others. In this way it helps us become more whole and relate more totally.

STRUCTURE OF A FEELING

Feelings have conscious and unconscious dimensions. Here we have shaded the less conscious elements of a feeling. Note how the conscious elements of a feeling are transformed when they are extended into the unconscious: Plans extended into the unconscious become wishes and impulses, perceptions become intuitions, predictions become expectations, reasoning and thought become dreams and fantasy.

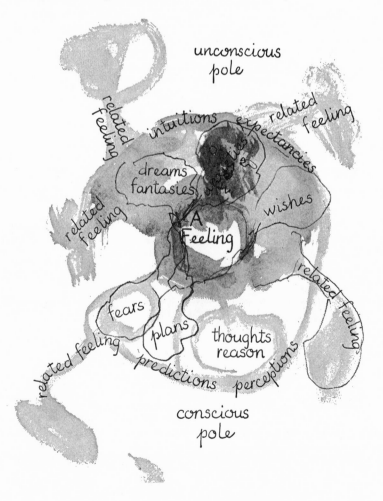

The Feelings Whip

Objectives

1. To get a quick census of how everybody in a group feels at a certain time (now) or concerning a certain issue.
2. To get people involved in the group process.
3. To prevent a small group of talkative people from taking over.

When Used

It can be used at the end of an activity as a quick evaluation or critique.

It can be used to increase group involvement, determine group direction, and get information at the beginning, middle, or end of any activity or meeting.

Rules

Same as Process Whip except that each speaker talks about his feelings.

The Feelings Focus

Objectives

1. To get a deep understanding of how everybody in a group feels about an issue, a meeting, a process, a happening.
2. To explore and get a deeper understanding of our own feelings.
3. To help us complete and clarify our feelings.

Where Used

The Feelings Focus is useful at the end of a meeting or a series of meetings, as part of an evaluation.

The Feelings Focus may be used as an independent game or activity to help discover and clarify feelings when we feel confused.

Rules and Procedures

1. If a large group has convened, break up into smaller groups of three to five members. The Feelings Focus takes too long to be conveniently used in a larger group.

2. One becomes focus and talks about his feelings.

3. The others act as facilitators and draw him out.

4. When the focus is completed, it passes on to another member until each person has had a turn.

Suggestions for Facilitators of Feelings Focus

AT THE BEGINNING OR WHEN THE PERSON NEEDS TO TALK

During the early stages of a Feelings Focus, or when the person is bottled up and needs to talk things out, a reflecting technique is best. (See "Reflection Game," page 14, for suggestions.)

WHEN THE PERSON IS CONFUSED, PARALYZED, OR HIGHLY EXCITED

If a person is confused, paralyzed, or highly excited, it often helps him get perspective if he becomes aware of all of his feelings, not just the few he is focusing on. Some questions that help a facilitator do this are:

Do you have any other feelings or reservations?

What is the best thing about it (alternative, issue, situation)?

What is the worst thing about it?

What is the best thing about the worst possibility?

What is the worst thing about the best possibility?

If you were angry, what would you be most angry about?

If you were happy, what would you be most happy about?

What is the most guilty feeling you have in this situation?

What is the most boring . . . happy . . . sad . . . tearful . . . tense . . . relaxed . . . painful . . . exciting . . . etc., aspect about the situation . . . subject . . . alternative . . . issue . . . event . . . possibility . . . etc.

In doing a survey of feelings, it is best to end with an exploration of the more constructive, peaceful or happy feelings.

WHEN A PERSON IS TIED UP BY A TIGHT, RIGID, DOMINATING FEELING

When a person is bound hand and foot by a rigid, unchanging feeling, it is often possible to undo the knots by breaking the feeling into separate elements or threads. A feeling feels like a single quality, but it is made up of many elements: fantasies, perceptions, past experiences, expectancies, wishes, assumptions, and plans. Some of these have never been examined and are not fully conscious. Asking about wishes, expectancies, perceptions, and fears makes a person more aware of the basis of his feeling, which permits the feeling to change. (A detailed and advanced version of this type of exploration follows: See "Insight into Feelings," page 69.)

Analysis of Feelings Leads to New Insights

We know that we can change our thoughts and opinions by reasoning and thinking, but feelings seem harder to change. If they change, they seem to change of themselves, taking their own sweet time, and it seems that there is little we can do about it. Feelings seem to have a basic irreducible quality about them. When we have gotten to our feelings, it seems as if we have gotten to rock bottom.

Feelings are difficult to change because they represent a broad psychic integration. They include needs, wishes, fantasies, plans, fears, loves, hates, expectancies, and assumptions as they relate to one's ongoing perceptions and activities. Feelings also integrate various levels ot awaredness. They include fully explored, rational thoughts, ideas, wishes, and fantasies which we are aware of but have never critically examined; and other ideas, wishes, fantasies, and sensations of which we are only dimly aware or are totally unaware. To make matters worse, all of these diverse elements of consciousness and levels of awareness are all integrated into a single feeling quality.

Sometimes one is unaware of one's feelings. One has a sense of anxiety, disconnectedness, alienation, and depersonalization. Focusing on the separate feeling elements, wishes, expectancies, fantasies, and perceptions will often bring the feeling again into awareness and reestablish contact with our inner life.

Sometimes we do not like the way we feel. While we cannot consciously and willfully change feelings (since feelings represent a broader integration than either consciousness or the will), we can create conditions enabling feelings to change of themselves, to become more unified, more rational, and more constructive. One can do this by considering one at a time the various elements that go into the creation of a particular feeling.

GAINING INSIGHT INTO FEELINGS
A More Advanced Feelings Focus

Objective

The object of this focus series is to gain understanding in depth concerning our feelings so that we are not controlled by first one feeling and then another.

The objective is achieved by systematically breaking a feeling down into its elements through a series of subfoci: (1) perception focus, (2) exploration of expectancies, (3) exploration of wishes, fears, and fantasies—and the needs they reflect as well as alternative ways of fulfilling those needs, and (4) elements of the self-concept involved in the feeling.

These subfoci may also be used independently for a variety of reasons, which will be stated as they are presented.

Where Used—Use of the Entire Sequence

The entire sequence of foci that make up the insight focus is best used in close-knit groups requiring a high level of commitment, such as the family, closely-knit social groups, people working very closely together on projects requiring a high level of cooperation.

The sequence may be used among friends when one person is confused or upset, but not sufficiently so as to need psychiatric help.

The entire sequence may be used as a culminating activity in a workshop or a course to help integrate the new learnings into the self so that they may be used in life.

Safeguards

Do not enter into such a focus unless you feel reasonably sure you can handle it.

Do not let the process go beyond your capacity to handle.

As facilitator, ask questions, but do not pressure the focus to answer.

Do not give interpretations unless qualified to do so.

Do not enter a focus as facilitator unless you are able to remain there as long as is necessary to come to a good stopping point. Do not leave the focus in the middle. Stop at a point when comfort has been reestablished.

Give positive feedback at the end of the session. Let the focus person know that you still like and respect him despite the feelings he may have expressed. If you feel that you will not be able to accept what the focus is likely to express, do not enter the process as a facilitator.

Use of Some of the Subelements of the Feelings Focus

The Perception Whip or Focus may be used in any group when there is a dispute among a few of the members as to what happened. (Follow the basic procedure described in "Feelings Whip" or "Feelings Focus.")

An Expectancy Whip or Focus may be used at the beginning of a course, workshop, meeting, project, club, marriage, partnership, project, etc. Knowing what everybody's expectancies are in advance can save a great deal of trouble.

An Expectancy Whip or Focus is also very useful when trouble arises. Conflict, frustration, disappointment, and anger are often the result of having one's expectancies disappointed. Finding out what each person's expectancies are, and agreeing on new, more realistic expectancies is a good first step in resolving the trouble.

The Wish Focus, or Whip, can be a fun focus. It quickly establishes an atmosphere of spontaneity and puts us in contact with the child within ourselves. It is good for parties and social occasions as a way of livening things up. It also has a serious aspect, for wishes sometimes give the illusion that they are needs. Fears are sometimes disguised wishes.

The Wish Focus is also very valuable in getting to the heart of things, when issues have been obscured with too many words, too many arguments, and too many rationalizations. For the wish exists at the border of consciousness and unconsciousness, where we are most direct, most honest, and most alive.

The Needs Focus, or Whip, is almost essential if one is going to make a successful change in attitude or behavior. In general it has two parts. In the first part, one tries to discover what needs are met by the attitude, wish, fantasy, way of behaving, etc. In the second part, one considers alternative ways of meeting those needs.

The Fear Focus, or Whip, is very valuable just before changing an old behavior or embarking on a new behavior. If one does not look at what one is afraid of, one's resolution to change usually remains unfulfilled. A consideration of possible difficulties and fears before embarking on something new often enables one to overcome those fears and difficulties.

Focus On the Self-Concept

Every feeling, every action or behavior, involves the self-concept. To understand a feeling or behavior it is necessary to know what part of the self-concept is involved. The way we think, feel, and behave is a part of our self-concept. To change any of these involves a change in one's self-concept.

The Focus on the Self-concept permits one to make changes in one's self-concept in order to allow one to change some specific ways of thinking, feeling, or behaving. There are three steps to changing one's self-concept.

a. Exploration of how one feels and thinks of oneself in respect to what one wants to change.

b. Decision as to what changes one wants to make in the kind of person one is.

c. Consideration of all the small changes that the larger decision involves, followed by a decision to make these secondary changes.

Procedures and Rules: Focus on Gaining Insight into Feelings

All the subelements of the focus on gaining insight into feelings can be explored either in a whip, a focus, or a discussion. The whip is preferable in a large group or when there is a shortage of time. If a focus is used, group size should be kept to five or below.

See the previous section for the objectives or use of any of the subelements of the insight focus. See also the following section for use of each element as a focus.

Using the Total Series

In using the total insight focus series, we start with perceptions, and go through each of the subgames in systematic fashion, integrating the insight gained as we go along.

Suggested procedures for doing this as an integrated sequence follow.

Step 1. The Perception Focus

The focus person explores his perceptions as related to the feeling, situation, etc.

The facilitators draw him out. Questions that draw out the focus on what he would feel if the situation were changed are very helpful in exploring the relation of feelings to perceptions. Some examples are, "How would you have felt if you had done what you wanted?" "What was the worst thing about it? . . . The best thing about it? . . . How would you have felt if Sally had sided with you rather than with Tom? etc."

Step 2. The Expectancy Focus

The focus explores his expectancies within the situation. The facilitator tries to help the focus define all of his expectancies as clearly and in as much detail as possible. The relation between the expectancies and the perceptions of the focus should then be related.

Step 3. Focus on Wishes, Needs, and Fears

The focus first talks about his wishes. The facilitator draws out the focus concerning all his possible wishes. He then asks questions to help the focus relate his wishes to his perceptions and expectancies: "Did the wishes account for any discrepancy between what was expected and what actually happened?"

The focus then talks about his needs as they were reflected in his wishes. If the wishes and the actions based upon them were unrealistic and failed to satisfy the needs they were intended to satisfy, one may brainstorm alternative ways of meeting those needs.

The focus explores his fears. What fears did he have in the situation? How did they influence his perceptions, expectancies, wishes, and needs? What fears might prevent him from using alternative strategies in meeting his needs? Were any of the fears really disguised wishes?

The facilitators help the focus by drawing him out and asking questions such as the ones above.

Step 4. The Self-Concept Focus

The focus explores the relation of his self-concept to his feelings, perceptions, expectancies, wishes, needs, and fears. What changes in his self-image would be necessary if he were to change his feelings and everything that goes along with them? What would be the good, the bad, the pleasant, the fearful, the difficult, the delightful aspects of such a change as a whole, and of each part of such a change?

The Concept of Focus
in Conflict Situations

When there is a clear focus, there is no conflict because it is accepted by the group that the needs of the focus person are dominant, while the facilitators' needs are subordinate. Conflict arises when there are two foci at the same time. This may be seen in conversation. As long as there is one clear focus at a time, as long as the focus moves clearly from person to person, there is communication rather than conflict. But as soon as two people are trying to be focus at the same time, communication is blocked and destructive conflict tends to develop.

All the modes of conflict resolution presented here require skill in shifting focus. One person takes a turn at being focus, while the other acts as facilitator; then the process is reversed. Basically, conflict resolution reduces itself to: The Rule of Shifting Focus (taking turns in focusing;) and The Rule of Focus Completion, (making sure you complete one focus before shifting to the next). The games in this chapter vary in that the focus and facilitator roles are somewhat different in each game.

Sometimes the two positions in a conflict are set so firm and so far apart that resolution is impossible in one, or even in several, confrontations. But even in these cases the technique of shifting focus with a process of drawing-out, reflection, or questioning between each change of focus leads to greater understanding, greater respect, and greater tolerance of opposing positions and persons. (See the Reflection Game for Conflict, page 78, for reestablishing communication when it has broken down.)

THE CHALLENGE GAME

Objective

When there is a conflict of beliefs, opinions, interests, or values, discussion often is fractured, and more heat than light is generated. People in conflict situations are likely to talk past each other. They are likely to cut off or ignore what the others are saying. Instead of listening, people tend to be thinking of what they want to say. If many people are involved, the focus shifts from person to person and from point to point so that it becomes difficult to get anywhere. The Challenge Game is an attempt to make confrontation constructive by facilitating communication.

Situations In Which the Challenge Game May Be Used

When two persons are fighting, the Challenge Game may be offered to each as an opportunity to clarify the conflict.

When a discussion becomes unruly or a group is engaging in argument, the Challenge Game may be suggested.

The Challenge Game can be played after somebody has presented a point of view, to give others a chance to air their differences.

The Challenge Game can be played if tension has been growing in the group and there has been no avenue for its expression.

Caution: If somebody is using games to facilitate instruction, some of the more positive games should generally be used before the Challenge Game is used.

Procedures

1. A person can open himself to challenge at any time, and may end the challenge at any time. He starts the challenge by saying, "Who would like to challenge me on this?"

2. The persons who are interested in accepting the challenge make themselves known.

3. The challenger then makes his statement or stand clearly, briefly, and completely.

4. The challenger chooses one of the volunteers to be the *foil*.

5. The foil states his objections to the challenger's position without interruption.

6. The challenger then asks questions, reflects feelings, and attempts to clarify the foil's position. This can be done by checking his understanding of what the foil said by restating it and asking if that is what the foil meant.

7. The foil must answer all of the challenger's questions as honestly as he can. He may not answer a question with a question. He may not shift the focus of the question even if he sees that answering the question gets him in a corner.

8. The challenger then has a chance to defend his position without interruption by the foil.

9. The foil now does what the challenger did as stated in the sixth and seventh paragraphs in this section on Procedures.

10. All of these steps may be repeated any number of times until either the challenger or foil calls it quits. This can be done only at the end of a round.

11. *Rating the Game.* A good challenge is one in which both players (*a*) understand each other's position better, (*b*) are more accepting of each other's position, and (*c*) have modified and clarified their own positions.

1. To what extent have you understood your opponent's position better?

    a. not at all   *b.* a little better   *c.* much better

2. To what extent do you accept your opponent's position more?

    a. not at all   *b.* a little more   *c.* much more

3. To what extent have you clarified and changed your own position?

    a. not at all   *b.* a little bit   *c.* a great deal

The total score in the game is the sum of the scores of both players.

12. If the challenger and the group wish, the confrontation may be repeated with another foil.

Note: Some drawing-out questions are:

1. How did you reach your conclusion?
2. Why do you feel that way?
3. What experiences have you had with this problem?
4. What evidence do you have for . . . ?

CONFLICTS OF EMOTION AND THOUGHT
A Variant of the Challenge Game

Conflict often arises because the same word, the same activity, the same request arouses opposed feelings and meanings in different people. Like the Reflection Game for Resolving Conflict, this game helps bring these differences of meaning and feeling out into the open, and makes accommodation more possible.

Rules and Procedures

1. Two people who have been in conflict about an issue in which feelings are involved, decide to play the game.

2. It is preferable for them to try to get a third party, whom they both trust, and who, if possible, is skilled in game play, to act as a referee and reserve facilitator. His function will be to enforce the rules and on occasion to draw out one or the other of the two participants concerning his feelings.

3. One volunteers to state his or her feelings first.

4. The other draws out the focus concerning his feelings. He asks questions in order to get an understanding of the totality of the feelings involved.

5. When both are convinced that they have an understanding of the feelings, roles are reversed. The process of reversal may take place a number of times. After the second reversal, the focus should begin to explore ways in which the feelings of both parties may be accommodated.

6. Use the Rule of Negative Feedback: Do not say what the other person is, that is, do not name-call or pigeonhole. Say how you feel toward his behavior. This mode of expressing negative feeling is much more likely to meet with positive results. Say, "When you do that, I feel caged in," rather than, "You are a dictator" or "jailer." The former kind of statement leads to a discussion of behavior, while the latter kind of statement usually results in anger and name-calling.

THE PREJUDICE GAME

We all see the world in terms of our past experiences. We tend to see men in terms of our fathers, and women in terms of our mothers. Our preconceptions of blacks, whites, Jews, and Christians depend upon our experiences and what we have heard. We all prejudge, depending on our past. But the error in our prejudgments is greater, the less we have experienced, and the less reliable is our source of information.

In the Prejudice Game, we will confront our prejudice toward another person.

Procedures

1. A group decides to play the game. It can be used with any size group within which there are differences around which prejudice may develop.

2. The group selects a difference among its members around which some prejudice may exist, i.e., differences of sex, age, race, background, profession, or person.

3. The total group is broken into pairs containing one member from each of the two subgroups. Those left over may join a pair as observers.

4. One person in the pair goes first. He states his beliefs about the group to which the other member belongs. The other draws him out. The other then states his opinion of his own group, and is drawn out.

5. The process is critiqued.

6. The roles are exchanged, and steps 1 to 5 are repeated.

Suppose prejudice concerning sex difference was being confronted. If in the first round the man gave his opinion of women, then, in exchange of roles, the woman would give her opinion of men to start the round.

REFLECTION GAME FOR CONFLICT

Game 1

Voting Questions (for introduction to voting questions, see Compliment Game, page 5):

Have you ever gotten into a relationship in which both you and the other person felt that you could not make yourselves understood no matter how hard you tried?

Have you ever found that in these circumstances, bringing up the subject, instead of leading to more understanding, led to more conflict? Less understanding? Withdrawal? Confusion?

This form of the Reflection Game is designed to help this kind of situation. (The basic form of the Reflection Game is in Chapter 1.)

PROCEDURES

1. Two people who are in conflict get together to play the game.

2. It is helpful if a third person who knows the rules is present to act as a referee. He helps to enforce the rules and keeps the process going.

3. The two players take turns being focus and facilitator.

4. A turn, at the minimum, will consist of several exchanges and may last as long as one or two hours.

5. The focus will make a statement as clearly and as honestly as he can.

6. The facilitator will try to reflect it (not interpret it) to the satisfaction of the focus.

7. If the focus is satisfied, he may make another statement. If not, he will help the facilitator repeat his reflection until he can do it without distortions.

Note: You might well shift to the use of this game when the situation suddenly calls for it, even though you have started a session using one of the other games. When the conflict has been reduced, you can return to the game with which you started if the players so choose.

Game 2

Rules and procedures are the same as in Game 1 with this modification:

Rule 8. The facilitator may reflect or draw out the focus.

Suggestion: It is better to reflect when the focus is excited; better to draw out when he has come down.

Game 3

Game 3 can be played when both parties to the conflict are calm and improvement in the relationship has begun.

Rules and procedures are the same as in Games 1 and 2, with this modification:

Rule 9. Both parties to the conflict agree to answer all questions asked as honestly and as directly as possible. Do not answer a question with a question.

The Reflection Game for Conflict: Some Expected Outcomes and Problems

One of the ways a person maintains his position in an argument is to not listen, to block, to destroy, to deny, or to reinterpret contrary positions. In this game you will find that the things one most hates to hear are hardest to repeat. This is because it is practically impossible to repeat something without hearing it. It is the very sentences, ideas, or feelings that we have most trouble in repeating that are crucial and must be faced if the conflict is to be resolved.

Here is both the value and the difficulty of the game. You will find it very hard to follow the game rules when it comes to ideas and feelings that are in basic conflict. You may find more than just reluctance or difficulty in repeating your opponent's position on crucial issues; sometimes it will seem impossible just to remember the words. Sometimes you may start a sentence and forget it before you finish, even if ordinarily you have an excellent memory. But if you win the struggle just to repeat accurately what the other person is saying, closed and seemingly insoluble problems become open and soluble again.

GAMES FOR GAINING STRENGTH IN CONFRONTING CONFLICT AND THREAT

Voting Questions

Have you ever collapsed when someone insulted you, ignored you, or seemed bored and uninterested in what you said?

In such circumstances, has it been difficult to answer appropriately, so that you felt defeated and misunderstood?

Have you ever felt depressed and anxious because of an insult or a remark?

Have you ever gotten so mad at a remark or a snub that you said or did destructive things, which you deeply regretted but found difficult or impossible to undo?

Have you ever found that you could not try to understand another's point of view, solve a problem, approach a difficulty, say, do, or discover what was right because you were too upset by something somebody said or did?

In this series of games you will learn to maintain your spirit in the face of insult or difficulty, so that you will be able to persist more happily in solving problems and in carrying through things you commit yourself to.

Game 1

Maintaining a mood, a feeling, a plan, an opinion, a course of action in the face of someone's negative remarks or feelings.

Introduction: Does it ever happen that you are happy about something and someone makes a negative remark and you lose your enthusiasm and joy in it? Does this happen even when the remark is not true or justified?

In this game you will learn to maintain your good feeling in the face of negative statements.

PROCEDURES

1. A group convenes to play the game. If it is a large group, it may be best to break into smaller groups of threes or fours.

2. Each person thinks of something that he is proud of or feels justifiably good about.

3. One person volunteers to be focus. The focus thinks about his good feeling, examines the basis of it, and attempts to hold it firmly in mind. He tells his good feeling to the group. The other members of the group make remarks attempting to undercut the good feeling while the focus attempts to maintain his good feeling despite what is said.

4. (Optional: May be used when the group has developed skill in maintaining a feeling resolution or idea in the face of attack.) The focus draws out and explores the reasons for the other person's negative feelings, and explains to the other person the grounds for his pride. In doing this, he maintains his good feeling concerning the subject.

5. After each round, the group explores with the focus the degree of his success in maintaining his good feeling.

6. Steps 1 to 5 are repeated with another focus.

Game 2

Admitting an error, a weakness, a problem, or a defeat without feeling that one is an inadequate person.

Do you ever feel inadequate, stupid, depressed when you find that you have made a mistake or done something wrong?

Have you ever lied to yourself and/or others concerning a mistake, problem, or difficulty?

Have you ever refused to admit a problem, difficulty, or mistake, and suffered afterward?

Are there any areas or situations that you avoid because you did poorly in them and cannot face the fact?

Introduction: Because you have all had the experience of being attacked or torn down for errors and weaknesses, you may tend to feel that you are no good when you make an error or betray a weakness.

This makes many of you avoid admitting or thinking about errors, which makes it hard to correct mistakes and grow.

Keeping this attitude limits or stifles growth.

In this game you will learn to admit mistakes and weaknesses without feeling inadequate or worthless.

You will learn to take pride in facing errors and correcting them, rather than ignoring them and forgetting them.

1. A group convenes to play the game. If it is a large group, it may be best to break into small groups of threes and fours.

2. Each player thinks of some error or mistake he has made. Think of the feelings of depression and inadequacy that the thought of the error provokes as invalid. Concentrate on feeling proud for facing the error and planning to do something about it if possible.

3. One player volunteers to be focus. He tells the group his mistake and relates his success or failure in feeling proud about facing the error.

4. The group helps the focus explore his experience in facing the error.

5. After the focus is finished, steps 1 through 4 are repeated with a new focus.

ROUND 2

The same as Round 1, but this time try to pick errors or failings that are more serious and have made you feel bad.

ROUND 3

Steps 1 through 3 are the same as in Rounds 1 and 2.

4. The group members attack and tear down the focus for his mistake. The focus concentrates on feeling good because he faced the error despite the attack.

5. After a few minutes of attack, the group explores how the focus handled the experience of admitting an error and being attacked.

6. Steps 1 to 6 are repeated with a new focus.

ROUND 4
(To be played with people who know each other)

Step 1 is the same as in other rounds.

2. One person volunteers to be focus.

3. The other members of the group think of some error or fault in the focus.

4. One by one the members tell the focus a fault. The focus draws them out and clarifies his position regarding the fault. During this time he concentrates on feeling worthwhile despite the fault or error.

5. Steps 1 to 4 are repeated with each focus.

Game 3

For gaining strength where needs are at stake.

SOME VOTING QUESTIONS

Have you ever wished that everybody loved you or thought you great?

Have you ever feared that nobody cared for you or appreciated you?

Have you ever used the reaction of one person or one event as a test to decide between your wishes and your fears?

Introduction: Frequently you may feel vulnerable and weak because you take the response of the other, or your success in a situation, as a test case to decide whether you are lovable and capable.

Examples of using the response of another as a self-test:

"I cannot live without Mary."

"If my good friend, John, cannot understand me, nobody can. I must be crazy."

An example of using a situation as a self-test:

"I can't understand this problem in algebra. I am no good in algebra. I better drop the subject."

If you use situations as a test of self-worth and you pass the test, you are likely to create another test situation for yourself, and place yourself in the same vulnerable, fearful, dependent position. If you fail the test, you probably feel depressed. Making a person's reaction to you, or your success or failure in a situation, symbolic of your worthiness as a human being, burdens you with a tremendous weight of anxiety and fear without giving any lasting satisfaction.

ROUND 1

In Round 1 you will practice getting the strength to face possible rejection or failure by remembering that no single situation or person is a test of what you are.

PROCEDURES

1. A group convenes to play the game. If it is a large group, it may be better to break into smaller groups of threes or fours.

2. Think of situations in which you took the response of another or your success or failure in a situation as a test of your self-worth.

3. As a player, now reconsider the situation. Consider what else your self-worth may depend upon. Try to get clearly in mind a basis of self-worth independent of that situation or person.

4. One person volunteers to be focus. As focus, he describes the situation to the group.

5. The group then draws the focus out concerning the situation, why he made it a test of himself, and how he might have approached the situation without making it a test of himself.

6. Steps 1 to 5 are repeated with a new focus.

ROUND 2

The same as Round 1, only instead of drawing-out in Step 5, the situation is role-played with the focus trying to feel that his self-worth was not at stake in the situation.

Game 4

Gaining strength when faced with an important issue.

Have you ever been anxious in taking an important test?

Has this anxiety ever led you to do more poorly than you ordinarily would have?

Have you ever been anxious in meeting somebody important?

Have you ever been anxious in applying for a job?

Introduction: In important situations, you may often freeze, appease, block because it seems as if your whole life depends on the outcome. You may have a feeling that you cannot risk or consider failure.

This may lead you to appease, to block out your own negative feelings, and ultimately to experience the failure you fear. Such painful defeats may lead you to avoid risking or asking for things that you really want.

In this game you will gain strength in facing such situations by considering what is the worst thing that could happen, and preparing for it.

PROCEDURES

1. A group convenes to play the game. If it is a large group, it may be best to break into smaller groups of threes and fours.

2. Think of situations in the past, or better, those that may be coming up in the future in which something important is at stake, and in which you feel fearful of being weak.

3. Consider carefully what could be the worst that can happen. Decide how you would handle this worst alternative. Do this without giving up or lessening your motivation to succeed in any way.

4. One person volunteers to be focus. He describes the situation. He then chooses someone to role-play it with him.

5. While role playing, the focus aims to succeed, but keeps in mind the fact that he will not be destroyed if he fails.

6. The process is critiqued with the group exploring how the focus felt during the role playing. Where needed, the role play process may be done several times.

7. Steps 1 to 6 are repeated with a new focus.

THE SOCRATIC GAME

Introduction and Objectives

Which would you rather have: power, wealth, status, truth, friendship, acclaim? Choose only one.

In playing the Socratic game, you choose the search for truth above all else. Remember, Socrates chose death because he would not compromise with truth. The agreement to face the possibility of self-deception is a painful thing. The object of the game is to confront your inconsistencies and self-deceptions no matter how painful that may be, for the sake of truth.

Do not play this game unless you and your partner feel strong and secure, are willing to go into sensitive areas, and can accept unpleasant and painful truths.

The Socratic game is based on the premise that no matter how high the price of truth, the price of error is higher. The Socratic method is the first Reality Game.

The Socratic method is seen by many as a model of good teaching—a way of clarifying thinking, revealing contradictions, and arriving at truth.

Most people who have read the works of Plato have attempted to use the method of Socrates on their friends. Some have tried it on their classes. But few have really succeeded. Though Socrates is known as the greatest of all teachers, his method is seldom adequately used.

It is my contention that the game theory can not only enable us to understand why the method of Socrates is so difficult to apply successfully, but can show us how to apply it. Basically the failure to carry on successful Socratic dialogues arises from failure to apprehend the true nature of the dialogue. We tend to see the success of the Platonic dialogues as dependent on the skill of Socrates. We fantasy that if we are only as skillful as he, we can apply his method. But such is not the case. In actual fact, the dialogue constituted a game with rules understood by both the questioner, "Socrates," and the "answerer," whoever he may have been. The proof of this contention is best approached indirectly by examining why our attempts to "play" Socrates fail.

We often fail to imitate Socrates in that Socrates stayed within the system of beliefs of his answerer. He let the dialogue follow the answers given and did not attempt to impose opinions of his own. However, though we may have avoided this simple and elementary failure, we may still have failed to recreate a Socratic dialogue.

The failure to apply the Socratic method successfully often rests not on the one who tries it, but on the person he tries it on. The person who is questioned may refuse to answer. He may stop the dialogue, or he may turn the tables and answer a question with a question. If any of these things happen, the process of exploration comes to an end or at least its direction becomes scattered and confused.

When the questioner (Socrates) is backed with the authority of a teacher, an employer, a lawyer, or a judge, the answerer cannot stop the dialogue or turn the tables, but he has other options. He can lie, be evasive, or be ambiguous in his responses. So while the dialogue continues, it gets nowhere.

The present-day incapacity to apply the Socratic method springs from the one-sided nature of the attempt. The Socratic method was successful originally because both parties to the dialogue followed a set of rules. In imitating Socrates, we try to recreate the dialogue without paying any attention to the role of the person being questioned by Socrates. If the person cast in that role doesn't wish to play or can't, a Socratic-type dialogue can no more take place than a chess game between one skilled player and an opponent completely ignorant of the rules.

The Platonic dialogue can be successfully carried out only when its game structure is recognized implicitly, or better explicitly. By this I mean when both the questioner and the answerer consent to play and both accept the rules of the game.

Procedures

1. The game is introduced to clarify an issue.

2. Two people volunteer to play and agree who will be questioner and who answerer.

3. The questioner must accept the answers of the answerer.

4. His questions may try to ascertain the opinions, beliefs, and theories of the answerer.

5. The questioner may present his own point of view in question form only as long as it meets with the agreement of the answerer.

6. The questioner may ask questions that point to contradictions between several answers the other had given.

7. The answerer agrees to follow the dialogue where it will go.

8. The answerer answers as honestly and truthfully as he can.

9. The answerer does not attempt to reverse roles and ask questions unless it is with the formal consent of the questioner.

10. Name-calling and insults are out by both sides.

11. When the rules are violated, the audience expresses disapproval.

12. The whole dialogue is evaluated afterward by the group.

13. Do not show nonacceptance of a response by repeating the questions, by mocking the answer, by showing a mock kind of surprise, that is, "Do you really think that? How interesting," etc.

The Socratic Game as a Lesson in Interaction

The Socratic Game succeeds in recreating Platonic-type dialogues while the attempt to play Socrates without the consent of the other fails, because the game strategy recognizes that all successful interplay between people requires skill and discipline on both sides.

We would laugh at a person who tried to start a chess game with a nonplayer without explaining the rules and the objectives of the game, or even knowing that a game was being played. It did not seem quite so laughable to try to start a Socratic dialogue with another person without explaining the rules or objectives of that game.

But would we laugh at all the one-sided attempts to impose relationships that need both cooperation and skill on both sides? Would we laugh at the teacher who one-sidedly tries to impose the learning game, or at the doctor who wishes his patient to get well but does not explain the hows or the whys, or the therapist who is opposed to his patient learning about therapy.

The problem is that most of our paired relationships are one-sided. Teachers, therapists, doctors, lawyers, husbands, wives, parents, have books written for them concerning what they can do in a one-sided way about a relationship. The one-sidedness of what should be a two-sided relationship is what makes relating more and more difficult and less and less satisfying. What is proposed in the game strategy is to make contracts that will define an agreement concerning all roles in a relationship, as we have done in the Socratic and other games.

THE PROBLEM-CONFLICT RESOLUTION GAME

See Reflection Game for resolving conflicts for a simpler version, page 78.

Voting Questions

Have you ever entered into a conflict and been sorry?

Have you ever avoided conflict and felt depressed? Angry? Trapped?

How many have surrendered to avoid conflict, and felt small, unworthy, or cowardly as a result?

How many have won a conflict and felt guilty or isolated?

Most conflicts with people are fought within the norms of our society, which are too often destructive. The object seems to be to tear down your opponent, to frighten him, to create guilt, to manipulate, to demean, till the opponent surrenders to avoid the pain.

Such methods result in tension, confusion, loss of relationships, buried antagonisms, manipulations, and secret revenge. This is why people avoid confronting differences that need to be confronted. The standard means for conflict resolution in our culture are too painful and unrewarding.

In the Problem-Conflict Resolution Game, you agree to play by a different set of rules. You agree not to attempt to hurt, punish, demean, degrade, or manipulate the other person. You agree to try to understand the other person, to help the other understand you. You agree to attempt to work out an accommodation based on mutual respect for each other's thinking and feeling.

Objectives

1. To help people to confront differences in such a way as to strengthen relationships rather than weaken them.

2. To increase understanding and mutual respect between people who have differences.

3. To help resolve and work through conflict in a manner that is constructive for all parties.

4. To increase conflict resolution skills so as to be able to prevent others from winning a conflict by tearing down, demeaning, or manipulating—without replying in kind; so that despite the lack of conflict resolution skills in one's opposite, the result will be increased understanding, a better relationship, and some degree of accommodation.

Forms of the Game

The game may be played in two forms:

Role Play—The game can be played with two people role-playing a conflict situation in which both are committed to use the conflict resolution skills. A third person acts as observer and helps critique the process.

Actual Use in Conflict Resolution—The game may be played by two people faced by a real conflict or problem who agree to try to use the conflict resolution skills. Here, also, it is helpful to have an observer who critiques the process and helps the players abide by the rules.

Convening the Game

ROLE PLAYING

1. Three people convene to play the game. If there is a larger group, it may be broken down into three's.

2. One volunteers to play a problem situation that he has faced. He describes the conflict and the character of his antagonist. He then chooses one of the other players to be his opposite.

ACTUAL USE IN CONFLICT RESOLUTION

In playing to resolve a problem, the two players both use problem resolution skills. Where possible, they try to get a third person who knows the skills to help remind them of the rules and skills.

Sequence in Problem Resolution

These skills are the same for all forms of the game. They are to be used by both players as agreed.

Definition: The person expressing himself is called the focus. His opposite, the person who is primarily listening, drawing out, and clarifying, is called the facilitator. These roles periodically reverse themselves in the course of the game.

STEP 1—THE POSITION STATEMENT

If you are focus, be sure that you state your position as your own, and not as some absolute. You can do this by using any one of the following beginnings: "As I see it. . . . My feeling is. . . . From my point of view . . . ," etc.

Your position statement will be most effective if your tone is calm, firm, and warm. A position statement includes two things, feelings and thoughts.

Feelings include: emotions, needs, and objectives or wishes.

Thoughts include: (a) present view of the situation and (b) background or point of view.

(Making a full Position Statement is a little more complicated and takes considerable skill. This skill can be learned by use of the Position Statement Game, which can be found in Chapter 1.)

STEP 2—AFTER THE FOCUS HAS MADE SOME STATEMENT OF HOW HE THINKS OR FEELS, THE FACILITATOR DRAWS HIM OUT CONCERNING HIS POSITION

In drawing out:

1. Ask questions that help the other person expand on what he said.

2. Ask questions that help get at some essentials that the other person has left out.

3. Try to get an understanding of his emotions, his thinking, his needs or objectives, his point of view on the particular problem.

4. Paraphrase when necessary, to check your understanding of what was said.

5. Ask questions designed to clarify the thinking, feeling, objectives, or promises of your partner.

STEP 3—THE UNDERSTANDING RESPONSE

After you as facilitator understand the other person's position, make a statement communicating your understanding. Make clear that it is your current understanding, and not necessarily the final truth about his position. You can do this by starting with one of the following: "As I understand what you are saying. . . . What I hear is. . . . It seems to me that you are saying . . . ," etc.

The understanding statement should communicate an understanding of all the other person's relevant feelings, and relevant reasoning. The statement should be clear, as short as possible, warm, and empathic.

An understanding statement is often sufficient to help resolve a problem or conflict. It helps a person to feel less alone, and to grasp his own thinking and feeling so that he is less apt to go around in circles.

Usually after an understanding response, the other person will ask some questions or make statements to help tie up some loose ends concerning what he said and your understanding of it.

Use of the Understanding Response when the focus is excited, loud, or repetitious:

People are often loud, excited, and repetitious when they feel that they are not being listened to or understood. At such a time, frequent brief understanding responses may help calm them down and move the communication process forward. It does this by convincing the person that he is in fact being heard, making it unnecessary for him to shout or repeat himself.

Sometimes an understanding response triggers a new flow of ideas in the focus, in which case the facilitator may listen and draw out, then give a new understanding response.

(Learning how to give understanding responses is valuable in many situations. To learn how to do this more skillfully and fully, see the Understanding Response Game in Chapter 1.)

STEP 4—REVERSAL OF ROLES

When the focus feels that he has been understood, the roles are reversed. The former facilitator becomes the new focus and states his position. The former focus becomes the new facilitator and steps 1 to 3 are repeated with the new roles.

STEP 5—SEARCH FOR RESOLUTION

After both positions have been clearly stated and explored, try to find a solution to the conflict or problem that will be consistent with the thinking, feeling, needs, and objectives of both. That is, the problem now is to find a mutually acceptable alternative.

At this point the communication pattern may not be in the form of drawing-out, position statements, or understanding responses, but will take the form of a keying-in response, which is briefer, but has the qualities of all three.

The keying-in response is a clarification, an addition, a modification of the previous statement, that tends to build a common solution which is sensitive to the feelings and objectives of all.

At this point, the focus may shift back and forth rapidly. (See "Keying-in Game" under Creativity Unit.)

Order and Length of Steps Not Fixed

In general, understanding response should end the process of drawing-out and precede a new position statement with role reversal. Drawing-out may be short or long, depending upon whether the initial response was complete, clear, consistent, and well-organized; or incomplete, contradictory, and confused.

When mutual understanding and rapport have been achieved, and the points of view are coalescing into a common viewpoint, the *keying-in response* may be given; mixed with occasional drawing-out, paraphrasing checks, abbreviated understanding, or position statement responses. (For "Keying-in" response and the closely related "Pulling-together" response, see the Creativity games.)

Critique the process. This should include the following:

1. An exploration by each of the players of how he felt during the process.

2. A statement by the observer of what he saw happening.

3. A discussion by all three players of how the skills were used and how they might be improved.

See also, on Conflict.

1. *Pulling-together and Keying-in: Creativity Unit.* These games are very helpful in developing a unified plan among a number of participants based on the areas of agreement.

2. *Cross Groups.* Cross grouping is helpful in healing communication gaps and conflicts that develop between subgroups in an organization.

3. *Large Group Participant Meeting.* Helpful in planning and carrying out any large group meetings in which members have conflicting feelings.

4. *Alter Ego Game.* Helpful in getting a deeper, more empathic view concerning oneself or the other in a conflict situation.

5. *Dealing with Various Modes of Behavior.* Helps a person acquire sensitivity to his own emotional state or that of another person when acting in a conflict situation.

6. *Helping Professions: Resolving Conflicts and Overcoming Barriers.* Provides some way of resolving problems within and between groups.

7. *Position Statement.* The position statement helps one be clear, precise, direct, and nonmanipulative in discussion. It thus helps avoid conflict. It also teaches one of the essential skills of the Problem Conflict Resolution Game.

8. *Understanding Response.* The understanding response helps one convey an empathic understanding to the other person. This often smoothes the way to conflict resolution. It is also an essential skill in the Problem Conflict Resolution Game.

CHAPTER 4

Task-Oriented Games

The task-oriented games address themselves to a variety of problems related to group planning, group decision-making, group production, leadership, and followership. At the left is a list of problems and issues, on the right some games dealing with them.

PROBLEMS AND ISSUES	GAMES
1. Needs assessment in planning, group decision-making.	1. Focus Game for Planning
2. Group and individual creativity. Stimulation in thinking of ideas.	2. Games for Creativity: *a.* Sharing New Ideas *b.* Freeing Thought *c.* Relevant Creativity *d.* Brainstorming *e.* Pulling-together Game *f.* Keying-in Game
3. Unification and integration of ideas or plans. These games also important in last steps of conflict resolution.	3. Games for Creativity *a.* Pulling-together Game *b.* Keying-in Game
4. Division of labor in planning and production.	4. Production Focus Game
5. Problems, issues, feelings and skills involved in leading, following, and supporting, in relation to action.	5. Obedience Game

6. Games for use in a variety of teaching situations.

6. Teaching Games
   a. Discussion Game
   b. Teacher Focus Game
   c. Expert Focus Game
   d. Positive Focus Game for Discussions of Subject Matter
   e. Group Learning Game
   f. Positive Focus Game for Young Children

USING THE DRAWING-OUT GAME OR POSITIVE FOCUS GAME FOR PAIRED OR GROUP PLANNING

Conflicts often arise in families or between two closely related people because of a lack of joint planning. In such cases, individuals see their needs or goals as opposed, with no way of compromising or integrating them. This activity, with the use of the focus or paired interaction games, enables two people or a group to integrate their goals as well as possible.

Procedures

1. Each person makes a list of his needs, and ranks them in order of importance.

2. These needs are discussed by use of the drawing-out game.

3. Both lists are combined and each person ranks the needs from the point of view of what is best for the total group.

4. Each person discusses his ranking by use of the Drawing-out Game or Focus Game. Then the ranking of both is averaged. This sheet with the averaged ranks is to be used in the next activity.

5. Each person makes a list of activities, routines, plans of action that will meet the needs of all involved, and ranks them from best to worst.

6. The lists are discussed, each taking a turn being focus.

7. The combined lists are then ranked and discussed, with the rankings averaged. This list with the average rankings is to be used in the next activity.

8. Each person makes a list of principles for choosing which items on the list to act on. The principles are ranked in order of importance. They are then discussed, using one of the game forms. A combined list is then made, ranked, discussed, and the final individual ranks averaged.

9. Each person makes a plan, using all the data accumulated so far. The plans should be designed to meet the needs of everyone involved, not just the person making them. The plans are then discussed. If agreement is not reached through the discussion, and more than two individuals are involved, the plans are voted on, using an elimination procedure. If

two individuals are involved, use the Challenge Game or Conflict Resolution Game until the points of view become close enough so that their difference is insignificant.

See also the Transcendental Game for Planning, p. 203, for a more advanced form of integration in planning.

GAMES FOR CREATIVITY

The first games in this series are designed to help free our imagination and creative intelligence. In the later games, we will practice not only originating, but pulling together and elaborating ideas.

SOME VOTING QUESTIONS

Have you ever felt in a rut?

Have you ever felt embarrassed about sharing new or crazy ideas?

Have you ever ignored your thinking because you felt it was too far out?

Have you ever felt tired of doing the same old things or thinking the same old thoughts?

Do you enjoy letting your imagination and mind run wild?

Game 1
Sharing New Ideas

PURPOSE

In this game you will let your mind and imagination run free.

The purpose is to have fun. The game will also stretch and free the creative imagination.

PROCEDURES

1. A group convenes to play. If it is a large group, it is best to break into smaller groups of between three and eight members.

2. One player volunteers to start. He tells the group an unusual imaginative idea, plan, perception, or way of doing things. The other group members draw him out briefly without being critical or judgmental. A time limit between five and fifteen minutes should be allowed per turn.

3. Other players volunteer until each player has had a turn.

4. The process is critiqued with a general sharing of how the players felt in both giving ideas and listening.

5. After the process has been critiqued, the game may go another round with steps 1 to 4 repeated.

Game 2
Freeing Thought

PURPOSE

Developing a quickness of response and thought.

VOTING QUESTIONS

Have you ever been stuck and unable to continue because you could not think of what to do?

Have you ever been caught with nothing to say?

Have you ever been so critical of your own thoughts that you could not get started?

We are often prevented from being creative or solving problems because our critical faculty blocks the flow of our creative thought. At such times we cannot get our thoughts out, so we cannot perfect them, evaluate them, or organize them. The result is that we are left with nothing.

In this game we will practice getting our thoughts out quickly by suspending our own critical judgment as well as that of others. After ideas are out, there is plenty of time to judge them and decide what to do with them.

PROCEDURES

1. A group convenes to play the game. A large group breaks into smaller groups of between three and eight players.

2. Seat yourselves in a circle.

3. The person closest to the window says the first thing that comes to his mind. The statement should be short. It may be a single word, at most a sentence or two.

4. Without pause, the person to his left says what comes to his mind. This need not be related to the first statement.

5. The process continues at high speed until at least three rounds have been completed.

6. (Optional) Pulling Together: Using some (not all) of the statements made in the three rounds, each player mentally tries to pull together a complete coherent pattern.

7. (Optional) Each player takes a turn giving his "pull together."

8. The process is critiqued with attention to the feelings of the players during the process.

Game 3
Relevant Creativity

PURPOSE

In Game 3 the abundance of creative thought is disciplined by the need for relevance.

PROCEDURES

The same as Game 2 with the following substitution for Step 4:

The Rule of Relevance: After the first person has spoken, each statement must be relevant to something a previous speaker has said. The relevance may be of any kind—an association, a contrast, an alternative, a continuation, etc. If the relevance is not obvious, show the connection verbally.

Game 4
Brainstorming

PURPOSE

In Game 4 we use free thought to produce a great many possible solutions to a problem. Some of these alternatives may then actually be used in solving the problem.

PROCEDURES

The rules and procedures are the same as those in Game 2, except that all statements should relate to the brainstorm task.

BRAINSTORMING DEFINED

In brainstorming we may do any one of the following:

1. State all the possible solutions to a problem—practical, imaginative, scientific.

2. State all the uses of an object—practical, new, imaginative, fantastic, etc.

3. State all the consequences or implications of an action or a situation—immediate, long-range, probable, or improbable consequences or implications.

4. State all the possible causes or influences that may have given rise to a certain problem or situation. The causes or influences may be direct or remote, obvious or subtle.

PROCEDURES FOR CHOOSING A BRAINSTORMING ISSUE

A specific problem or issue for brainstorming may be presented by the game organizers or organizer.

Or a member of the group presents an issue or problem for brainstorming. Every subsequent player states his preference for an issue to be brainstormed, with sensitivity to the needs and feelings of all the players that preceded him. This process is continued in a clockwise manner until general agreement is reached.

Game 5
Pulling Together

VOTING QUESTIONS

Have you ever had so many ideas that you couldn't think of what to do?
Have you ever been in a group where so many ideas were produced that nothing could be done?

PURPOSE

In the "Pulling Together" Game you will learn to pull together a number of ideas into a unified whole.

APPLICABILITY

This skill is useful in group and individual planning or creative work. In group planning it serves not only to help build a unified plan, but also to help commit the planners to the carrying-out of their joint conception.

PROCEDURES

1. This game is best played when a group problem or project has been identified. It is therefore best for the organizers of the game to have some problem or project in mind before convening the group. However, if no problem or project has been identified, the problem or project may be identified as well as solved, using the pull-together response.

2. A group convenes to play the game. If it is a large group, it is best to break into subgroups of between three and fifteen members.

3. When the problem or issue has been identified, the first volunteer will state his solution to the problem.

4. Each subsequent player will state his solution or plan. In doing so,

make use of as many ideas of previous speakers as you can, giving credit to the individuals who thought of them.

5. But in the event that your plan is identical to that of a previous speaker, say so and pass. Similarly, if your plan differs from that of previous speakers in only one respect, say, "My plan is the same as X with the exception of Y." Do not repeat in detail the plan of previous speakers because this takes too much time.

6. This process is continued until a plan generally acceptable to all the players is arrived at.

Game 5B
Pulling Together Solitaire

Sometimes it is difficult to come to a decision. This is true when one is faced by too many needs, too many alternatives, too many possibilities. In such a situation, one often tends to polarize by presenting oneself with choices each of which tends to fulfill certain needs while denying others.

In "Pulling Together Solitaire" you learn to arrive at a solution that integrates your needs, objectives, feelings, assumptions, and thoughts.

WHEN USED

This game is best used when one is faced with the need to plan some action in which one is involved emotionally and intellectually.

PROCEDURES

1. Take four sheets of paper. Label one "feelings," one "needs and objectives," one "thoughts concerning the situation," and one "assumptions."

2. On the appropriate sheets, list your feelings, your needs, your objectives, your assumptions, and your thoughts concerning the situation or problem.

3. Rank the items going from the most meaningful to the least meaningful.

4. State the item of greatest importance to you.

5. Look at the next highest-ranking item. Insofar as it is consistent with the first item, make a statement including the first and second items. If the second item is consistent with the first, drop it.

6. Go down the list of items in the order of their rank. Add each one to your statement if it is consistent with those previously added.

7. The last statement will have pulled together into a single coherent whole as many of the elements of your first list as is possible.

8. Check over your statement. Is there anything that is inconsistent that should be left out? Check over your list. Is there anything that should be included that has been left out?

Game 6
Keying-in Game

PURPOSE

The Keying-in Game is designed to enable two people or a group to build together. It requires the ability to share, trust, and support each other, so that you may build and elaborate on each others' thoughts, feelings, ideas, and actions rather than negating or destroying them. In advanced play, "keying-in" may be done in terms of joint projects in living as well as working together.

PROCEDURES

1. At the beginning, the game is best played with between two and five players. If a larger group has convened to play, break up into smaller groups.

2. One person starts by stating a thought, feeling, or idea.

3. All the subsequent players elaborate, building on what has previously been said. They do this with sensitivity toward the feelings, thoughts, and intentions of the previous players. In addition, they are sensitive to the content and style of what has been previously said. They do not destroy the work of other players.

ALTERNATIVE MODES OF PLAY

The Keying-in Game may be played with the group writing a poem, telling a story, painting together, planning a project, improvising music, improvising a dance, etc.

Here the same rules apply: Elaborate, but do not destroy the work, mood, feeling, or style of the others.

Game 6B
Keying-in Solitaire

Can be used to create a unified work.

1. Perform the first act of creation.

2. Every subsequent act should be consistent with the mood, style, intentions of all the creative acts that went before.

1. Write the first line of a poem or story. Use the rule of keying-in and let the story or poem finish itself.

2. Play a phrase of music. Use the rule of keying-in to complete the composition.

3. Make a shape on a sheet of paper. Use the rule of keying-in to complete the picture.

THE PRODUCTION FOCUS GAME

Have you ever been in a group faced with completing a task? Has a conflict ever entered the group? Has there been insufficient time to discuss each point? Has the discussion sometimes wandered into unrelated areas? Have you felt that the group should return to the task, but were you uncertain as to how to bring attention to this fact? Often a group will shy away from completing a task because the members are unsure of how to proceed.

Objective

The objective of the game is to complete a task efficiently with all members feeling a satisfaction with the group product.

Procedures

1. A group of two to six persons agrees to play the game.

2. A task is introduced. This task can be an outside task or a group-chosen task.

3. The task is divided into parts with each group member responsible for planning a part.

4. Members then agree to complete their part of planning. Time limits may or may not be set.

5. The group reconvenes to critique each partial plan. Use the Rule of Product Critique (below).

6. Each member may then incorporate suggestions into his part of the plan.

7. The group again convenes and critiques the plan. Each member of the group has responsibility and makes the final decisions for his part of the completed plan.

8. The same procedure is then followed in carrying out the plan. Here each person is responsible for carrying out or coordinating some aspect of the plan. The group gives support, feedback, and criticism to the member. The member may use or may not use this help as he sees fit.

9. The process is critiqued. What things helped? hindered? What made you feel good? bad?

Rules

1. *The Rule of Problem Solving.* Solutions are to be arrived at on the basis of available evidence, a weighing of the advantages and disadvantages, rather than a reference to subjective feeling, opinion, or authority. Maintain an open mind and a willingness to hear all arguments. Avoid win/lose confrontations. Solutions are to be arrived at on the basis of complete understanding and consensual agreement. Avoid compromise solutions. Work for the best solution, which, in a sense, lets everyone "win."

2. *The Rule of Clarifying.* Whenever you are not clear about the focus person's meaning and/or feelings, communicate your present understanding in such a way as to check out his real meaning or feelings, or ask him a question that will help to clarify the situation. Try to develop further understanding.

3. *The Rule of Keying-in.* Constantly attempt to see and understand the focus person's point of view. Put yourself in his shoes. What does he feel? And why? Express your understanding of his position and feelings. State areas of agreement.

4. *The Rule of Identifying Alternatives.* During this period of game activity, the emphasis is on thinking of all possible alternatives, solutions, consequences, no matter how way-out they may seem. Do not express value judgments, either verbally or nonverbally. This is not the time to evaluate.

5. *The Rule of Product Critique.* The work of an individual has a style, a life, and an energy which reflect that person's essence. In giving advice and critiquing, people often reduce the product of another to a dull, uniform texture, like dishwater. Try to help the person find his style, sharpen his expression, reveal his own kind of glow, whether it be jewel-like, a steady warmth, or flashing.

6. *The Rule of General Facilitation.* Generally maintain and reflect in your game participation an attitude of facilitation—an attitude of helping others, including yourself, grow, learn, and relate more effectively.

THE OBEDIENCE GAME

Objectives

1. To learn how to be a better leader.
2. To learn how to be a better follower.

3. To get necessary things done quickly without hurting feelings, vying for leadership, and wasteful competition.

4. To learn to work under external discipline as well as self-discipline.

5. To help one identify and overcome authority problems.

Appropriate Occasions for Play

The Obedience Game may be played as a fun game at parties, for it permits each player to organize interesting experiences for the group, and it permits each player to participate in experiences that other players have organized.

The Obedience Game may be played in a family, social, or work group to coordinate and organize work that has to be done.

The Obedience Game may be used as a training game in schools or businesses to teach leadership, followership, and the ability to work under external discipline as well as self-discipline. In this connection it is useful in identifying and overcoming difficulties that individuals may have with authority.

Introducing the Obedience Game to a Group

The facilitator or person introducing the game reads the following out loud:

"I am going to ask you some questions. Raise your hand to the degree that the answer is true of you. For 'very true,' raise your hand very high. For 'very untrue,' lower your hand as far as it will go. For the rest, somewhere in between.

"How many of you have ever disliked school or teachers because you were told what to do?

"How many still dislike having to learn from somebody?

"How many still feel so rebellious about certain things that you have trouble concentrating on doing them even when you want to?

"Like putting certain things away?

"Like being on time?

"Like doing dishes?

"Like resting when sick?

"Spelling correctly?

"Not eating too much?

"Not eating too little?

"Not eating unhealthy foods?

"Not drinking?

"Not smoking?

"These questions point to the first objective of the game. In this game we learn to lead in such a way that we do not create resentment or rebellion, and we learn to obey others, which is sometimes necessary before we can obey ourselves. For example, sometimes we cannot carry out our plans because we rebel against the demands we make on ourselves.

"The following questions point to another objective of the game.

"Have you ever been in a group in which nothing could get done, because nobody would accept the leadership of anybody else?

"Has it ever happened that what was finally decided was a compromise that pleased no one, that lacked unity, style, or coherence?

"Has it ever happened that by the time your group decided to do something, it was too late to do it?

"The second purpose of the game is to provide means of coordinating activity in a group, without endless discussion and without establishing differences of rank or power."

Playing the Game

Each player should have a copy of this portion of the game. A facilitator introducing this game to a group may skip this portion and go on to rules and procedures.

Game Objectives Summarized

We often lack the self-discipline to do what we really want to do because we cannot obey ourselves. This happens because we often continue to rebel against ghosts. We have never learned self-discipline because we have never accepted the discipline of others graciously.

Groups often fail because everybody wishes to lead, but no one wishes to follow, or vice versa.

This game is designed to increase our skills in leadership, followership, discipline, and self-discipline. It is also helpful in identifying and overcoming problems with authority.

Rules and Procedures

1. A group gets together to play the game. The best size for beginning players is between two and five members. If a larger group has convened, they should split up into smaller groups before proceeding further.

2. Look over and discuss the critique sheets with suggestions for leaders and followers that follow this section.

3. Discuss the limitation you wish to put on the leader focus. Time limits and range of permissible activities should be clearly defined. Group objectives and activities may be defined generally or left to the discretion of the leader.

4. One volunteers to be the first focus leader. (See Rules and Critique Sheet for leader.)

5. The others obey him within the limitations set. (See Rules for Followers.)

6. When the time is up, the round is critiqued. This should include a discussion of the process and of the feelings of each group member during the process. This should be followed by an evaluation of leader and followers using the critique sheets. Problems or strong feelings that interfered either with leading or with following are important. Where these arise, they may form the basis of a subfocus.

7. Steps 1 to 6 are repeated with a new focus-leader until everyone has had a chance at being focus-leader.

Rules and Critique Sheet for Leader

This sheet serves the dual function of providing certain rules to the focus-leader and of serving as a leader evaluation sheet. For use in evaluation, mark where the leader falls on each continuum.

1. Be realistic concerning objectives, plans, and procedures. Do not ask anybody to do what they cannot or will not do.

Successful (leader) _____ Unsuccessful

2. Consider the strengths, weaknesses, desires, needs, and limitations of your followers.

Successful _____ Unsuccessful

3. Be polite, firm, courteous, and supportive.

Successful _____ Unsuccessful

4. Do things that are challenging, interesting, and, if possible, successful.

Successful _____ Unsuccessful

5. Consider all possibilities and get the advice of your followers in making decisions.

Successful _____ Unsuccessful

6. Make your decisions on what is best for the group, not what is easiest or most popular.

Successful _____ Unsuccessful

7. Be firm in your decisions, but change if they are really wrong.

Successful _____ Unsuccessful

8. Use encouragement and praise frequently, criticism sparingly.

Successful _____ Unsuccessful

9. Set an example of trying as hard as you can to fulfill group objectives.

Successful _____ Unsuccessful

Rules and Critique Sheet for Followers

For use in evaluation, mark where the follower falls on each continuum.

1. Be supportive of the leader and other group members.

Successful _____ Unsuccessful

2. Obey your leader in both spirit and words.

Successful _____ Unsuccessful

3. If you feel that your leader is making a mistake, talk to him privately. Whatever his decision, do not undermine him, or go along grudgingly, critically, or complainingly, but give him your full support.

Successful _____ Unsuccessful

4. If the going is hard, do your best without complaints or backbiting.

Successful _____ Unsuccessful

5. Only when absolutely necessary, or when there has been a serious violation of the spirit of the game, may you withdraw in the middle of a round.

Successful _____ Unsuccessful

TEACHING GAMES

In the following series we have a variety of games that can be used where teaching is needed. They may be used by teachers or anybody else engaged in a teaching role.

GAME	PURPOSE
1. Discussion Game	Focuses discussion and makes it more effective.
2. Teacher Focus Game	Helps a person improve his teaching skills. Helps a group make use of the special abilities of all its members.
3. Expert Focus Game	Permits a group to make use of an expert to fulfill their own needs.

4. Positive Focus Game for Discussions of subject matter

An example of how a Focus Game can be adopted to a particular subject area.

5. Group Learning Game

Describes how a group can learn through reading consensus on common problems.

6. Positive Focus Game for kindergarten and first and second grades

Describes how the Focus Game can be used with very young children.

The Discussion Game

Discussions frequently become fragmented, fractured, diffused, and shallow, with everyone speaking and no one listening. This happens for one or more of the following reasons:

1. There is frequently no clear decision as to what is being discussed. The process of determining what subject or aspect is to be discussed is carried on in the midst of the discussion, to the confusion of everybody.

2. The topic keeps on shifting from one issue to another with no thought even being looked at, explored, or developed.

3. People do not listen to each other. Statements are made without any relation to one another.

4. Where there is confrontation, focus is on defeating or changing each other's views rather than exploring, understanding, and exchanging points of view. This results in a musical crescendo with the themes being repeated with ever greater volume, but with no development, deepening, or elaboration.

OBJECTIVE OF THE GAME

The Discussion Game helps make discussion a way of exploring a topic in depth, communicating with and understanding others.

PROCEDURES

Deciding on Topic:

1. The topic may be assigned by the game leader or teacher. Assignment of the topic by a leader, however, rather than by choice of the group fails to give the group a common experience, which is helpful in developing a good discussion.

2. The group chooses a topic or subtopic to discuss in the following way:

   a. By whipping around a circle of people with each contributing an idea for discussion in brief. This can be done more than one time.

b. When most group members feel the list is long enough, the various ideas are voted on until a consensus is reached on which idea to discuss first. Before voting, one can go around the group with each person briefly stating the reason for his choice or choices. More than one idea can be discussed at once.

c. When consensus is reached, discussion begins.

RULES FOR DISCUSSION

1. A few minutes of silence should precede the discussion, while people relax.

2. Stick to the idea at hand. If others wander, bring them back to the subject agreed on.

3. Try to refer back to what has previously been said. It is best to address the particular person who made the original point to which your statement is related. Where possible, it is best to refer back to the last speaker.

4. Don't interrupt. Confirm, elaborate, and ask questions about things that have been previously stated.

5. Don't deny or give evidence against what has been previously stated.

6. Be sure you understand what each person says and feels about an idea. This can be done by asking questions and by restating one's opinion of what was said and felt, so that the other person can tell us if our understanding was right.

7. Do not bring up new aspects of the subject until older aspects are exhausted.

8. When a new aspect of the subject is brought up, it is best to relate it in some way to what has already been said.

The Teacher Focus Game

In most groups in which members are on an equal level, members avoid confronting differences of skill and status. Group members relate to one another on the basis of common feelings, ideas, feelings, attitudes, activities, and skills. The assertion of differences, uniqueness, special abilities or skills by any member is seen as a threat to group unity. It is frowned upon and punished by the other group members. The result is that the unique contributions that any individual can make to the group in terms of feelings, sensitivities, insight, knowledge, or skill is for the most part lost to the group.

Because the shared feelings, attitudes, skills, and knowledge that all members hold in common are simpler, more primitive, and less effective than those of any group member, most groups institute a kind of formal or informal leadership which introduces new ideas to the group and initiates the action that the group will take. Leadership permits the expression of the unique and highly developed qualities of at least a few individuals within the group. The individuality of the other group members remains repressed and they tend to become apathetic, conforming, or rebellious. The potential contribution of all of these apathetic, conforming, or rebellious group members is unfortunately lost to the group.

In the Teacher Focus Game, each individual is given a chance to make some unique contribution to the group process. The game also leads the group members to reevaluate the experiences, feelings, values, habits, and prejudices that prevent group members from accepting and confronting differences in perceptions, sensitivities, values, knowledge, and skills. The game will utilize growing through differences to promote growth. In the game, we practice growing through sharing, understanding, and mastery of differences.

If this way of relating, practiced within the game, were transferred to any working group, that group would be able to utilize the resources of all the individuals within it. Since the unique contributions of each individual would be received by the group instead of being punished and excluded, the individual growth of each group member would be stimulated instead of being discouraged by the group process. Groups in which individuals relate in this fashion are extremely rare in history. Where they have arisen spontaneously, they have been associated with a creative flowering in the arts, sciences, or religion.

OBJECTIVES OF THE GAME

The game is designed to enable individuals within a group to learn from each other to a maximum degree. This permits individual differences of feelings, sensitivities, intuition, thinking, knowledge, and skill within the group of players.

PROCEDURES

I. *A group of between four and fifteen people get together for the purpose of playing the game.*

II. *The group members discuss the following questions:*

1. *What do teachers do to block the learning process?*
2. *Why do teachers block the learning process?*

The following is the author's contribution to the discussion of these two questions. This may be read before, during, or after the group discussion, though it is preferable that the group have its discussion *prior* to the reading. If the members of the group wish, the passage need not be read at all.

1. The teacher often remembers how his teachers or parents scared, threatened, and humiliated him into learning. He tries to get his revenge by doing the same to his students. People don't like being threatened or humiliated into learning, so they either rebel against learning and refuse to learn, or submit and give an outer show of learning which they inwardly reject.

2. Because teachers have been made to feel inadequate or inferior, they will frequently attempt to make their students feel inadequate or inferior. They will do this by asking questions that the students can't answer or presenting problems that the students can't solve. They will rationalize this attempt to diminish their students by saying, "People learn from their mistakes and must be challenged." Unfortunately, people are discouraged by being made to feel inadequate; some withdraw and become apathetic, some become anxious and withdrawn, and some become angry and rebellious.

3. It seems to enhance the importance of the teacher's knowledge if students fail to understand it, or understand it with extreme difficulty. In order to make learning difficult and thus important, unnecessary and time-consuming tasks are assigned. The students are required to master unclear, trivial, or unnecessarily complicated ideas. Simple and trivial notions are made obscure and difficult by the use of meaningless jargon designed to make learning difficult. This makes some students feel inadequate, some feel indifferent, some feel angry, and some amused. It enhances the learning of no one.

4. Some teachers withhold the answer to questions in order to make the knowledge they impart seem important. They exact a price in humiliation for the knowledge they impart by asking questions designed to demonstrate the students' stupidity or ignorance in front of everyone. This is rationalized by asserting that they are trying to draw the student out. Most students refuse to pay this price and learn not to ask questions.

5. Some teachers enjoy being in the limelight. They enjoy asserting their thoughts, feelings, and attitudes. This makes them insensitive to the thoughts and feelings of the group members. They don't listen: they cut the student off and override him. Some students resent not being listened to, and get their revenge by not listening in return.

6. Some teachers express their need to be loved and dependent by becoming demanding, authoritarian, and controlling. Since love and attention do not come as free gifts, they attempt to use their authority to get what they need. They feel that they can force the students to meet their needs. This makes them insensitive to the needs, interests, desires, and limitations of their students. This insensitivity leads the student to become alienated from the teaching/learning situation.

III. *The group next discusses what the teacher can do to facilitate rather than block the learning of the group.*

Following are the author's contributions to this discussion. If the group wishes, they may be read before, during, or after the discussion. If group members prefer, they need not be read at all.

AUTHOR'S SUGGESTION FOR TEACHER

1. Make your students feel adequate about themselves. Do not try to prove that their ideas are wrong or stupid in order to get your ideas across. Do not attempt to motivate learning by proving your students' ignorance.

2. Present what you are teaching in such a way that it is understood. Check frequently by asking questions to make sure you are coming across. Provide an atmosphere in which the student is free to speak up immediately when he doesn't understand.

3. Permit students to integrate what is being presented by giving frequent opportunities to ask questions or present their thoughts, feelings, or perceptions.

4. Encourage your students to be creative by giving them an opportunity to present contrary, parallel, or related ideas, feelings, skills, etc.

5. In particular, be sure there is opportunity for group members to express their feelings of inadequacy, anger, or opposition. These feelings should be dealt with openly and in a way that doesn't lead to withdrawal, hidden resentment, embarrassment, or destructive opposition.

6. Do not assert superiority. Share your role with those who are willing and able to share it.

7. Be aware of your students' needs as well as your own.

8. Break into smaller groups to facilitate exchange and communication.

IV. *The group should next discuss why students are blocked in learning.*

The following is the author's contribution to this discussion. As before, the group may utilize the author's contribution if, when, and how it wishes.

1. We all depend upon others or need to depend upon others at various times in our lives. Since we are more dependent when we are very young, depending on others often makes us feel like children again. This may make us feel inadequate, angry, or both, by recalling the times when we were little and were pushed around with no power to defend ourselves. Recalling this makes us feel bad, so we avoid situations which make us feel dependent. Unfortunately, learning from others is one of these situations. As a consequence, we often avoid learning. But this unfortunately makes us mentally rigid and old before our time.

2. Students often avoid learning because learning may involve competing with and challenging their peers, which may cause anger.

3. Students often won't try to learn because they don't want to risk feeling inadequate.

4. When subject matter arouses strong emotions that the student has no opportunity to express, the student will often forget what is being said and think about his own feelings.

5. Often a student won't learn because it means asking a question that might expose him to ridicule.

6. Sometimes a student is angry at the teacher. If the anger is not directly dealt with, the student might withdraw or not learn out of revenge.

V. *The group discusses what the student should do to help unblock his learning.*

The following are the author's contribution to this discussion. Feel free to use it or not, as you wish.

RULES FOR THE STUDENT

1. Try to understand what the teacher is saying. Remember that learning from someone is not an admission of inferiority, nor is being temporarily dependent on the teacher the same as being a helpless child, though it may sometimes feel that way.

2. Be sure you understand everything that is being said. If not, ask questions and insist that they be answered.

3. If you are made to feel inadequate or angry, express your feelings and deal with them.

4. Express your positive feelings toward the teacher as well as toward other members of the group.

VI. *After the discussions, one member of the group volunteers for focus.*

This volunteer will teach something to the group, using the discussions as a guide. One or more people may volunteer as process observers. They will not participate until the end. They will try to understand what is going on during the teaching session.

Those that are neither focus nor process observers are the student group. They will try to act as ideal students, using the discussion as a guide.

VII. *When the teaching session is over, the process observers will talk about what they saw going on.* The focus teacher and the other group members may come into the discussion to clarify what they felt while the teaching process was going on. In this discussion, everyone should try to discover what facilitates and what blocks learning.

When the game is replayed, only procedures VII and VIII need be repeated.

VIII. *Coping with feelings.* Since coping with withdrawal, anger, feelings of inadequacy, dogmatism, and rebellion, as well as encouraging freedom, spontaneity, and creativity are part of the objectives of the Teacher Focus Game, it may be desirable to discuss these issues before playing other sessions of the game.

The author's contribution to the discussion follows. As before, his contribution may be used or not used as the group or individual players choose.

1. *Coping with withdrawal.* Withdrawal may reflect boredom, anger, or feelings of inadequacy. People usually withdraw for one of two reasons: (*a*) They feel that the expression of their own feelings would be destructive to others; or (*b*) they feel that others would destroy them if they expressed their feelings. Sometimes we are not even aware of the strong feelings hiding behind withdrawal. We discover that they are there when we are prevented from withdrawing and suddenly get angry or depressed.

To overcome withdrawal in oneself takes courage in the face of fear. One must risk all. Just try out a partial expression of your feelings.

Passive waiting is not enough to help a person get over withdrawal. One must actively approach and encourage the person to express the feelings he is hiding. Often it is important to persist even if the person gets angry, for if this anger remains unexpressed it functions as a prohibited area in the relationship. It is probable that relationships go sour because the failure to express or cope with anger leads to ever larger areas of withdrawal until there is nothing vital left within the relationship and it ends.

Divorce, "dropping-out," and breaking diplomatic relations are examples of this behavior.

2. *Coping with anger.* There are two ways of responding to anger that will quickly destroy a relationship or group. The worst thing possible is to withdraw in the face of anger. The pattern of withdrawing in the face of anger leads to the gradual constriction of the relationship of the group, leading to its dissolution. Submitting to the anger and doing what the angry person wants, even if we do not feel we should or want to, is almost as destructive. If we yield to anger out of fear, we ourselves become angry and eventually withdraw from the relationship.

It is far better to fight back than to withdraw or submit. In countering anger with anger, it is important that the counter anger not be so intense as to cause the first person to withdraw.

If one remembers that most people get angry when they are feeling inadequate themselves, more effective responses to anger may be found. Listening and accepting the anger without submitting to it and then offering help is perhaps the most effective response.

3. *Coping with inadequacy.* The three most frequent responses to

inadequacy vie with each other for effective destructiveness. The most frequent destructive way of responding to an expression of inadequacy is to deny it. "No, you weren't so bad. Yes, you can do it, just try." How can a person solve the problem of feeling more adequate, if simply posing the problem is prohibited?

Very similar is the response of offering help in such a way that the inadequacy is perpetuated. Like, "Let me do it for you." "Just don't worry, I'll take care of it." In more culturally stereotyped form it may come out, "Let me do that, it's a man's job. Women don't understand anything mechanical." Or, "Let me take care of that for you. A man just doesn't understand that." (Aside to herself: "They are like children.")

Even less relevant a response is the intellectualizing of the inadequacy. Instead of helping the person overcome the inadequacy, one intellectualizes about reasons, feelings, and causes. Demanding a creative solution from people who are feeling inadequate is a simple way to make them feel more inadequate.

Most helpful in overcoming inadequacy is showing the person what to do in a step-by-step fashion; having them practice and master it one step at a time.

It is also very important to give the person who is feeling inadequate a great deal of support and positive feedback while he is in the process of overcoming his inadequacy.

Caution: One should distinguish between feelings of inadequacy and simple ignorance. If a person simply does not know but feels confident about his ability to learn, he needs less support. Feelings of inadequacy arise when not knowing is coupled with fear or anxiety concerning one's ability to learn.

4. *Coping with dogmatism and rigidity.* When you have mastered your anxieties, fears, and inadequacy by learning one way of doing something, you hang on to it like a drowning man. This is dogmatism and rigidity. You may more easily overcome dogmatism in yourself by remembering that you do not have to give up the way you are used to in order to try something new.

In helping another person to overcome dogmatism, it is most effective not to demand that they give up the ways they are used to, but to suggest that they try to consider other ways as well. An intellectual attack on a dogmatic way of thinking or acting is effective if one tries to listen and understand as well as argue. Personal attack or withdrawal only strengthen dogmatism.

5. *Coping with defensiveness and rebellion.* It is much better to rebel than to submit against our better judgment and our feelings of what is right. Similarly, it is much better to be defensive than to pretend to accept criticism, which in actual fact is ignored or rejected or acted upon contrary to our better judgment. If we are able, it is better to give

balanced criticism than to rebel, and to give objective consideration to criticism directed against us than to become defensive.

Similarly, in dealing with the rebellion or passionate criticism of others, it is better to be defensive or counterattack, than to ignore the criticism. In helping a person move from a rebellious, overly critical position or a defensive position to one of constructive criticism and cooperation, the most effective way is to consider thoughtfully, openly, and honestly what is being said.

6. *Coping with creativity.* Concerning our own creative ideas, we do best not to show them to others who will be overly critical, defensive, or hostile concerning them, unless we are willing to cope with their criticism, defensiveness, or hostility. This may be difficult in the early stages of the creative process. At an early stage we do best to approach people who can be open, accepting, and encouraging.

We can encourage the creativity of others best, if we can respond to their new ideas openly, with genuine interest. We may be encouraging or neutral, but not defensive, hostile, or overly critical. Where we are anxious or inadequate, it is best not to look at the creative efforts of others.

THE EXPERT FOCUS GAME

Often a group wants to learn the skills of an expert, but in some way he puts them off. He communicates it in a way, in an order, at a level, that they cannot understand. The result is that the learners feel frustrated, inadequate, and lost. The structure of this game is to put the control of learning in the hands of the learner.

Procedures

A group and an expert come together for the purpose of meeting the needs of the group.

The focus person makes himself available to meet the needs of the group and its members by:

I. Answering questions on the level, in the way, and in the order that the individuals within the group desire.

II. Giving evaluations, demonstrations, role play, etc., if asked to by the group.

THE POSITIVE FOCUS GAME FOR DISCUSSIONS OF SUBJECT MATTER

The focus technique can be used for small group discussions in the classroom or in informal situations. The technique is viable with any subject matter; the authors have trained teachers to use it for discussions of German, mathematics, English, history, science, etc.

The game that follows was used extensively in the college classroom for discussions of poetry and drama. It is presented here as an example of applying the focus game in a particular subject area. The game can be easily adapted to other subject matter by substituting the appropriate subject focus in place of the section "Specific Rules for Playing the Game with Literature."

(See essay in Chapter One, p. 46, for a statement of the author's experience in the early use of games in the classroom.)

THE POSITIVE FOCUS GAME FOR DISCUSSIONS OF LITERATURE

We sometimes have trouble expressing or exploring our thoughts and feelings about literature in group discussions. Many times we hesitate to speak in class because we think that others might consider us stupid or awkward. We may still lack confidence in speaking out, though in fact they may think us intelligent and perceptive, since they rarely give us their positive reactions.

In the Positive Focus Game, people do tell us their positive feelings when they find our comments stimulating or insightful or meaningful. Sometimes they are interested if we express our true thoughts and feelings simply because they are *our* true thoughts and feelings. Knowing their positive reactions, we feel more courageous and confident in expressing ourselves, and we gain a deeper rapport with the others in our group.

In this game, we needn't worry about negative reactions of others because the players are held to the rule of giving only positive feedback. Should the focus wish to invite negative comments and differences of opinion and interpretation, the group can play the Challenge Game or some other game that encourages expression of differences.

The person acting as focus does not have to compete for attention— the group gives him its total concentration for as long as he wants it. He may feel safe about exploring his views and feelings, for the group's purpose is to try to understand him, to draw him out so that he can further clarify his own thoughts, and to give him genuine positive response for the insight and pleasure which he gives them.

Objectives of the Game

It is the objective of the game to understand the literature that is being discussed, and the impact of the literature on the focal person. The focus may decide in any particular game to shift the discussion either to the literature or to his feelings about the literature. In either case, attention remains on him—on *his* interpretation or *his* reactions.

General Rules

1. The ideal size for a group is four or five. If the game is played in the classroom, break into several groups of this size, with students forming their own groups.

2. In the Positive Focus Game, any group member may have the focus for any topic for as long as he wishes to keep it, unless limitations of topic or time are agreed upon in advance. Limitations are to be avoided if possible.

3. When the focus slips from the person who has it, either through inadvertence or because someone else takes it, a group member should bring the focus back to the player to whom it belongs.

4. When the focus person feels that he has had enough, he should announce that he is relinquishing the focus. He should not let it gradually slip away.

5. Keep to the issues raised by the focus. Let the focus determine the direction of the discourse.

6. Honesty is important. Overstatements are to be avoided. The effectiveness of the game is seriously impaired when group members cannot trust each other's communications.

7. Each group member has responsibility for enhancing the group climate. Each should take initiative within the limits of the other rules to help others feel secure, appreciated, and understood.

8. No leader is required for the game and no privileges or penalties are permitted for any group leader who happens to be present.

Specific Rules for Playing the Game with Literature

I. Instructions for the focus person.

As the focus, you may discuss one or more of the following topics. However, you need not feel restricted to these. Whatever you choose to discuss, announce your intention to the group at the start.

Topics for the focus:

a. The author's intention or purpose.

b. The poem or play as an aesthetic experience: your perception of the artist's vision, sensitivity, and form.

c. The poem or play as a personal experience: how the work made you feel; ideas or issues that stimulated your thinking and perhaps gave you new insight into your world and self.

d. If the subject is drama, you might discuss:
the plot
the theme
your attempt to understand each character,
and your attitude toward each of them

language
symbolism
literary tradition
historical background

e. If the subject is poetry, you might decide to focus on some particular aspect of the poem's texture or technique such as tone, diction, imagery, use of figurative language, rhythm, sound.

II. Instructions for the group.

After the focus has finished speaking, the group will draw him out in order to explore and clarify his ideas and feelings. The group should concentrate on drawing out the focus on what he has already said, that is, help him to pursue the main drift of his thought. They should not bring up new topics or aspects.

The focus person can pass any time he does not wish to answer a question, but if he chooses to answer, he must be honest.

As a member of the group, you can draw out the focus in a number of ways:

a. Reflect the feelings or content of the focus and then check by asking him if you have understood him.

b. Summarize what you think he has communicated, and then ask him if you have gotten his main drift.

c. Ask the focus to summarize what he has said.

d. Ask why he believes something he has said, or why he feels a certain way. Ask him what evidence or experience has led him to his conclusions or feelings. Ask him to expand on parts of what he has said.

e. Follow through in getting him to clarify—pursue a line of questioning in some depth.

f. Give positive feedback to the focus. This might be done in a number of ways: Let him know that you understand him and how he feels. Tell him of thoughts or experiences of your own that enable you to understand him. If he has shown good qualities such as openness, sensitivity, thoughtfulness, praise him.

Challenge Phase

The focus may ask for challenge at any time. (Other players should never initiate the challenge.) The challenger will bring up facts or interpretations that are counter to the views of the focus person. The challenger is to be permitted to speak without interruption, and for as long as he wishes. The focus should attempt to understand the position of the challenger, and can facilitate this by drawing him out further after his initial statement. The process is then reversed: The focus replies and defends his own views, also without interruption, and then the challenger draws him out. Several exchanges may take place if the focus wishes.

THE GROUP LEARNING GAME

Many times people have common problems that they cannot solve, or that they solve poorly, because they cannot work together, understand each other, or learn from each other. People are often too defensive about their status to learn from one another, and too jealous of their knowledge to teach one another.

This game is designed to help a group of people work together, learn from each other, and teach each other. It is best played with a group of people who are all about equal, who are faced with a common problem or task to which there is some clearly defined objective solution.

The game may be played by a group doing a homework assignment together or studying for a test together.

The game may be played within the classroom where a group of students work together on a common assignment.

It may be played with a group coming to a vital decision that affects them all.

At a first or second grade level, the game may be played to enable a group of children to read together with little or no help from the teacher.

At a high school or college level, the game may be used to help a group learn how to use and understand complicated mathematical problems.

Procedures

1. A group of from two to six people get together with some common task or tasks to accomplish.

2. When the game is first introduced, the task or tasks should be such that some definite answers are possible.

It is best to start with problems that have one answer, such as $15 + 10 = 25$. Later one may move to problems that have more than one answer, such as, "List the causes of World War II." Finally, one may progress to problems that have no right answer, such as, "Is it better to be very poor or to be deformed?"

3. Before the group starts working, each person should do a previously agreed-upon portion of the task independently. To save time it is permissible for the entire task to be done before the group meeting by one or more members.

4. Each person presents his solution or solutions to the problem, and the process by which he arrived at them. He describes how he got the answer, his thinking, his feeling, his reasoning.

5. The other members of the group attempt to understand each member's solution.

6. If some members of the group understand how to get an answer and the others don't, be sure to help the others to understand. It is not enough that they put down the same answer. They should know how to get it and why it is right.

To explain an answer, start out where the other person's understanding is clear. Explain new ideas or facts one at a time, being sure that the other person understands fully before you go on to the next point. If a number of ideas have to be fitted together to understand the problem, review all the old ideas before presenting each new one and fit them together one at a time.

7. Where answers are different, one should not try to prove the other person wrong. Instead, one should try to understand how each person got his answer. By doing this, the mistake often becomes easy to see without argument.

8. If there is disagreement about a simple fact, look it up.

9. If nobody in the group understands how to do something, ask somebody outside the group to explain it.

The Positive Focus Game for Young Children: Kindergarten, First Grade and Second Grade

Step 1. Start with the old standby, "show and tell."

Here the child is asked to bring something to school and talk about it. The kinds of things that can be brought are toys, rocks, leaves, a picture the child drew, etc.

While it is easier for the young child to talk about something he can touch, he should not be restricted to this. Permit the child to talk about anything he wants to talk about: things that happened to him, pets, the birth of a new baby, his mother or father, accidents, dreams, TV shows. All of these should be permitted.

Step 2. After the child has finished telling the story, the teacher draws him out by asking questions about his account or reflecting some of his feelings.

When she is through, she asks if the class has any questions to ask.

In time, the children, modeling themselves on her behaviors, will also find questions to ask.

Step 3. When the children have finished asking their questions, the teacher says several positive things about what the child who was focus said or did. She then invites the other children to say nice things about the focus person.

After several sessions, the children, modeling themselves on her, become skilled in giving compliments.

Step 4. After four or five sessions, when the children have become fluent in asking drawing-out questions and giving compliments, she suggests that more children could have a turn being focus if there was one "show and tell" person at each table or group. At this point, there should be about eight or nine children in a group.

The teacher then selects focus persons from volunteers for each group. She moves from group to group, keeping the process going.

Step 5. The teacher introduces the concept of turns, so that each group member gets a turn to be focus if he wants it. This removes the responsibility for choosing focus persons from the teacher, and makes the group self-sufficient in this.

Step 6. The groups are further subdivided into groups of four or five so that more people can have turns being focus.

It is a good idea to continue occasionally playing the focus game with the class as a whole, even after the children have learned to do it in small groups. This permits the teacher to continue modeling drawing-out and giving positive feedback. It also helps create group coherence.

See also, on Teaching Games:

1. *Creativity Games.* The Creativity Game series is not only useful in stimulating divergent thinking, but stimulates carrying through and integration in creativity.

2. *Socratic Game.* This is an advanced teaching game that recreates a Socratic-like dialogue.

3. *Uses and Modifications of Focus Game.* A number of suggestions on how the focus game can be modified for various problems in teaching.

4. *First Use of Games in the Classroom.* A discussion in depth of the use of the focus game to teach English on the university level.

See also, on Task-Oriented Games:

1. *Free Choice Game.* A group helps an individual choose the best approach to solving a problem.

2. *Uses and Modifications of the Focus Game.* Various ways of organizing communication are presented. Some of these are suggestive of how a group may approach various kinds of tasks.

3. *Teaching Games.* Wherever there is a problem of expertise in sharing or communicating as part of a task, the teaching games become relevant.

4. *Transcendental Game for Planning.* In transcendental planning, conflicts in interest are overcome through the participants taking a broader, more general point of view.

CHAPTER 5

Coping

This series of games deals with various levels of adjustment and creativity in ourselves and others.

Objectives of This Program

1. *Understanding.* This program will help you to understand better your own behavior as well as the behavior of others.

2. *Helpful Behavior.* This program will help you to know what to do to help yourself and others.

3. *Professional Effectiveness.* If you are a member of the helping professions, or if you work in supervision and administration, the program will help you to know how to encourage creativity and freedom without creating anxiety, insecurity, and chaos. It will do this by helping you to distinguish more clearly and precisely where freedom is called for, where limits are necessary, and where support and help are essential.

ACTIVITY 1. USING ONE'S OWN EXPERIENCE TO UNDERSTAND HUMAN REACTIONS

Most often we tend to do to others what was done to us. We tend to bring up our children as we were brought up. If we are teachers, we teach the way we were taught. Sometimes the results are good, sometimes bad. If the results are to be good on a better than chance level, we can't just do what was done to us uncritically, we have to recall what the results of these actions were. Did they help us? Did they hinder us? How did we really feel? In Activity I of this program, you will explore in depth what helped you and what hindered you in becoming the kind of person you want to be.

Objectives of Activity I

In Activity 1 you will explore and share how you have felt about being treated the way you were treated by different people, as a child and as an adult. You will do this to help yourself to become:

a. More aware of your own real feelings.

b. More sensitive to the effects your behavior may have on others.

c. More aware of how your upbringing and your responses to it are similar and how they are different from those of other members of your discussion group.

Directions

This program can be used with large groups. Parts of it have been used with groups as large as several hundred individuals. With large groups, and even with smaller groups, the program needs a facilitator to lead individuals through its various phases. The facilitator will read the directions and facilitate the large-group interaction.

It is also possible to use the program individually by skipping the sections involving group discussion.

If the group is large (over 12), use a facilitator and proceed as follows:
The facilitator reads aloud:

"I would like you to take several minutes to consider the kind of person you would like to be, your ideal. Jot down a few notes to help you remember. [Wait about 5 to 7 minutes.]

"Now consider how you were helped or hindered from becoming the kind of person you want to be by parents, teachers, friends, and others. Jot down notes. [Wait about 5 more minutes.]

"Would anybody like to tell us the kind of person he would like to be, and how he was helped and hindered in becoming that way?"

When a person volunteers, the facilitator may ask several questions to draw him out. The attitude of the facilitator should be accepting and encouraging, not challenging or condemning. When the facilitator has finished drawing out, he asks if anyone else has any questions for the focus. In this way he sets the mood, tone, and structure of the focus techniques that are to follow.

After the mini-focus on one volunteer is finished, the facilitator calls for other volunteers and proceeds in the same way.

Where there are differences in what different people see as helpful, the facilitator asks some voting questions to get a group census of feeling. As facilitator, be sure you are receptive to all feelings and differences in feeling. Asking voting questions creates a shared experience with the large group, no matter what its size. It creates an atmosphere of accepting differences and owning one's feelings. This is essential if the program is to be successful.

When an accepting atmosphere has been established through voting questions and the mini-focus, the group should be broken down into groups of four to discuss in depth the notes that persons have made.

Facilitator: "I want you to break into groups of three or four with each of you taking a turn telling the kind of person you want to be, and how others helped or hindered you from becoming that kind of person. The other group members draw out the speaker by asking questions and reflecting back to the speaker what they understand him to be saying. In explaining the kind of person you want to be, and how you were helped or hindered, you may use your notes as a guide."

If the group is small (12 or under), the facilitator's role can be minimized. Break into groups of three's and four's almost as soon as individuals are through jotting down notes, and discuss, using the focus technique, with members drawing each person out.

For People Working Individually

Since you cannot participate in the group processes, it would be advantageous if you spent more time in exploring just what kinds of human behaviors helped or hindered you in becoming the kind of person you want to be. If at all possible, get a small group together and share your perceptions.

ACTIVITY 2. RANKING BEHAVIORS FROM MOST HELPFUL TO LEAST HELPFUL

Objectives:

1. To bring to mind a larger number of behaviors for evaluation as helpful or hindering.

2. To help the persons participating to organize and evaluate these behaviors through the process of comparing and ranking in terms of their own values.

Facilitator: "Think again about the kind of person you want to be.

Now in terms of your own experience, I want you to rank the following behaviors of others toward you from most helpful to least helpful in becoming the kind of person you want to be.

_____A. An interested, understanding, and encouraging attitude.

_____B. A firm, clear stand, limiting freedom. If punishment is involved, it is in the nature of a natural consequence, administered without anger.

_____C. A punishing, angry attitude, harsh physical punishment, embarrassing, shaming, insulting, diminishing.

_____D. Reward or praise.

_____E. A challenging attitude. The challenges may be of many kinds. They may include criticism or a pointing out of inadequacies; but they do not involve name-calling or shaming.

_____F. An ignoring or uninterested attitude.

_____G. A babying and strongly protective attitude.

Optional: For Large Group

After everybody in the group has finished ranking the behaviors, the facilitator takes a census as to how each item was ranked. He notes the ranks in the following way for each of the categories:

If ten people ranked item A first, he writes: 10 (1).
If three people ranked it second, he writes: 3 (2).
If six people ranked it third, he writes: 6 (3), etc.

He then multiplies the rank by the number of people and adds the result for every rank. For rank A, the numbers are as follows: 10 (1), 3 (2), and 6 (3), which by multiplication and addition becomes $10 + 6 + 18 = 34$. He does this for all the categories. The resulting sums give a group rank from most constructive to least constructive behavior. (The smaller the sum, the more constructive the behavior.)

After a brief discussion of the results, the facilitator asks: "Is there anybody who would volunteer to tell us how he ranked the items and explain why he ranked them as he did?" When the person has finished giving his ranks and explanations, the facilitator should do the following:

1. Draw out the person with a few questions concerning his reasons. Be sure that you accept anything the person says as valid for him.

2. Ask the general group if they have any questions for the focus. At times members of the group will try to take the focus away by giving their own experience. Bring the group back to the person who is actually on focus.

3. Watch the group for nonverbal cues concerning their response to each focus. When there is an emotional reaction, try to explore its nature

by a series of Voting Questions. For example: How many feel the same way? How many feel the opposite way? How many sometimes feel one way, sometimes the other?

After one or more persons have had this mini-focus, the facilitator will ask the group to break into three's and four's. He will instruct them to use the focus technique to give each person a chance to explore in depth all the feelings and thoughts excited by the large group discussions.

In addition, the groups may wish to discuss the following data:

In general, most groups going through this program ranked the items from most to least helpful in the following order.

1. An interested, understanding, and encouraging attitude.
2. A challenging attitude that does not invoke name-calling, shaming, or demeaning of any sort.
3. Reward or praise.
4. A firm, clear stand, limiting freedom. If punishment is involved, it is in the nature of a natural consequence, administered without shaming, demeaning, or tearing down.
5. A punishing attitude, physical punishment administered with strong anger, demeaning, shaming, insulting, tearing down.
6. A babying, protective attitude that will not permit one to try things or do them for oneself.
7. An ignoring, uninterested attitude.

This information can be discussed in terms of the following questions.
1. Why do you think that people on the average rank the items in this way?
2. In what way does each item show respect or disrespect to a person? Which show more and which show less respect?

Medium-sized Group: (4–12)

After everybody in the group has finished ranking the behaviors, break into three's and four's. Using the focus technique, give each person a chance to explore in depth all the feelings and thoughts excited by the earlier focus discussion (Activity 1), and by the ranking (Activity 2).

About ten minutes before stopping time, the facilitator announces that the groups should finish in five minutes. Save the last five minutes for discussion. A good opener might be:

"When we have explored what kinds of behaviors have helped us and what kind have hindered us, we are able to know what the effect of our behavior will be on others. We will go into this in greater detail in subsequent sessions. For the present, how have you found the experience? Any comments or criticisms?"

ACTIVITY 3. HOW WE USUALLY RESPOND TO OTHERS

When we feel in certain ways and are in a particular state of mind, we tend to act in certain ways. At the left of the table below are descriptions of ways of feeling and being. Imagine yourself feeling and being in the way described. How would you behave? How would you respond to others?

Look to the right of the table. Pick out those behaviors that would be most characteristic or natural for you in each state of feeling and being described. Jot down other behaviors not listed.

WAYS OF FEELING AND BEING	WAYS OF BEHAVING OR RESPONDING
1. When you are feeling creative and curious.	1. Questioning, clarifying, inventing, suggesting.
2. When you are feeling rebellious.	2. Rewarding, praising, limit-setting.
3. When you are convinced and feel comfortable and secure in your conviction.	3. Challenging, interrogating, arguing.
4. When you are feeling rigid and tight about something.	4 Punishing, getting angry, acting overprotective.
5. When you are feeling pressured, frustrated, out of balance, losing control, anxious.	5. Rewarding, praising, limit-setting.
6. When you just want to forget, rest, close your eyes, withdraw.	6. Ignoring, daydreaming.

Procedure

Get into small groups of about three or four and discuss your answers and their implications, using a focus technique.

Look at the As-Is chart on page 128 and discuss its implications.

Activity 3A. Appropriate and Inappropriate Inner States

We all to a greater or lesser degree:

1. ignore and withdraw.
2. lose control, feel inadequate, fearful, or angry.
3. are firm, clearly convinced, and very definite.
4. are challenging, rebellious, and critical.
5. are self-motivated, creative, and constructive.

All of these behaviors are part of the human nature of everybody. Under what circumstances are each of these behaviors constructive and appropriate, or destructive and inappropriate?

Discuss the positive and negative aspects of each of these behaviors in your group, using the focus technique for every item. After each item has been discussed, compare your conclusions with the opinion of the author, and discuss.

WITHDRAWING AND IGNORING

Appropriate ignoring: We all ignore things in sleep. To concentrate or pay attention to some things means that we ignore other things. We ignore things when our need for them has been met. Such ignoring is appropriate and necessary.

It is also appropriate to ignore unimportant behaviors in others (children) that we would like them to stop. This will work provided the behavior we are ignoring is not very important to the person, and that we don't ignore the whole person instead of just a part of his behavior.

Ignoring becomes inappropriate and dangerous when important things are ignored out of feelings of inadequacy or fear. When we ignore important needs, perceptions, realities, or dangers, we are in trouble. Such ignoring is constricting and growth-stopping.

LOSS OF CONTROL, FLOODING BY FEELING, LOSS OF TEMPER, FEELINGS OF INADEQUACY, FEAR, OR CONFUSION

Appropriate: If we are faced with something really new, or if we face something that we have ignored out of fear, then feelings of anger, confusion, fear, and inadequacy are likely to arise. It is usually better to face these feelings than to run from the situations and problems that give rise to them. If we work slowly and cautiously on the causes of these feelings, then they will gradually retreat and we will solve our problems with increasing control and confidence.

But if, instead of working on these problems and slowly gaining mastery, we blame others, then the anger, fear, and inadequacy become destructive. What happens is that the feelings we want to get rid of are provoked in others so that they either withdraw, feel inadequate, or fight.

FIRMNESS, CLARITY, AND A SENSE OF CONVICTION

These attitudes are often very important in seeing something through. When one feels insecure, these attitudes are important as a way of hanging on to something that works.

Convictions that are too firm, too clear, and too definite become a hindrance to growth and constructive change when applied at a time when there is no pressing need. When there is no pressing commitment

THE AS-IS DIAGRAM. A DIAGRAM OF HOW THINGS USUALLY ARE

Usually we respond to others as they respond to us. If they get mad at us, we get mad at them. If they ignore us, we ignore them. If they encourage us, we encourage them. This is shown in the *as-is* diagram.

OUR STATES OF MIND	MOST LIKELY RESPONSE WE MAKE	STATE OF MIND OUR RESPONSE CREATES IN OTHERS	MOST LIKELY RESPONSE OTHERS MAKE
creative, curious	questioning, encouraging, accepting	creative, curious	questioning, curious
rebellious	challenging, critical	rebellious	challenging, critical
flexibly conforming, convinced, feel comfortable and secure	rewarding, praising, limit-setting	flexibly conforming, convinced, feel comfortable and secure	rewarding, praising, limit-setting
rigid, conforming, tight, a little insecure	rewarding, limit-setting, punishing	rigid, conforming, tight a little insecure	rewarding, limit-setting, punishing
loss of control, anger, frustration, anxiety	inadequate, punishing, overprotective	loss of control, anger, frustration, anxiety	inadequate punishing overprotective
forgetting, repressing, had too much, want to get away, bored	ignoring	forgetting, repressing, had too much, want to get away, bored	ignoring

The horizontal arrows indicate the most likely consequences. The diagonal arrows indicate a somewhat less frequent consequence.

to a task, or a rigidity springing from insecurity, a more open and less dogmatic approach would be better for growth.

CHALLENGING, REBELLIOUS, CRITICAL BEHAVIOR AND ATTITUDES

These are appropriate when something goes wrong. Rebelling is saying "no" to something. Saying "no" is a step in all change. But if this is the only attitude shown, it suggests a sense of insecurity. The person would like to break with conventional, rigid, dogmatic behavior, but is unable to do so. He sees much that is wrong, but feels unable to change things. So instead, he criticizes what everybody else is doing.

One of the reasons that the overcritical person cannot undertake and carry things through on his own is that he tends to apply the same overcritical attitude to his own behavior as he does to everybody else's. This is often so discouraging that it paralyzes him from doing anything.

THE SELF-MOTIVATED, CONSTRUCTIVE, CREATIVE AND INDEPENDENT WAY OF BEHAVING

This is obviously good in most circumstances. Creativity and innovation are sometimes inappropriate when things have to be done quickly and there is no time for innovation.

ACTIVITY 4. SEEING THE MODES OF BEHAVIOR IN TERMS OF NEEDS

All human behavior is motivated by various needs. To mention a few, there is the need for achievement, for recognition, the need to be liked, the need to move around, the need for sleep, the need for food.

When a person is withdrawing, losing control, being rigid, rebellious, or creative, it is important to know which needs are motivating his behavior.

All of the examples that follow involve child behavior. This is because the behavior of children is much more transparent and honest, and hence easier to understand. The same principles apply to adults, but to unravel the need dimensions involved would require too unwieldy an analysis for this book.

Example one: Suppose a child gets into a fight at 11:30 A.M. Looking at this behavior, we see that he has clearly lost control. It is important to know whether he lost control because he could not meet his need to be liked, or because he was getting too hungry to contain himself, or because he attempted a task he couldn't succeed in.

If he is hungry, he probably should be given milk or crackers some time before 11:30.

If he doesn't have friends, he needs to be helped to make them.

If he is upset because he couldn't achieve some task, he needs to be given tasks he can succeed in.

Example two: A third-grade girl, instead of turning in her spelling words, drew a beautiful picture. How would you classify her behavior? What would you have to find out, and what could you do for her?

The girl was being creative in respect to art.

What was her attitude toward spelling? It is important to know whether she was withdrawing from spelling because she was discouraged and fearful, or because she was rebelling against an assignment she thought useless.

If she didn't do her spelling because she was fearful, she would need to be given easier words that she could learn for her spelling.

If she knew her spelling very well, she was probably rebelling against the assignment. The teacher could ask her what alternative assignment in spelling would be fair. She could then work out an agreement about work during spelling time that would meet the needs of the child.

There is still another aspect of the child's behavior we have to look at.

What were her needs in respect to the teacher? Were these needs more important than the spelling itself in the child's failure to do spelling? Did she have a need to assert independence? If so, how can she be helped to be independent in more constructive ways? Was she perhaps angry at the teacher, and getting revenge by being disobedient? If this were so, she would have to be helped to learn better ways of expressing anger and resolving conflict.

How can one find out which is the need behind the behavior? One can do this by talking to the person. One can do this by seeing the behavior against the background of all we know about the person. For example, if the girl in question had usually gotten 100% in spelling, it would be unlikely that she refused to do spelling because she was fearful and inadequate. We would then have to look to motives of rebellion and independence, or anger.

If we can identify the level of behavior and the motive behind it, and if we can keep ourselves from reacting automatically, we are most likely to act in a helpful way.

See the chart on page 131 for further detail on understanding levels of behavior in terms of needs.

ACTIVITY 5. THE IDEAL RESPONSE TO INNER STATES

In this section you will consider what responses are best for you when you are in various states of feeling and being.

Imagine yourself feeling and being in the ways described to the left

DIAGNOSTIC CHART: SEEING LEVELS OF BEHAVIOR IN TERMS OF NEEDS

If we know the behavior, the internal state of mind, and the needs that are pressing on a person we will be best able to make the ideal response to the situation. In this chart, we are considering the behavior, state of mind, and needs of a child. The chart, with only a little modification, is applicable to adults as well.

CHILD'S BEHAVIOR	STATE OF MIND	THE NEEDS MOTIVATING THE BEHAVIOR			
		Food	Achievement	People	Safety, etc.
Explores, builds, creates.	Creative	Let him prepare it.	Encouragement, interest, freedom.	Be honest and open.	Explain or discuss dangers.
Challenges, questions.	Rebellious	Give him some choice, negotiate.	Same as under "food."	Be honest, open, not defensive, don't patronize.	Ask his opinion, explain. Negotiate, set limits.
Does what he is told; does it well.	Flexibly conforming	Give him something different at times.	Challenge him. Ask questions. Get him to think.	Ask about his feelings. Express your feelings. Be honest.	Leave well enough alone.
Gets upset at any change. Likes routine.	Rigidly conforming	Give alternatives, but respect his rigidity.	Give alternatives. Make them such that he can succeed.	Give him new but safe experiences. Don't take away his security.	Let him approach things he fears in as slow and safe a manner as possible.
Is destructive, breaks things, cries.	Loss of control	Feed him. See doctor if this doesn't help.	Easy work. Help. Structure limits.	Protection. Limits. Support helps.	Limits. Emotional security. Use force if needed.
Ignores.	Withdrawn, frightened. Feels inadequate.	Give food. Call doctor.	Encouragement. Help. Structure.	Encouragement. Protection.	Set limits. Protect.

of the table below. What responses in others would help you most while you are in each of the described states?

Look to the right of the table. Pick out the behaviors of others that would help you most for each state of being and feeling. Break into small groups and share your answers using focus technique.

WAYS OF FEELING AND BEING	WAYS OF BEHAVING AND RESPONDING
1. When you are feeling creative and curious.	1. Questioning, clarifying.
2. When you are feeling rebellious.	2. Rewarding, praising, limit-setting.
3. When you are convinced and feel comfortable and secure in your conviction.	3. Punishing.
4. When you are feeling rigid and tight about something.	4. Challenging.
5. When you are feeling pressured, frustrated, out of balance, losing control, anxious.	5. Arguing, interrogating.
6. When you are feeling so discouraged, ashamed, or defeated that you simply want to withdraw and forget.	6. Removing threats.
	7. Providing a sense of security by limit-setting, guiding, and helping.
	8. Approaching, reducing fear, helping.
	9. Ignoring.
	10. Offering alternatives, instructing, helping without being critical.

ACTIVITY 6. AUTHOR'S CONCEPTUALIZATION OF IDEAL RESPONSE TO EACH INNER STATE

Coping With Withdrawal or Loss of Control

In general, if a person is withdrawing out of fear or inadequacy, or if he is upset and losing control, he needs support. In such circumstances, one can best help by taking the lead.

With the withdrawn person, it is important to make him feel safe. If it is a child or a person in one's charge, one may demand that he take a few safe steps in overcoming his withdrawal, while offering encouragement, help, and protection.

There is a natural tendency to ignore or get angry at people who withdraw or ignore us. This tendency must be overcome if one is to take the lead in helping the person overcome his fears. This is particularly true because most often the person who has withdrawn is not capable of taking the lead himself.

With the person who has lost control, it is important not to follow the natural tendency to get angry and lose control oneself. One must remember that a person loses control when he is upset. It is important to calm the person and reestablish security.

You are best able to help a person who has lost or fears that he will lose control, if you remain calm and strong yourself. Find a safe way for the person to express his feelings. Remove the pressure that is upsetting the person. Make clear what you want the person to do or not do without being angry, punitive, or threatening. Explain calmly. Do not get involved with arguments, threats, or challenges.

Coping With Rigidity

When a person is rigid, it is because he feels too insecure to give up the way he knows of doing things. In dealing with such a person, the natural tendency is to become rigid oneself, and attack his way as dogmatically as he defends it. This usually makes the person more insecure and rigid in his defense.

It is better to accept the procedures of the rigid person as valid, and suggest that other alternatives are possible as well. If one offers support and help in learning these other alternatives, the person is most likely to overcome his rigidity.

Coping With Rebellion

When a person rebels, he is saying "no" to something. If what he is saying "no" to deserves a "no," the best thing one can do is support the rebel. In helping a person who can only respond in a critical way, our natural tendency is to become defensive and argue. This tends to confirm the person in a nonconstructive, rebellious attitude. The best thing is not to rebel against the rebellion, but to ask the rebellious person to present alternatives to what he doesn't like. If these alternatives are reasonable, they should be accepted; if not, the flaws in them should be pointed out. In this way the rebellious person is helped to transcend himself and become creative.

Dealing With Creativity

We are often tempted to respond to the creative person defensively and critically. This often makes a person rigid and inflexible concerning his creative ideas. It is far better to respond with an interested, questioning attitude. This is most likely to maintain the creative thrust while helping the person achieve balance and objectivity concerning his creative ideas.

The following chart is a convenient summary of our discussion of the ideal response.

THE IDEAL RESPONSE

While our automatic impulse is to respond to others as they respond to us, this is far from ideal. Ideally, our action should always be under the control of the creative portion of ourselves, which creates an overall plan of approach. The other portions of ourselves should be under the control of the insightful, planning part of ourselves.

We should be critical and rebellious against what is destructive, inept, or cruel.

Our plan should include a flexible determination to carry it out with some elements of rigidity to prevent us from compromising essentials. It should include an awareness of when we or others may lose control or withdraw so as to resolve problems and set limits without things coming to this point.

Given these, we have the Ideal Response Diagram.

STATE OF THE OTHER	THE IDEAL RESPONSE
Creative	Questioning and clarifying. Challenging. Providing a sense of security by limit-setting, guiding, and helping.
Rebellious, challenging	Questioning and clarifying. Rewarding, praising, limit-setting. Providing a sense of security by limit-setting, guiding, and helping. Approaching, reducing fear, helping.
Flexibly conforming	Challenging.
Rigid conformity	Removing threats. Providing a sense of security by limit-setting, guiding, and helping. Approaching, reducing fear, helping. Offering alternatives, instruction, and help without being critical.
Loss of control	Rewarding, praising, limit-setting. Providing a sense of security by limit-setting and guiding and helping. Approaching, reducing fear, helping.
Withdrawal	Removing threats. Providing a sense of security by limit-setting, guiding, and helping. Approaching, reducing fear, helping.

GAMES FOR COPING

The games in this section may be played after the program "Dealing with Various Modes of Behavior," earlier in this chapter, or independently of it.

GAME FOR OVERCOMING DEFENSES OF IGNORING, WITHDRAWING, AND FORGETTING

There are many things we would like to be able to forget, but can't. We are afraid of things that we have no reason to fear. We feel we can't do something even though we know that we are smart enough or strong enough to do it. We have feelings of fear and inadequacy, though it makes no sense to have them; and we know no way to get rid of them.

Procedures

1. Meet in a group to play the focus game.
2. The focus person volunteers to talk about his fears.
3. All the group members relax before the focus person speaks. This is done by breathing deeply, holding the breath on the intake, and breathing out completely. This exercise reduces the carbon dioxide in the blood. This in turns slows the heart rate. The unpleasant sensations which fear, anger, or anxiety produce in us are thus reduced. If tension rises too high or if a more complete relaxation is desired, getting up, stretching, tensing and relaxing each muscle, stretching every part of the body as far as it will go in every direction, may be done prior to the breathing exercise, for more complete relaxation. This is helpful because it relaxes the muscles and uses up the adrenalin in the blood and thus permits a more complete relaxation.
4. The focus person talks and thinks about the things that bring on the fears, the feelings of inadequacy, or the anxiety and worry. As soon as he feels himself getting tense or worried, he should stop and breathe deeply, holding his breath on the intake, and breathing out completely. He should do this until he feels calm again, and then he should resume talking and thinking. He should do this until he can talk and think about the subject without feeling bad.
5. The members of his group should also try to be in as calm and relaxed a mood as possible. If they notice the focus person getting tense and worried, they should ask him to stop and do breathing exercises

again. If a group member finds himself getting tense, he should do the breathing exercise described above until he calms down.

6. Group members may ask questions and give support to the focus person. This should be done in a calm, relaxed, and nonthreatening way.

7. The group members should not make the focus person feel better by jollying him along or denying his problem. Saying, for example, "I also get nervous and tense when I have to clean my room" or "Everybody freezes up on tests," doesn't help.

8. It may take several sessions before a focus person can talk about things that have made him worry without feeling the physical signs of anxiety, such as increased heartbeat and sensations in the stomach and around the throat. It is best to approach talking about things that make us feel badly a little at a time, and use as many sessions as are needed. This gives rise to a more certain cure and gives everybody a turn to talk about their fears.

9. When we have learned to talk and think about things that make us feel badly without physical signs of anxiety, fear, or worry, then it is time to start doing the things that make us worried. Here the problem should be approached gradually, just as talking about the fearful was approached gradually. If, for example, one is trying to get over the fear of water, the first thing he would do is enter shallow water until he was comfortable with that. Only then would he go into deeper water.

When we are attempting to overcome or forget our fears, it is important not to do things that would increase them, such as trying to swim in water where we can't stand. If one had a fear of reading, he would start with things he can read easily and gradually go on to harder materials as his fears were reduced.

a. The key notion is to start where you are not afraid.
b. Move gradually into an area where you are slightly afraid.
c. Stop until you have no fear in this new area.
d. Then move again into an area where you are only slightly afraid.

GAME FOR LEARNING TO WITHDRAW

The facilitator reads the following voting questions:

Are there any things that you would like to forget, but can't? Perhaps these are things that keep going around in your mind and won't let you sleep.

Have you ever done things that were unpleasant or unhealthy, but that you were not able to stop, like smoking cigarettes or watching a dull television program?

Did you ever persist in situations that were dull, meaningless, unpleasant, or destructive because you didn't know how to pull out of them?

Did you ever remain in a boring conversation from which you wanted to escape?

In this game we will explore the reasons why we do not withdraw when it is appropriate, and what we can do about this.

Procedures

1. Make a list of four or five situations in which it might have been better to withdraw than to remain.

2. Under each situation, make a note of the reasons that prevented you from withdrawing.

3. Choose one or two of the situations listed in which you would really like to be able to withdraw.

4. Meet in groups of four, using the focus technique to explore:

a. Reasons why you were unable to withdraw appropriately.

b. How you might succeed in withdrawing appropriately in the future.

5. After you have finished a round of focusing, discuss some general ways in which people might help themselves or others withdraw when it is appropriate.

GAME FOR OVERCOMING FEAR

Sometimes there are things we want to say or do, but can't. We feel paralyzed, angry, inadequate, churned up inside. At such times, life seems to pass us by. We start daydreaming, feel depressed, or stop feeling altogether. Sometimes we get to feel mean and get into fights with everyone so that we begin to feel useless, and life starts feeling empty. Such feelings may often be avoided if we could learn to act and face what is bothering us instead of withdrawing. If you want to learn to do this, continue with this program.

1. Have you ever wanted to say something to someone, but kept your mouth shut because you were afraid that they would get mad or be too hurt? Or that they might laugh at you, reject you, or simply not understand? On a separate piece of paper, make a list of examples of cases where this has happened to you.

2. Play the Focus Game, Discussion Game, or Action Game with a group and discuss some of the examples you have listed. Where fears are involved, use the procedures of breathing and action to overcome them, as outlined in the Game for Overcoming Defenses of Withdrawal, page 135.

3. Have you ever wanted to try something, but didn't, because you

were afraid that you would act clumsy, fail, or get laughed at? On a separate piece of paper, make a list of times when this has happened to you.

4. Play the Focus Game or Action Game with some of the examples that you have listed.

5. After the game is completed, find somebody who knows how to do what you want to do and is patient. Start your learning where you can succeed easily without fear or tension. Have your teacher move in very small steps. Be sure you are comfortable with each step before taking the next.

There may be times when your confidence will grow and you will want to take much larger steps. Do not increase the size of the learning steps too quickly. Even when you are taking large steps, be sure you are comfortable and relaxed about each thing you learn before going on to the next.

One becomes comfortable with a learning step by repeating it in different ways, using it for different purposes, and understanding its meaning, and causes in as many ways as possible.

GAME FOR OVERCOMING RIGIDITY

Have you ever been in a rut?
Have you ever wanted to change, but were afraid to?
This game is designed to help you overcome rigidity.

Procedures

1. Three to five people convene to play the game. If the group is larger, break into small groups.

2. Make a list of four or five areas in which you are rigid.

3. Select one or two in which you would like to change.

4. One person volunteers to be focus.

a. Talk about fears, pressures, or feelings of inadequacy that might make change difficult. The group draws out the focus.

b. Focus and group share in thinking up alternative ways of acting or thinking.

c. The focus chooses two or three alternatives to talk about, and the group draws him out.

d. The process is reversed with the focus drawing out the group for suggestions and help.

5. The process is repeated with a different focus.

Coping With the Problems of Creating and Maintaining a Free Safe Group

Activity 1

We have all been in or had experience with groups that were relatively safe and free. A group where one can feel safe enough to be free is an ideal for many people.

Despite the universal attraction of a free safe group, most people or institutions that have attempted to create such an environment have found difficulties. Often these difficulties are so great that there is a drift back to a less free, more authoritarian structure.

Think back to your experience with such groups and make a list of several difficulties or problems that you encountered.

PROCEDURES

1. Make a list of several of those difficulties.

2. Break into groups of four or five members. Each person takes a turn reading his list, with others drawing him out with clarifying questions. In the drawing-out process, do not relate your own experiences; wait your turn.

3. When everybody has had a turn, compile a list of difficulties or problems encountered. Put your list on ditto sheets so it can be shared with the other groups.

DO NOT READ ON UNTIL THE START OF ACTIVITY TWO, WHEN YOU WILL HAVE THE RESPONSES OF EACH GROUP, PLUS THE AUTHOR'S OPINION.

Author's Opinion I

1. The first problem that most people think of in establishing a free and safe atmosphere is that it usually results in a lot of limit testing. This is only one of the problems that arises.

2. In a safe, free atmosphere, many feelings that have been buried or kept under cover tend to come out. Unfortunately, buried needs emerge together with the rage that one felt at the time they were buried. Also, because they have been buried, they tend to be distorted, untested, and very intense. One would expect feelings of inadequacy and rage to be among the first to come forth. See the accompanying diagram of a buried feeling, page 145. These feelings are themselves sometimes so frightening that they cause a person to withdraw.

3. The freedom to express negative feelings may make the atmosphere unsafe for others, so that it is difficult to maintain a safe atmosphere.

4. The absence of strong authoritarian controls may lead some group members to try to fill the power vacuum and create an authoritarian structure of their own.

5. Insofar as the program is successful and the above-mentioned problems are solved, people become very confident and their level of aspiration goes way up. This introduces two new dangers:

a. The high levels of aspiration are maintained by a great deal of fantasy, and people start living in an unreal world.

b. People become frustrated and depressed when they cannot immediately meet the high levels of aspiration that they set for themselves. This may result in withdrawal and regression, wiping out all the gains made.

Activity 2

1. Read the list of difficulties compiled by all groups in Activity 1, also the preceding section entitled "Author's Opinion I."

2. Make some notes as to what should be done to overcome or minimize these problems.

3. Meet in new groups of between four and five members, so that no member of the new group was in your old group (where possible).

4. Each person takes a turn reading his list with the others drawing him out with clarifying questions. In the drawing-out process, do not relate your own experiences; wait your turn.

5. When everybody has had a turn, compile a list of strategies for overcoming these problems.

DO NOT READ FURTHER BEFORE THE START OF ACTIVITY 3, AT WHICH POINT YOU SHOULD READ "AUTHOR'S OPINION II" AS WELL AS THE LISTS OF RESPONSES OF ALL GROUPS INVOLVED.

Activity 3

Read "Author's Opinion II" as well as the lists of all the small groups from Activity 2. Also examine the two diagrams on buried needs, page 142.

Meet in a large group to discuss and evaluate.

Author's Opinion II

1. Introduce the freedom and safety elements gradually so that no one is called on to handle and integrate more freedom and more of the

feelings which freedom and safety release than is possible at one time.

2. Let the participants know at the start that feelings of inadequacy, anger, and rage, as well as a great deal of fantasy are likely to emerge before they can get the full benefits of the program. Knowing at the start that this is likely to happen will enable the participants to cope better with the results.

3. Some of the limits controlling behavior are based on feelings of fear and inadequacy. As these are removed, it is important that people learn to set limits for themselves in a conscious, rational way. Statements like the following, repeated frequently, may help individuals do this.

a. You know what you can handle. Do not go over your head. If you feel you are in too deep, stop and come back to it when you are better able to deal with it.

b. Do not try to undertake more than you can do with reasonable comfort.

c. In a free atmosphere such as this one you are likely to feel inadequate at times and angry at others. When you feel this way, there is a tendency to blame yourself or somebody else. Do neither. These feelings are unpleasant and painful, but if you talk about them with others rather than act on them, they will gradually get less. You will find yourself able to do many things you were not able to do before.

4. Provide opportunities to talk about and work out the feelings released by the safe and free atmosphere.

5. If the free and safe atmosphere is introduced gradually, it will discourage people from trying to fill the power vacuum. Structures that permit but do not force cooperation so that group restriction on individual freedom is minimized are also helpful. Making the group participants aware of the problem of individuals trying to take over is another way of discouraging the growth of an authoritarian structure from the bottom.

6. Opportunities for practice and reality testing should be provided so that levels of aspiration are kept on a reasonable, realistic level, and fantasies do not substitute for reality.

EXPLANATION OF DIAGRAMS: "STRUCTURE OF A BURIED NEED"

Movement into the circle of inner needs is facilitated as each layer or ring of frustration is eliminated by setting rational limits which are explained and enforced without punishment or ridicule. When the inner circle is penetrated, creativity is released. The frustration ring immedi-

STRUCTURE OF A BURIED NEED

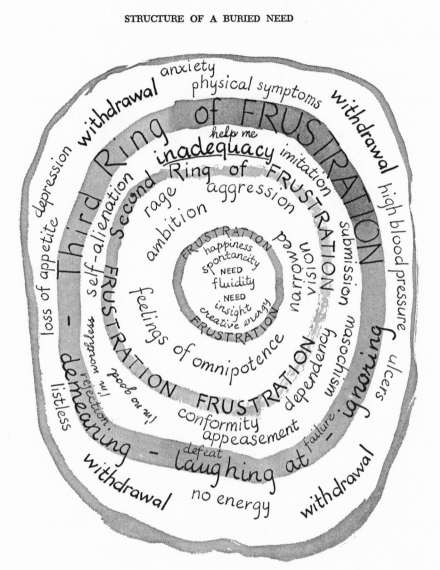

ately outside the inner circle is filled with feelings of aggression that are negatively expressed as rage and feelings of omnipotence. Here the individual is ready to fight and demonstrates irrational feelings.

SEE CHART: "LIMITS SET BY FEAR VS. LIMITS SET BY RATIONALITY"

page 144

If the aggression is unlimited, it leads to defeat, and the buried-needs state is reestablished. The result is feelings of defeat, depression, withdrawal.

If rational limits are set to contain the aggression, then inadequacy is permanently eliminated. Aggression changes from hostility to creative energy.

SEE CHART: "TRANSFORMATION OF NEEDS BY FRUSTRATION"

page 145

This chart shows how specific needs change as they go through successive layers of frustration. It is thus a more specific version of the buried-needs chart.

A free-safe atmosphere removes the rings one by one. As one gets closer to the center one has to deal by turn with withdrawal, inadequacy and rage before getting to constructive creative feelings and ideas. There is danger of being flooded with strong unacceptable feelings. How can this danger be met?

LIMIT-SETTING

Limit-Setting I: How Good Are You in Setting Limits for Others?

I. Consider the following questions and answer them in writing as thoughtfully as you can.

Sometimes you find your privacy or responsibility invaded by someone else. Are you able to set limits to prevent this?

Sometimes you have responsibility for a group that requires some limitation on individual behavior. Are you able to help the group use limits to prevent problems and solve what problems do come up?

Do you sometimes hesitate to set limits where you should?

Do you frequently wait until you grow angry before setting a limit?

Are you calm and supportive in your limit-setting of others?

Are the limits you set for others thought out?

Are you clear and firm in your limit-setting?

II. Meet in a focus group of three to five members. Draw out, discuss, clarify.

LIMITS SET BY FEAR vs LIMITS SET BY RATIONALITY

Limits through Fear

Limits through Rationality

1.

Withdrawal
Inadequacy
Aggression
Frustration
Fear
Fear
Hostility
Hostility

**Inner Need
Exploration
Fluidity
Joy**

Frustration
Fear
Aggression
Fear
Inadequacy
Withdrawal
Withdrawal

Creative Energy

Limits Explained

Aggression Becomes

Rational Limits

Inner Need

Needs of Others

Part of Nature

Creative Energy

Empathy
One with Man

6.

2.
Safety strips away the layer
of inadequacy
and withdrawal.
Aggression is *unbounded*
feelings of
omnipotence
a readiness to fight.

4.
If aggression is
left *unlimited*,
it leads to
defeat.
    The buried state
is reestablished.
Feelings of
depression
and withdrawal
result.

3.

Aggression
Frustration

Inner Need

Aggression
Unbounded Aggression

Frustration

Unbound
Aggression

5.
If rational limits are set
if they are explained
and enforced
without the punishment
that makes for
fear;
then the inadequacy
is permanently
eliminated.
Aggression changes to
creative
energy.

5.
But if rational limits are set

TRANSFORMATION OF NEEDS BY FRUSTRATION

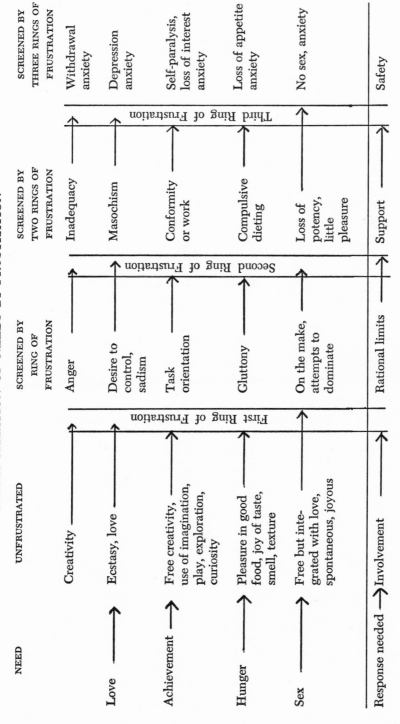

NEED	UNFRUSTRATED	First Ring of Frustration → SCREENED BY RING OF FRUSTRATION	Second Ring of Frustration → SCREENED BY TWO RINGS OF FRUSTRATION	Third Ring of Frustration → SCREENED BY THREE RINGS OF FRUSTRATION
	Creativity	Anger	Inadequacy	Withdrawal anxiety
Love	Ecstasy, love	Desire to control, sadism	Masochism	Depression anxiety
Achievement	Free creativity, use of imagination, play, exploration, curiosity	Task orientation	Conformity or work	Self-paralysis, loss of interest anxiety
Hunger	Pleasure in good food, joy of taste, smell, texture	Gluttony	Compulsive dieting	Loss of appetite anxiety
Sex	Free but integrated with love, spontaneous, joyous	On the make, attempts to dominate	Loss of potency, little pleasure	No sex, anxiety
Response needed →	Involvement	Rational limits	Support	Safety

Limit-Setting II: How Good Are You at Accepting Limitations That Others Set?

I. Consider the following questions and answer them in writing as thoughtfully as you can.

Sometimes a person or group feels that you are imposing on them. At other times the leader or the activity of a group places restrictions on you. How are you able to handle this?

Do you accept the reasonable limits that others set for you?

Are you disturbed when someone sets a limit for you?

Do you often feel rebellious and hostile when a limit is set on you?

II. Meet in a small group of three to five members. Play the Focus Game on the basis of the responses.

Limit-Setting III: How Good Are You at Setting Limits for Yourself?

I. Consider the following questions and answer them in writing as thoughtfully as you can.

Sometimes health requirements, ambitions and goals, or obligations require that you restrict your impulses, needs, or habits. Are you able to set your own limits and live by them?

When setting a limit on yourself, do you consider the obstacles and ways of overcoming them?

When setting a limit on yourself that closes one way of meeting a need, do you provide other alternative methods for meeting the need?

Are you firm and clear in setting limits for yourself?

In what ways would you like your limit-setting behaviors to change?

What can you do to help implement the changes you would like to make?

II. Meet in a small focus group. Use written answers as the basis for focusing.

Criteria for Adequate Limit-Setting

The limit established is seen as:

1. Rational: The reasons for the limit should be explained fully and objectively. Alternative ways of meeting the need blocked by the limit should be explored. Where possible the person being limited should participate in the limit setting.

2. Clear: Limits should be carefully explained and clarified before the occurrence of behavior. They are designed to prevent the occurrence of certain behavior, not to punish the behavior once it has occurred. Ambivalent or unclear statements of limits invites violation.

3. Firm: The limit should be firm, and where possible, impossible to violate. You can't smoke cigarettes if you've thrown them away. A child can't open a refrigerator if you put a lock on it.

4. Non-punitive: Limits should be enforced with as little use of punishment as possible. Punishments that create feelings of fear, insecurity, or inadequacy should be particularly avoided.

5. Humane: The limit should be enforced in respect to action only. The person's right to feel and think negatively concerning the limit should be respected.

CHAPTER 6

Games for Integration

In the integration section we learn to pull together qualities that better unify our lives. There are four parts to this series.

I. *Values Games*, in which choosing, prizing, and acting are integrated.

II. *Creativity Games*, in which one practices first producing ideas and then pulling them together, or making them relevant to each other. (See Chapter 4 for games.)

III. *The Game of Feelings, Knowledge, and Skills*, in which these three elements are unified to make for more spontaneous, more powerful, and wiser action.

IV. *Five-fold Life Plan Game*, in which one integrates one's values and those of one's primary group in a life plan.

V. *Position Statement*, in which one integrates feelings, objectives, point of view, and thinking in a single statement on some issue. (See Chapter 1 for game.)

VI. *Understanding Response*, in which one integrates one's understanding of another's position including their thinking, feeling, objectives, and point of view. (See Chapter 1 for game.)

VALUES THEORY

If you are working individually, answer the questions below. If this program is being done in a group, it is best to read the questions with the following introduction.

Facilitator reads: "I am going to ask some questions to find out how people in the group think and feel about certain issues. If you strongly agree, raise your hand very high. If you agree a little, raise it less high. If you disagree, lower your hand. If you disagree strongly, lower it as far down as you can reach.

"Have you ever been confused about any of your values?

"Do you think that most people practice what they preach?

"Are the values shown on TV, the movies, and in newspapers consistent with the values we want our children to have?

"How many really enjoyed what they did this Saturday?

"Have you done anything this week that you are proud of?

"Is there anything you did this week that you did not choose to do and didn't like doing?

"How many feel bored when they have to do something they neither chose nor like?

"How many feel rebellious when they are forced to do something that they like?

"How many feel angry or rebellious when they are forced to do something they neither chose nor like?

"How many feel dragged down at times by routine?

"How many feel exhilarated when they decide to do something and actually carry it out?

"How many have decided on their own to do something this week and actually carried it out?

"How many of you feel good about it?

"How many find their values become clearer when someone tells them what to do?

"How many find that their values become clearer when they go through the process of making a difficult choice?

"How many find that their values become clearer when someone tells them what's right or wrong?

"How many find that their values become clearer when they discuss the consequences of different ways of acting?

"How many have found that moralizing helps them clarify their values?

"How many felt that understanding listening helps them more than moralizing?

"How many have been helped by being asked a good question?

"How many find their values become clearer when they consider what they really want to do or be?"

Answer the following questions in writing. Take ten minutes.

1. Describe how you feel when your values are unclear or are not involved in a situation in which you find yourself.

2. Describe how you feel in a situation in which your values are clear and are fully involved.

3. How can you know that a person holds a value strongly and completely?

4. Must he have chosen it freely, or can he have just grown up with it for it to be held completely?

5. Must he be willing to identify himself openly and publicly with his value, or may he be ashamed of it?

6. Is it necessary for him to act on it consistently, or is it sufficient if he just talks about it?

If you are doing this program alone, go over your answers and see what meaning they have for you in your present-life situation.

If this program is being done in a group, break into subgroups of four. Each person takes a turn reading his answers. Afterward discuss briefly. Total discussion should take twenty minutes.

Definition of a Clear Value

It is not sufficient to be open. To live vitally, one must be together; and this is difficult in a world fragmented by conflicting demands. The resulting confusion and fragmentation leads to apathy, listlessness, drift, or surrender to dogmatic rigidity.

Values represent a very high level of psychic integration, making a directed, vital existence possible, despite the fragmenting pressure of society.

A value held completely, one that serves this integrative function most completely, must meet the following seven requirements: (1) It should be freely chosen (2) from among alternatives (3) after a thoughtful consideration of the alternatives. (4) It should be something one feels good about, (5) is proud of, willing to talk about publicly, (6) is acted upon, and (7) is part of a total pattern of one's life. The order of criteria given here is the order of the Values Games given in this chapter.

To get an experiential feeling for this material, try these exercises.

Directions: Identify some values in your life. List them across the top of the following chart and check to see how many of the seven criteria of a complete value they fulfill.

VALUES CRITERIA	VALUE 1	VALUE 2	VALUE 3
1. Chosen freely			
2. From among alternatives			
3. After careful consideration			

VALUES CRITERIA	VALUE 1	VALUE 2	VALUE 3
4. Feel good about it			
5. Is publicly affirmed			
6. Is acted on			
7. Forms part of pattern of one's life			

Now get into groups of four. Each person takes a turn in reading his answers with the other members of the group drawing him out. Take forty minutes for discussion.

The answers to the following questions are to be done individually at a later time. The group can now go on to some of the other Values Games.

1. Do you see any unique qualities in your life when you are dealing in areas integrated by complete values?

2. Think of some of your *complete* values in each of the following important life domains:

> money
> friendship
> love and sex
> religion and morality
> leisure
> politics and social organization
> work
> family
> self

3. Were there some areas in which you had trouble stating complete values?

4. Would you like to develop more complete values in some of these areas? Which ones? In what way do you want them more complete?

5. Have you thought of any ways to do this? In which domains?

Opportunities to Assess Your Understanding of Values Theory

1. Informally

You have achieved the objective of this lesson if you now have a sense of what a complete value is and of how it functions to make life more unified and meaningful.

2. Paper and Pencil Test

Write your answers on a separate sheet. Our answers are below each question, so cover them with a sheet of paper as you do the test.

a. How many of the seven values criteria can you recall?

Answer: A value should be (1) chosen freely, (2) from alternatives, (3) after thoughtful consideration. It should be something one (4) feels good about or is proud of, (5) is willing to talk about, (6) acts on, (7) repeatedly as part of the pattern of one's life.

b. If the seven criteria are present, is the value complete?

Answer: Yes

c. Is a complete value a more forceful influence on one's life than an incomplete value?

Answer: Yes

d. If a person has chosen to buy a bicycle after careful consideration, has told everybody that he intends to buy it, but doesn't, what must he do to make his choice a value?

Answer: Buy a bicycle.

e. Which of the seven criteria was missing in the above situation?

Answer: Action

f. If, in fact, the person does buy a bicycle, will his life be more integrated?

Answer: Yes

g. What values criteria are shown in the following statement? "I like the Republican candidate."

Answer: (1) Public announcement (2) and feeling good about something.

h. What value-rich area does each of the following questions get at?

1. How did you spend your allowance this week?

Answer: Money

2. Where have you met most of your friends?

Answer: Friendship

3. What would you want in a boyfriend or girlfriend?

Answer: Love and sex

4. Do you have any idea of God?

Answer: Religion

5. Who would you vote for? Do you belong to any club?

Answer: Politics and social organization

6. How do you spend your weekends?

Answer: Leisure

7. What kind of job would you like to have?

Answer: Work

8. How do you overcome disagreements with brothers or sisters?

Answer: Family

9. What kind of man or woman would you like to be?

Answer: Self

i. Can you name some value-rich areas?

Answer: Money friendship, love and sex, religion and morals, leisure politics and social organization, work, family, and self are some of the areas we think important. (Questions focusing on these areas may help clarify values.)

Focus Game for Asking Personal Questions

Most important issues are excluded from conversation. Communication tends to be bland because it avoids personal, emotional, involving questions. Questions of love, life, death, ambition, sex, family, marriage, hatred, sadness, depression, fantasy, dreams, joy, ecstasy, and religious feeling are avoided in many social interactions. This leaves most of us relatively isolated and alone in dealing with questions that count. In the Personal Question Focus Game we attempt to break out of this isolation.

Procedures

A group gets together to play the game. It breaks into groups of between three and five members each.

Each person takes a turn being focus.

The members of the group ask the focus important questions concerning central life issues that they are interested in. They also express the positive feelings they may have toward the focus person.

The focus person tries to answer the questions as honestly as possible. If he feels he cannot or does not want to answer a certain question, he may pass.

After each person has had his focus, he and the group discuss how they felt about the process.

Values Continuum Game

1. A group comes together to play the game.
2. Each member thinks of pairs of extreme position on issues, such as:

complete freedom of individual	1 . . . 2 . . . 3 . . . 4 . . . 5	complete dedication to group
miserliness	1 . . . 2 . . . 3 . . . 4 . . . 5	impulse buying
atheism	1 . . . 2 . . . 3 . . . 4 . . . 5	fundamentalism

3. All of the pairs are read, and the group determines which pair is most relevant or intriguing.

4. When one pair is chosen, each group member realistically places himself somewhere between the extremes on the continuum. (Use a blackboard or a large sheet of paper for the continuum.)

5. People take turns telling where they placed themselves and why.

6. They then place themselves where they would like to be and discuss why.

7. There can be a general discussion of the continuum, using the rules of the discussion game.

Some Suggested Continua

a. Orderly vs. disorderly

b. Radical vs. conservative

c. Outgoing vs. withdrawing

d. Conforming vs. nonconforming

e. Forgiving quickly vs. holding a grudge

BE REAL GAME

Many times we do things or say things which we do not intend—we seem to drift into them, respond to the expectations of others, or act out of habit. All of these ways of acting make us less real. In each case, we cannot be blamed since we neither wanted to do it, nor got the credit. It is as if we had no responsibility; it is as if we did not exist at all.

It is only when we have chosen among all the alternatives, knowing full well the consequences, and have acted upon the choice, that we are real. We may be wrong in our choice, but we have acted of our own free will.

Procedures

The game is introduced and members agree to play.

As a group, decide to do something that requires full group participation and which takes you beyond the confines of the group setting to carry out the action.

Now do it. When finished, return. DO NOT READ FURTHER.

Each group member is to be the focus and answer the following questions:

a. How did the group choose? With deliberation, spontaneously, or impulsively?

b. Were you active in the process? Or did you drift into acting, responding to the expectations of others?

c. What alternatives did the group consider? What others did you consider, but not mention? Why?

d. Did you consider the consequences? What are they?

Rule: During this last step, the focus person should say only what he has chosen to say, not what he is expected to say.

VALUES DISCUSSION GAME

1. A group gets together to play the game.
2. Old magazines or newspapers should be provided.
3. Each member finds a short controversial passage—or writes one of his own.
4. Each player takes a turn reading his passage.
5. All the group members answer in writing these questions concerning the passage.

a. What issues or problems does this passage bring up?

b. Which do you think most important?

c. What ways are there for solving or living with this problem?

d. What ways have you used? What ways do you prefer? Are your actions in keeping with your preferences?

e. What do you intend to do about this problem in the future?

6. Group members take turns reading and talking about their answers.

Note: If desired, a person may use a different set of questions with the passage he chooses. If so, it is best for questions to be involving, to get at feelings and possible action that the reader can take.

GAME FOR CLARIFYING VALUES

Round 1

Each player thinks of something he enjoys or values.

The players take turns telling what they enjoy or value, and add one sentence concerning what they did or plan to do about it.

Round 2

Each player writes something he recently did.

The players take turns stating something they recently did. They say whether they feel good about it, whether they drifted into it, or deliberately chose to do it after considering alternatives.

"FREE CHOICE" PROGRAM

Objectives

This lesson tries to give you some experiences in thinking about some of your attitudes, feelings, and patterns of action in regard to free choice. In doing this you may be able to sense why we believe that free choice is an important element in living.

Directions

If you are working individually, answer the questions, do the exercise, but ignore all directions concerning groups.

If this program is being done in a group, the group facilitator reads the following aloud: "I am going to ask some questions to find out how people in the group think and feel about certain issues. If you strongly agree, raise your hand very high. If you agree a little, raise it less high. If you disagree, lower your hand. If you disagree strongly, lower it as far down as you can reach.

"How many sometimes find it difficult to make a free choice?

"How many are sometimes very worried that they made the wrong choice?

"How many sometimes choose impulsively to reduce the tension of choosing?

"How many become very involved emotionally in the process of choosing?

"How many find a sense of renewal when they have ceased to drift and have begun to choose and decide?

"How many hate to·have other people make major decisions that affect them, without their being involved?

"How many make decisions affecting others?

"How many like to make decisions quickly?

"How many have stayed awake all night because of a decision they had to make?

"How many spend time learning about alternatives before making a decision?

"How many made a decision and discovered that there was another alternative that they would have liked better?

"How many ask others for advice before making a decision?

"How many get angry when they are given the advice they asked for?

"How many usually follow advice?

"How many follow advice even when they have an inkling that it is wrong?

"How many later blame those who gave them advice?

"How many like to make family decisions?

"How many prefer that the husband or wife make them?

"How many consider the consequences of the various alternatives?

"How many consider their immediate feelings only?

"Now read the following silently and break into groups to do the exercise, after which we will have a brief discussion of the experience."

The process of choice is a stimulant. It awakens the mind and enlivens the circulation.

In any significant choice, latent dreams and fantasies come into play. Needs long neglected find entry into awareness. Parts of ourself long dead awaken in the process of considering choices.

Free choice is a way of becoming whole, for many parts of ourselves are involved in making them. Free choice is a liberator of energies encased in routine. It is an effective antidote to apathy, boredom, and depersonalization.

Free choice can be painful, for it can be a powerful therapy. It brings up latent conflicts and puts us face to face with anxiety that routine has put in chains. To choose freely is to be alive, but it takes courage to live fully.

Think of one complex choice you made recently.

1. How did you go about weighing the various alternatives?
2. Were you happy with the way you thought the issue through?

After every member of your group has finished his answers, or when ten minutes are up, read your answers and start the discussion.

Individual Program

Everyone does the rest of this program individually. Consider the following continuum between free choice and routinization:

1. Delight in free choice.
2. Like it somewhat.
3. Have no preference between routine and free choice.
4. Dislike to choose freely.
5. Hate choice; prefer routine.

Place yourself on the above values continuum as you now are.

Are you satisfied with your position on the routine-free choice values continuum?

Where would you like to be on that values continuum?

Can you think of any ways in which you can get your "choosing" behavior more in keeping with your ideals?

The questions above involved you in a values-clarifying lesson. How did they make you feel?

Can you see ways of applying the technique used in this lesson?

Note: The "Values Continuum" can be used to help people clarify and identify their values.

Opportunities for Assessing Your Understanding of "Free Choice" Program

1. If you have thought through the material above, you may have obtained some sense of what the issue of free choice involves for you.

2. If you can see or feel how such involvement can improve your zest in living, you have achieved the purpose of this lesson.

3. If at this point you have not obtained a feel for the importance of free choice and would want to, you might like to get involved in one of the interaction games.

4. Consider the following stretch questions:

What portion of your life have you chosen freely?

Which statements about life make for a wider area of free choice?

a. I am what I am and can do nothing about it.

b. I am what I have chosen to be. I can change my mind and be what I am not.

c. One should try to be as natural as possible.

d. One should try to do what one chooses, even if it feels strange at first and everyone calls it unnatural.

e. What is called natural is a prison we cooperate in making for ourselves.

f. Consider the above five statements (1 to 5) and choose those that you have been living your life by.

g. Now choose those that you would like to govern your life by.

h. Are the choices the same? If not, would you like to test out doing something about it?

In answering the following questions, cover the answers with a sheet of paper.

5. The seven criteria for a complete value are:

Answer: (1) chosen freely, (2) from alternatives, (3) after thoughtful consideration, (4) feeling good about the choice, (5) publicly affirming it or talking about it, (6) acting on it, and (7) integrating it in a pattern.

Which of these criteria are most closely related to free choice?

Answer: The presence of alternatives and thoughtful consideration.

6. Can there be free choice if there are no alternatives?

Answer: It is hard to see how there can be any kind of choice without alternatives.

7. Can there be free choice without thoughtfulness?

Answer: No. Thoughtfulness may be slow and deep as a river, or quick as lightning, fire, and spontaneity. Free choice may be spontaneous or deliberate, but it is never impulsive or routinized.

Quick thought is spontaneity; slow thought, deliberation. No thought, impulsiveness or routinization. Impulsiveness or routinization are the negation of free choice.

8. Which of the following statements does not get at free choice?

When did you decide that?

How old were you when you decided?

Is it something you wanted to do?

Did you ever consider doing something else?

Is it something you want to do, or are you doing it not to lose face?

What have you done about it?

Answer: The last question is the only one that does not involve free choice.

FOR FURTHER UNDERSTANDING OF ACTING AND CHOOSING

Actions have conscious and unconscious elements. While the conscious reason for an action may be a need or a value, its unconscious side may reflect wishes and fantasies. While the conscious side may be based on reason and observation, its unconscious aspect may be determined by wishes and hunches and intuitions.

When the unconscious aspect of an action is excluded or repressed, the action will be mechanical, graceless, and rigid. When the conscious and unconscious aspects work together, the action will be spontaneous, organized, and balanced.

When the unconscious is primary but the conscious continues to exercise some control, the action is playful, spontaneous, and intuitive. But if the unconscious is primary and controls the conscious, the action becomes demonic and destructive.

When the distinctions between conscious and unconscious are resolved, the action becomes prophetic, wise, or heroic. When conscious and unconscious are opposed, action becomes disorganized, destructive and impulsive.

See "Structure of an Action" on the next page.

Our feelings, our imagination, and our intuition are the best clues as to what is going on in our unconscious. If we have strong feelings or intuitions that a course of action is to be avoided, we should respect these intimations even if the course seems to be correct from the point of view of reason. It is important at such a time to examine one's feelings and intuitions and try to understand them before taking action.

STRUCTURE OF AN ACTION

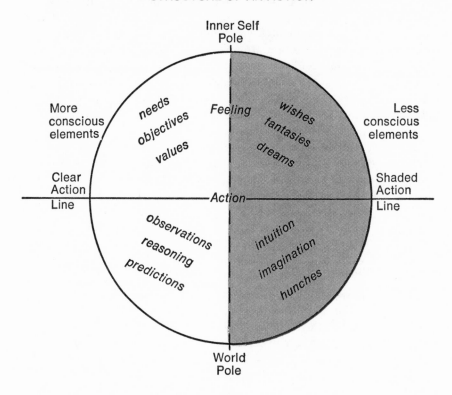

Inner Self Pole

More conscious elements

Less conscious elements

needs *objectives* *values*

Feeling

wishes *fantasies* *dreams*

Clear Action Line

Shaded Action Line

Action

observations *reasoning* *predictions*

intuition *imagination* *hunches*

World Pole

If our feelings and intuition favor a course of action that is also affirmed by our reason, then it is a course of action we will be able to pursue most energetically and undividedly.

If our feelings and intuition favor a course of action, but our reasoning is opposed, we should be cautious and examine feelings, intuitions, and reasoning further until we no longer feel inwardly divided.

GAME OF EXPLICATING ALTERNATIVE VALUES

Members think of some trait or issue or way of acting, like orderliness vs. messiness, courage vs. cowardice, facing vs. withdrawing, free choice vs. fidelity, accuracy vs. inaccuracy, etc.

The members decide which issue to discuss.

In the discussion an attempt is made to explore the immediate and long-range consequences of each position on the issue. The rules of the discussion game are used to do this.

Rank Order Values Game

We are often faced with value choices. Would we rather be loved, admired, or free? Would we rather be strong, clever, or popular? Sometimes the choices are negative: Would we rather be blind, deaf, or mentally deficient? Would we rather be robbed or killed? Background values such as these may be involved in the day-to-day choices we all make. Rank orders represent an opportunity to practice value decisions in the absence of any consequences.

How to Play

A group of people get together.

Each writes down three alternative choices, usually related to one or more of the value areas.

After most people are finished writing, one volunteers to read his list.

Each group member arranges these *in order of preferences.*

People read their choices and explain why they made them.

At any time, a person may choose not to read his list; or may read his list and choose not to explain why. This is accomplished by simply declaring, "I pass."

Avoid repetitious responses such as "same as before" during the game. It's usually better to have each person read his list.

Steps 1 to 7 can be repeated with others reading their lists.

Some Rank Orders

Following are a few rank orders that we have found useful in the past. Perhaps you might like to try using them along with your own.

wealthy	movie star	charming
intelligent	millionaire	reliable
respected	president	insightful
watch TV	American Negro	rose bush
go on a date	Mexican Negro	cactus
study	African Negro	lily
monkey	sickly	sword
porpoise	crippled	gun
bird	dwarfed	atom bomb
listless	teacher	teacher's pet
flighty	accountant	class clown
uncertain	writer	teacher's scapegoat

happy and average	mixed racial marriage
intelligent but tense	mixed religious marriage
powerful and hated	unhappy, unmixed marriage

This game can be used at parties, as a family diversion, or in the classroom. It's fun and helps people to know themselves and each other.

THE "FREE CHOICE" GAME

Choosing is difficult. Avoiding decisions and the pain of free choice is easy. We follow advice unthinkingly. We take the path of least resistance. We conform. We drift.

The Free Choice Game helps us take better hold of our lives and maximize the wisdom of our decisions.

Objective

A group helps one of its members to think through an issue that contains an element of free choice and to make a decision.

Procedures

1. *Introduction.* A group of two or more persons convenes and agrees to play the game. One person asks to be the focus person. He then begins by telling the group about something that presents a choice to him.

The choice issue may involve an impending decision. Should I get married to Bill? Should I drop out of school? Should I take a job? What should I do about my sister's request for a loan?

Or the choice may be whether or not to continue an existing pattern of behavior, perhaps a behavior one repeats routinely or impulsively. Should I give up smoking? What shall I do about my stinginess? Shall I continue my current work? Am I doing what I want in life? How can I make my friendship patterns more satisfying? Can I lose weight?

2. *Understanding the issue.* After introducing the issue, the focus person talks a bit about it, explaining how he feels about it, what led up to it, what his motivations are in the present, what his purposes are for the future, etc.

After the focus person has talked about this, he invites group members to make contributions from their own perceptual positions, and to ask questions in an effort to round out and fill in for the focus person an understanding of the elements that impinge on the issue.

If the issue deals with an existing pattern of behavior, it is useful for the focus to talk about why that pattern has persisted. He may try to answer the question, "What problems does the existing behavior solve or reduce?"

3. *Alternatives.* When the group, especially the focus person, feels as if the issue is pretty well understood, the discussion turns to a search for alternative actions the focus person might take. This step of the game has a brainstorming quality to it. The emphasis is on thinking of possible choices, not on evaluating the choices identified.

First the focus person tries to list alternatives. When he is ready, he invites the group to help him add new alternatives. A list might be kept of alternatives mentioned.

If the issue deals with an existing pattern of behavior, it is useful for the group to search for alternative behaviors that accomplish the same purposes as do the current pattern.

4. *Consequences.* When the group and the focus are ready, the discussion turns to an examination of what each of the most promising alternatives would lead to. Which would produce the most desirable results for the focus person?

First the focus person examines the consequences of the alternatives as he sees them, then he asks the group for their help in extending his understanding.

Sometimes this step can be combined with step 3 above.

5. *Decision.* When the focus person feels as if he has as much information about alternatives and consequences as he can handle or is likely to obtain, he announces his decision publicly.

If the issue deals with an old pattern of behavior, he says whether or not he will continue it; and if not, what, if anything, he will substitute for it. For new behavior patterns he intends to adopt, he also announces whether his decision is for the foreseeable future, or is time-limited (such as a trial for a specified period of time.)

The group hears his decision, accepting it. The group reacts only in response to direct questions from the focus, for the focus may find it useful to retrace with the group some of the steps above, perhaps in more detail, before a decision is made.

This step sometimes requires patience and some group silence. If the focus fails to announce a decision, the group is free to point out what it sees as the consequences of such a failure to announce a decision.

Rules

1. One person has the focus for as long as he chooses to keep it. If one meeting is not enough, he may ask if a group would be willing to reconvene and let him continue to be on focus.

2. A group member (this includes the focus person) should bring the focus back to the original person if it slips to someone else.

3. The focus person should announce when he has had enough. He should not let the focus slip away. After he has relinquished the focus, another person takes it or the group ceases play.

4. Group members should bring the topic back to the original one if it drifts.

5. Game players should be maximally honest.

6. Each should do what he can, within the limits of the other rules, to enhance the group climate, to make others feel comfortable and happy.

7. No leader of the group has any special privileges.

8. The group and individuals in it should not try to pressure the focus person toward any particular decision, either openly or covertly. The focus is to be viewed as someone with his own private perceptions and experiences, who must live with himself and be responsible for his own behavior.

VOTING GAME

This game is good for finding people's opinions on all sorts of questions. It is easy to play, and can be used at parties, at school, or at home. It opens up all sorts of questions for discussion and makes an interesting time for everyone.

How to Play

A group gets together to play.

Each player writes two or three questions that are revealing but require only a "yes" or "no" answer.

People take turns reading their questions and the other members indicate their answer by raising their hands for "yes," lowering their hands for "no."

If members wish, there can be a brief discussion of the answers.

PRIZING
GROUP AND INDIVIDUAL PROGRAM

Objectives

Being proud of what one does usually makes one feel good. Being proud is a pleasant feeling. This unit will consider the place of feeling good about and being proud of what we do.

Instructions

This program is designed for both individual and group use. If you are doing the program individually, skip those sections titled "For group only." If the program is being done in a group, it will be helpful if every group member has a copy of the program. Certain sections should be read by the person leading or facilitating the program.

For Group Only

The facilitator reads: "I want everyone to think of something he has done in the last week that he is proud of or feels good about. [Wait about two minutes.]

"Now we are going to go around in a circle with every person taking a turn telling the group what he has done in the past week that he's proud of or feels good about. If you are not in the mood to say anything to the group, say, 'I pass,' when your turn comes. No one should feel compelled to talk if he does not feel like it."

When everyone has had a turn, the facilitator continues: "I am going to ask you some voting questions. [For introduction to Voting Questions, see Compliment Game, page 5.]

"Have you ever felt overloaded by routine?

"Have you ever felt that you didn't enjoy most of the things you did?

"Have you ever been forced to do something because it was right, but it made everyone miserable?

"Do you think your life has some duties or activities that give you no satisfaction?

"Do you ever feel compelled or driven to do things that give you no satisfaction?

"Do you ever take pride in doing difficult things?

"Do you ever take pride or pleasure in some of your routines or habits?

"Are there some duties that you enjoy fulfilling?

"Are there some things you feel proud to accomplish, even if they are difficult, tense, or unpleasant?

"On a sheet of paper, write some of the possible reasons why you feel good about some hard, difficult, and unpleasant jobs and bad about others."

The facilitator now asks, after waiting two or three minutes, if there is anybody who would be willing to tell the group the differences he perceives. He draws out each person who volunteers with a few questions. This activity may go on for as long as twenty minutes. When the activity loses its interest, the facilitator continues:

"In general, things which we do without pleasure or pride, things which we feel driven to do, are things which we have swallowed as necessary or right uncritically. They are resented because they were never freely chosen, and hence are not felt to be truly meaningful to us. If there are too many things in which we take no pleasure or pride, we are not living our own life. We may be living the life of our parents, our spouse, our children, our friends, but not our own life.

"A life without pleasure or pride is a dull, boring, tight, mean existence.

"How many have felt inadequate, guilty, or depressed when they were doing too many things in which they could feel neither pleasure nor pride?

"How many have gotten angry and mean, and made others miserable under those conditions?

"How many have done both?

"Values theory suggests that the only solution is to do more things one feels good about, and to feel good about more of the things one does."

ACTIVITY I

Write a list of things that you could do which would make you feel good.

Are there any of these that you would like to commit yourself to doing?

Make a list of the obstacles to the activities you want to commit yourself to, and the resources you have in overcoming these obstacles.

For groups only. Break into pairs or focus groups and discuss your plans.

ACTIVITY II

Make a list of activities that you have to do, but dislike and take no pride in.

Look over the list and see if any of them are really unnecessary.

Check the few that bother you most.

Explore your feelings concerning them. Try to understand why you feel that way. Now look at the problem freshly. What might you do to make the activity your own, so you could feel better about it or take pride in it?

For group only. Break into groups or pairs. Each person takes a turn exploring what he can do about the activities he doesn't like.

Opportunities for Assessing Your Understanding of Prizing

Some questions testing your understanding of the role of prizing in values theory follow below.

DIRECTIONS: Cover the answer until you have read and answered the question.

1. Is anything that is prized a value to which one is completely committed?

Answer: Maybe. For something to be a value, it is not sufficient for it to be prized: It must be chosen freely and acted upon.

2. To what other three value categories should prizing be related?

Answer: Prizing should be related both to choice and to action. We tend to prize what we choose freely, and to choose freely what we prize. Choices made on the basis of prizing become values when they are acted on and talked about freely.

3. If someone mentions something that he prizes, how can we help clarify his values?

Answer: By asking whether he chose it freely, or by asking whether or not he acted on it.

Stretches Toward Prizing

Stretch A. During a set period of time, whenever you think of something you prize, ask yourself how you can act on it.

Stretch B. Whenever you find yourself doing something you have not consciously chosen to do, ask yourself if there are any alternative courses of action you might prize more.

Stretch C. Whenever someone mentions something he prizes, ask him some questions to find out if he is acting on it.

Stretch D. (This one might make enemies for you.) When someone is doing something you doubt that he values, ask a question getting at whether he has considered alternatives.

These four stretches may be done separately or all together for periods as short as an hour or as long as two days. The stretch may be too intense an experience for most values learning. It may present one with too much to think about, but it is a way of getting into the values frame of reference in a very short time.

PUBLIC STATEMENT
AN INDIVIDUAL AND GROUP PROGRAM

Instructions

This program is designed for both individual and group use. If you are doing the program individually, skip those sections entitled "For group only." If the program is being done in a group, it will be helpful if every group member has a copy of the program. Certain sections should be read by the person leading or facilitating the program.

The facilitator reads:

"I am going to ask you some voting questions. [For introduction to Voting Questions, see Compliment Game, page 5.]

"Have you ever found that you committed yourself through silence?

"Did this ever create anxiety, misunderstanding, or tension?

"Have you ever seen anything definitely wrong or unfair at work or at school that you spoke up about?

"Did you feel a little afraid when you spoke up?

"How many found that you had good reason to be afraid?

"Is there anyone who would like to tell us about it? [If there are volunteers, the facilitator listens to each, drawing them out with a few non-judgmental questions.]

"How many felt good that you spoke up despite the criticism that followed?

"Did you ever see something very wrong and not speak up?

"How did you feel about it? Is there anyone who wants to tell us? [If there are volunteers, the facilitator listens to each, drawing him out with a few questions.]

"Are there any of you who have been in a situation where you or your values were attacked unknowingly?

"How many always speak up?

"How many always let it pass?

"How many sometimes do one, sometimes the other?

"When you let it pass, did you feel small, disturbed, or angry?"

ACTIVITY I

FOR GROUP ONLY

"Now I would like you to do the following. Think of beliefs or values you hold strongly which you have recently acted upon. Pause for about two minutes. Select one of these to tell the group about.

"We will go around in a circle with each person taking a turn speaking. If your turn comes, and for some reason or other you are not in the mood to talk to the group, simply say, 'I pass.' It is very important that no one feel compelled to talk if he doesn't want to."

After the group goes around, the facilitator reads the following:

"Most of us have experienced the pleasure of finding someone with whom we could feel free to share our feelings, beliefs, ideals, plans, etc. But even when perfect conditions are not present, it is beneficial to talk about these things for the following reasons:

"1. Standing up for what we believe makes us stronger and more together.

"2. Talking about our values brings us closer to people.

"3. The responses of other people may help clarify or stimulate our thinking, or may open up new alternatives.

"4. The attention, interest, and concern of others in what we do is pleasurable and helps one maintain one's own interest.

"5. Even when the first response to what we say is negative, speaking is not as destructive as being ashamed or scared of being found out when certain topics come up."

ACTIVITY II

"Now I want you to do the following:

"Make a list of things you should bring up and confront. Rank them and select those that you would really seriously consider opening for discussion with the appropriate person."

For Group Only

"Think of alternative ways that you might bring up the issue most constructively. Close your eyes and try to imagine the consequences of each of your plans.

"Break into pairs or groups of four. Take turns in discussing each of the plans. What is the best and most constructive way of opening up the subject?

"Take turns in role-playing the introduction and discussion of the issue."

For Individuals Alone

Think of alternative ways that you might bring up the issue most constructively. Close your eyes and try to imagine the consequences of each of your plans. Select the plan that seems most appropriate and try it when the occasion arises.

To Be Done at a Second Session

Countering Some Disadvantages of Sharing Values

Despite the advantages of talking about one's values, beliefs, and activities, one often hesitates for fear of being laughed at, condemned, or misunderstood. While some of these fears may be realistic, they are often exaggerated. Negative reactions can often be invited by being suggested. When one starts out a statement with "you won't agree with this . . . ," the introduction is often a self-fulfilling prophecy.

A simple, honest, forthright statement of one's position tends to minimize negative reactions and win respect.

Have you ever been apologetic, indirect, or unclear in presenting yourself or your beliefs and ideas?

Think of some occasion where you have been less forthright, less clear, or less honest than you would have liked to have been?

Close your eyes and try to imagine a better way that you could have handled the situation. What dangers did you imagine? What benefits?

For Group Only

Get into pairs. Explain the situation to the other member of the pair. Role-play new ways of presenting yourself or your beliefs.

Can Be Done Individually Or in a Group

Are there things you feel good about but seldom talk about? Why?

Try talking about one of these. Choose something of which the feared consequences are mild at worst. Say it nonapologetically and proudly, if possible. After doing this, go on to the next question.

How did the experience of being more open make you feel?

Did you notice you had more energy? This is often a result of the removal of the fear that kept you quiet.

Stretch to Public Statement.

Take every opportunity to talk about what you value, your ideas, plans, activities, etc., and encourage others to do the same for a set period of time. Choose an hour or two to start; afterward try a period of several days.

Self-assessment

(Since this section covers a portion of values theory, you might want to test yourself to see if you understand it.)

This exercise is designed to give you a feeling of why and how talking about what one does tends to make one more integrated.

If you do not yet have an experiential sense of this, try the integration games, particularly the Interview Game.

Here are some assessment questions that should help clarify some issues concerning public statement (use a sheet to cover author's answer until you have worked out your own answer):

1. Question—Forcing people to reveal themselves will make them more open and better adjusted.

Answer—Being forced to do anything may be destructive to the person's sense of himself.

2. Question—If a person chooses to reveal part of himself in public, the results are almost certain to be beneficial.

Answer—No. This will depend in part on how others respond to him. If the response is punishing or rejecting, then the person will be less likely to reveal himself in the future. Revealing oneself or helping others to reveal parts of themselves requires judgment, caution, tact, and courage. One should consider the consequences and be willing to accept the worst as well as the best outcome.

3. Question—If one wants people to be more open and talk about their values, what kind of atmosphere should one set up?

Answer—A free and safe atmosphere.

Revealing Opinions to Which Others May Respond Negatively

4. Question—In revealing a feeling that others may respond to negatively, is it best to be apologetic, attacking, or calm? Rank these in order, and give a reason for your ranking.

Answer—Calm: If people feel that you are confident concerning your belief, they are more likely to consider it and respect it. Otherwise they are likely to attack you for it.

Attacking: An attack is sometimes the best form of defense. Unfortunately, it may often lead to superficial acquiescence, or simply turn others off.

Apologetic: Hardly ever. This is simply an invitation for others to vent their sadistic urges on you.

5. Question—Ideally one should say everything one thinks to everyone. Do you think this is a wise policy?

Answer—It is the best way of losing one's freedom in a very short time.

6. Question—What are the conditions under which public statement is wise for oneself or others?

Answer *a*. When you have a receptive, understanding, and nonpunishing audience.

Answer *b*. When you can handle the negative feelings aroused by your statement constructively.

7. *Caution:* Question—In telling what you think, feel, and know, is it important to consider the desire of the other person to hear, understand, and handle what you say?

Answer—Yes.

8. *Caution:* Question—Can being honest and open become an excuse for being dominating and inconsiderate?

Answer—Yes. If the person, on the basis of honesty, insists on saying everything that comes into his head, not only does he violate his unwilling listener, but he also prevents anybody else from talking.

9. *Caution:* Question—Can being honest be used as an excuse for being destructive?

Answer—You bet it can. One has an obligation to find constructive ways of expressing negative feelings.

THE GAME OF GROUP WHIP AND MINI-FOCUS

Objectives

1. Good for sharing experiences quickly on a wide variety of subjects.
2. Good as a get-acquainted game.
3. Good for stimulating exchange and opening up topics.
4. Can be used to get a group started by enabling all the members to give their feeling or thinking in brief.
5. Excellent for critiquing a group process.
6. Useful when a group gets stuck, for deciding on a new direction for movement.

Procedures

A group convenes to play the game. Four to fifteen members are ideal. Each person takes a turn asking a question.
The question should involve personal meaning.
Examples:

a. Name something you did that you are proud of.
b. What do you feel about (a current issue)?
c. What was the most interesting thing that happened this week?
d. Who are you? etc.

Whipping around the group, each person answers the question. (A time limit of two or three minutes may be agreed on.)
Optional: Rule of Mini-Focus. Each person may be briefly drawn out with several questions concerning his answer.

THE GAME OF PUBLIC INTERVIEW

Objectives

The first purpose of the Public Interview Game is to give the interviewee a chance to reveal more of himself in public in order to help him become more himself, more open and secure with his peers.

The second purpose of the game is to enable members of the audience to learn more about the interviewee, so that they may more deeply and honestly and sensitively relate to him.

The third purpose of the game is to raise value issues so that people may think about them if they so choose. This is accomplished by revealing issues of concern to one person or aspects of one person's life for all to consider as alternatives for themselves.

Procedures

A group of three or more persons convenes and agrees to play the game. The first step is to choose the interviewer. This can be done by having group members take turns, by asking for volunteers, or in any other way the group decides.

The interviewer then asks for volunteers to be interviewed. Whenever possible, the interviewer waits until there are at least two volunteers from whom to select the interviewee.

The interviewer then begins and follows the rules outlined below. At the completion of the interview, all members regain their seats and may, if they choose, discuss the interview. The game is then discontinued, or a new interviewer chosen.

Rules for the Interviewer

1. The interviewer takes a position in the group furthest away from the interviewee, so that the conversation traverses the group. He asks the interviewee to take a position in front of the group or in some other "special" place.

2. The interviewer tries to make the group and the interviewee feel as comfortable as possible. The first step is often to make certain that the interviewee understands the rules of selecting topics, passing questions, and terminating the interview. (See rules for interviewee below.)

3. Usually questions should begin in a relatively safe area and become more penetrating or personal only when the interviewer perceives the situation as ready for that. Begin by asking if the interviewee would like to have questions focused on a particular topic.

4. The interviewer may use neutral questions (i.e., "What are your favorite colors?") and/or an early termination of the interview to reduce anxiety. It is sometimes useful for the interviewer to talk about his own life or values during an interview; this has a tendency to reduce pressures on the interviewee by temporarily diluting the focus.

5. Usually the best questions to ask are those that are not ordinarily asked in public, especially those that help reveal persons and that raise important issues. Value-rich areas often useful to explore are family,

friends, money, work, leisure, love and sex, religion and morals, politics, and self.

6. Sometimes the interviewer will find it useful to offer to respond to any questions that he asked of the interviewee. This helps assure the interviewee that he will not be asked questions that the interviewer would not answer.

Rules for the Interviewee

The interviewee, within the limits of honesty and prudence, tries to make his experiences, feelings, and ideas publicly known. Since the purpose of the game of Public Interview is to bring humans together in closer and more real relationships, one should not answer a question nor make a statement that will not further those purposes. If a question is asked that makes you feel too uncomfortable, or if you think an honest answer might hurt yourself or other members of the group, you may (a) discuss this problem with the interviewer, (b) avoid answering a question by saying, "I pass," or (c) terminate the interview by saying, "Thank you for your interview." You may pass any question. You may terminate the interview at any time.

Rules for the Audience

1. The audience is to be silent unless the interviewer (a) requests volunteers from the audience to direct a question to the interviewee, or (b) offers the opportunity for the interviewee to direct a question to any member of the audience. In such cases the rules of answering honestly or being able to "pass" apply.

2. Using anything a person says in an interview in a way that might be harmful is prohibited.

Alternate Forms of the Interview Game

1. Persons are paired by lot, by volunteering, or by having one person volunteer to be interviewed and to choose the interviewer. The interview then progresses according to the rules stated.

2. One person volunteers to be interviewed and the whole group asks questions.

3. Each member of the group takes a turn asking one question in rotation. Every member of the group, including the interviewer himself, has an opportunity to answer it.

4. The interviewee-volunteer chooses a panel to interview him.

Acting On One's Values
An Individual and Group Program

Instructions

This program is designed for both individual and group use. If you are doing the program individually, skip those sections titled "For group only." If the program is being done in a group, it will be helpful if every group member has a copy of the program. Certain sections should be read by the person leading or facilitating the program.

The facilitator reads:

"I am going to ask you some voting questions. [Give some explanation of voting questions when necessary. See Compliment Game, page 5.]

"Are there some things you have wanted to do for a long time, but have never done?

"Do you think of those things as often as you used to?

"Do they continue to seem real to you?

"Have any parts of yourself ever died because you failed to act on them?

"Do you ever use outer actions to mask your inner self?

"When you do this, does it ever feel as if you have lost yourself?

"Do you feel more real when your actions reveal yourself?

"Are you doing any things that have no relation to what you want to be?

"How many sometimes feel frightened when they act in accord with what they are on the inside?

"How many feel a sense of pride or inner strength, when they make their actions reflect what they feel, think, and choose?

"Have you ever brought the lesser into being at the expense of the greater?"

The action program is designed to help you explore the place of action in your total scheme of values. According to our theory of values, a value to which we are fully committed is one that has been chosen from alternatives, which we feel good about, are willing to stand up for and publicly affirm, and finally, and most importantly, consistently act on.

This is not only because others judge us more by what we do than what we say; but it is because only in action can our inner world become real, be real-ized. In our action, we not only shape the world, but we also create what we really are. What we do, we are. What we do not do, we cease to be.

Now do the following in writing.

FOR GROUP OR INDIVIDUAL

1. Make a list of things you would like to do, but have not gotten around to doing. Rank the items from "most want to do" to "least want to do." Decide which ones you are ready to commit yourself to.

FOR GROUP ONLY

2. Discuss what difficulties or obstacles you foresee in carrying out your commitment, and what resources or skills you have or can develop to carry your desires to completion. Use Focus Game or Paired Interaction. Discussion may take from forty minutes to two or three hours.

FOR INDIVIDUAL ONLY

2. Take a sheet of paper for each action you committed yourself to. Fold the sheet of paper in half. On one side write down all the obstacles in the way of doing your action; on the other side make a list of ways of overcoming these obstacles, and/or resources and skills which you need to bring your action to completion.

FOR GROUP OR INDIVIDUAL

3. Make a list of activities that you are currently doing which you would like to stop doing. Rank the items from those you want most to stop, to those you are indifferent to. Choose some of them and commit yourself to stopping.

FOR GROUP ONLY

4. Discuss the difficulties or obstacles you foresee in carrying out your commitment, and the resources or skills you have or can develop to stop doing what you don't want to do. Use Focus Game or Paired Interaction. Note: You may have to do considerable exploration of the needs your unwanted activity meets, and of alternative means of meeting those needs, before you can stop successfully.

FOR INDIVIDUAL ONLY

4. Write down the difficulties or obstacles you foresee in carrying out your commitment. What resources or skills do you have or can you develop to stop doing what you do not want to do? Note: You may have to do considerable thinking about and exploring of the needs your unwanted actions or habits meet, and of alternative means of meeting those needs, before you can successfully stop.

To Be Done Individually

In this section you will evaluate your knowledge of the place of action in values theory. The section will consist of a series of questions with the answers immediately beneath them. Get a sheet of paper and place it beneath the first question. Answer the question and then check it by moving the paper down.

1. Our actions always show our true values. True or False.

False. Sometimes our actions do not truly reflect our values. We might act out of the impulse of the moment, or we might yield to pressure. At such times our actions do not reflect the rest of our values system. Engaging in such action is weakening and dividing. It makes us feel helpless, guilty, and mad.

2. Doing is better than talking. True or False.

False. On the contrary, values theory states that when we are completely committed to a value, we are willing to own it openly even when this may cause some rejection or conflict. Once we have decided on a course of action we really want to engage in, it is best to carry it out in an open, nonsurreptitious fashion.

3. For our actions to be part of a total commitment to a value, the following should take place before we act:

a. We should choose our action from available alternatives.

b. We should consider the consequences of each alternative.

c. We should be willing to stand up for our choice publicly. True or False.

False because incomplete. Complete commitment to a value involves free choice after careful consideration of alternatives and consequences. It involves a willingness to stand up for our choices. It also involves feeling good about our choices. Actions that we feel bad about, ashamed of, which we do not like to think about or talk about, do not involve a fully integrated commitment to a value. For full commitment, it is important that we *like* what we do.

4. Actions that are immediate and spontaneous responses to situations cannot be part of a truly integrated values system, because they do not involve choosing, consideration of alternatives, and announcement of good feelings about them. True or False.

False. The choices and consideration of consequences may take place instantaneously and without conscious awareness when we know through previous self-exploration what we are, what we believe, and what we want. When we are spontaneous, there is instant consideration. When we act impulsively, we have not explored ourselves or considered alternatives.

THE ACTION GAME

Do you ever preach things that you do not practice? Do you sometimes fail to act on things you cherish and prize? Are there some things that you always wanted to do, but never did? If so, you may enjoy the Action Game.

Objective

The objective of the game is to have group members help each other bring their behavior more in line with their intentions, ideals, or desires.

Procedures

1. A group of two or more persons convenes and agrees to play the game. One person asks to be the focus person. He begins by telling about one of the following:

a. A hope or wish or goal he has that is not reflected much in his behavior.

b. Something he often talks about, but about which he seldom does anything.

c. Something that would make him feel proud or feel happy, that he has never satisfactorily acted upon.

2. After one focus person has introduced the issue, he talks about ways in which he might bring his actions more in line with his ideals, words, or feelings. Can action be taken? How?

First the focus person talks about action possibilities. When he is finished, he asks the group to help him examine those ideas further or find alternative ideas to consider.

An effort is made to consider as many alternatives as possible for bringing the focus's actions more in line with his ideals-words-feelings. The consequences of each alternative are explored to help the focus weight the alternatives.

3. Finally, when the focus feels as if he has as much information as he can handle, or is likely to obtain, he announces a decision, what he will or will not do.

The group accepts his decision. If asked to do so, group members may comment on the decision announced. The focus person then thanks the group and offers the focus to anyone else who wishes to play the game.

This step sometimes requires patience and group silence. If the focus fails to announce a decision, the group is free to point out what it sees as the consequences of such a failure to announce a decision.

Rules

1. One person has the focus for as long as he chooses to keep it. If one meeting is not enough, the focus may ask if the group is willing to reconvene and let him continue with the focus.

2. A group member (this includes the focus person) should bring the focus back to the original person if it slips to someone else.

3. The focus person should announce when he has had enough. He should not let one focus slip away. After he has relinquished the focus, another person can ask for it or the group can cease playing the game.

4. A group member should bring the topic back to the original one if it drifts.

5. Game players should be maximally honest.

6. Each should do what he can to enhance the group climate, to make others feel comfortable and happy, within the limits of the other rules.

7. No leader of the group has any special privileges.

8. The group, or individuals in it, should not try to pressure the focus person toward any particular decision, either openly or covertly. The focus is to be viewed as someone with his own private perceptions and experiences, who must live with himself and be responsible for his own behavior.

FEELINGS, KNOWLEDGE, AND SKILLS INTERPRETATION OR SPONTANEITY FORMS GAME

In this game we deal with three elements: feeling, knowledge and skill. These qualities in their interaction give rise to other qualities as well. Some of these interactions and the new qualities generated are shown in the diagram. The vertices represent the original qualities. The sides represent the new qualities resulting from the interaction of these qualities. The inner triangles represent further qualities generated by the interaction of the derived qualities. In the text following the diagram we trace out some of these interactions.

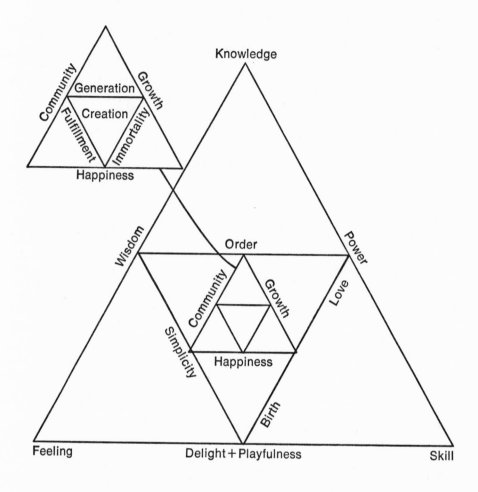

(First-order interactions: Vertices give rise to sides.)

Knowledge alone is pedantry.

Knowledge combined with skills is power (right leg of triangle).

Combined with feeling it is wisdom (left leg of triangle).

Feeling alone is anxiety.

Combined with skill it becomes delight and playfulness (base of triangle).

Wisdom alone is sadness.

Power alone is dangerous.

Wisdom, power, and playfulness combined give rise to creation (center).

(Some second-order interactions: Vertex and two sides give rise to third side of each of the next smaller triangles.)

Knowledge, wisdom, and power combine as order.

Delight, feeling, and wisdom combine as simplicity.

Skill, delight, and power combine as love, or birth.

Simplicity, love, and delight combine in happiness.

Simplicity, wisdom, and order combine as community.

(Some third-order interactions: The same process is repeated with next smaller sized triangles.)

Love, power, and order combine as growth.

Happiness, love and growth combine in immortality.

Happiness, simplicity, and community combine in fulfillment.

Community, order, and growth combine in generation.

Procedure

This game is played like any focus game with these differences:

1. The focus person thinks of a feeling or emotion.

2. The focus plays with the feeling, thinking of all sorts of ways that it can be beautifully or cleverly expressed. Other players encourage this with their own ideas in a playful nonjudgmental way.

3. The focus tries to get an understanding of the feelings. Here the other players help by drawing out the focus with questions, as well as relating relevant experience.

4. When the feeling has been understood and is becoming wisdom, the focus considers what skills are needed to turn this wisdom to creative action. The other players draw out the focus and also present their own ideas.

5. After the game is completed, the group and focus discuss the process and the unexpressed feelings they had during the process.

Another Form of the Game

This game can also be played as a Discussion Game. (See rules of Discussion Game, page 107.)

The steps are as follows:

1. Decide on a feeling to be discussed.

2. The group plays with the feeling, thinking of all kinds of ways to express it.

3. The group discusses the meaning of the feeling. Here the focus is on understanding the meaning of the feeling for each group member rather than agreeing on one meaning.

4. The group then discusses the skills needed to apply creatively the wisdom they have gained through the discussion.

5. The players then discuss what each might do to acquire the skills he needs.

6. The players discuss the process as well as their unexpressed feeling or thinking which went on during the discussion.

FIVE-FOLD LIFE PLAN GAME

This game is to be played with a family group or with very close friends.

1. Make a weekly plan to include these elements:

a. Meeting immediate goals, needs, and problems.
b. Meeting some long-range needs.
c. Some activity that will give pleasure to oneself.
d. Some activity that will contribute to the group.
e. Some activity that will contribute to the world.

2. At the end of the week, each person takes a turn being focus. The focus discusses where he succeeded and where he failed.

3. Other members of the group draw out and give feedback.

4. The focus then makes another weekly plan.

See Also: Games of Integration.

1. *The Pulling-together Game* and *the Keying-in Game* in the creativity section are ways of integrating a number of ideas with each other.

2. *Position Statement.* The Position Statement Game helps integrate one's feelings, objectives, plans, wishes, thinking, and point of view on a topic.

3. *Understanding Response.* The Understanding Response helps us integrate what we know of the thinking, point of view, feelings, objectives, and wishes of another person in an empathic understanding of their position.

PART TWO

SPONTANEITY AND SELF-EXPANSION

CHAPTER 7

Role Play,
Nonverbal,
and Physical Games

ROLE PLAY

Have you ever clenched your teeth and tightened your muscles and felt like killing someone?

Have you ever felt joyful, full of love, and giving?

The sinner and saint is in each of us. We all have the potential of countless lives within. But the reality is that we can live but one life.

We are all faced with the tension arising from the myriad of inner possibilities and the finite limits of time and space and circumstance within which we choose or are forced to live this life. This aspect of being is made sharper through role playing.

In what sense does the actor playing a saint become a saint? Is he expressing a portion of himself that finds no other room for expression within his life? That is my view. In role playing, portions of ourselves that are excluded by habit, role, or circumstance, are partially expressed. Such expression enables us to know parts of ourselves that were hidden. This knowledge in turn permits us to know others more empathically.

When we play a part well, we call on real capacities to think, to feel, to respond, to be. In this sense, the part expresses our real self. Role playing makes very thin the wall between the life we live and the lives we might have lived had circumstances, choices, and experiences been different.

This is both an opportunity and a danger. It is an opportunity because it provides a chance to know how to bring more of our inner selves into our real lives. But this new richness is a danger if we bring out these newly discovered capacities in a confused and disorganizing way. Then we run the risk of being like the actress who lives her many parts, but has no commitment to her one real life.

ROLE PLAY GAMES

Objectives

1. Role play may help you to get in touch with your feelings.

Explanation: By expressing a feeling outwardly, we are sometimes made more aware of our inner feelings.

2. Role playing may help you to express your feelings more freely so as to better meet your needs.

Explanation: Sometimes you may feel angry, lonely, friendly, uncomfortable. If you are not in the habit of showing your feelings, you may say nothing. In failing to express your feelings and the needs they represent, you may lose the opportunity to meet those needs. In role playing you can learn to express feelings and needs more freely, so that your needs may be better met.

3. Role playing may help you gain insight into yourself and others.

Explanation: In putting yourself in another person's place so as to act as he would, you are practically forced to understand him better.

When someone else role-plays you, you are enabled to see yourself from another point of view and thus to gain more insight into yourself and into how the other person sees you. This is particularly true where the other reflects your tone of voice, posture, and gesture.

4. You may learn and practice new, alternative ways of behaving in a safe role-play situation. This may lead you to broaden your behavioral alternatives in a real situation.

5. Role playing may lead you to be more aware of and more responsible for your actions. Sometimes people deny responsibility for what they do by claiming that they cannot help it. They may say that they are only being themselves, that it is their character or personality that makes them do what they do. When you role-play different ways of behaving, you may see that you do, in fact, have control, and that you can behave differently, should you choose to. You may see that it isn't your character or personality that made you act in a certain way, but that in fact you chose to be that way for a variety of reasons.

6. If a group stays together and practices a number of the role-play games, they may achieve professional or semiprofessional levels in acting as well as the rewards of personal expansion and insight.

Series I—Role Playing of Feelings

Getting in touch with feelings.

In this series you will be expressing some of the feelings listed below, or others that you may choose.

One may choose freely the feeling he wishes to express, or it may be chosen by chance. One way of choosing by chance is to use a single die. Toss it to determine the column. Toss it again to get the number of the feeling within the column.

1.	*2.*	*3.*
1. pride	1. love	1. sadness
2. happiness	2. loneliness	2. depression
3. glory	3. interest	3. elation
4. determination	4. warmth	4. freedom
5. joy	5. fascination	5. confidence
6. elation	6. adulation	6. pushed

4.	*5.*	*6.*
1. hate	1. bored	1. heavy
2. frustration	2. confused	2. light
3. anger	3. indifferent	3. dark
4. trapped	4. playful	4. colorful
5. inadequate	5. tired	5. anxious
6. weak	6. energetic	6. sadistic

GAME 1

1. A group of five to thirteen people gather to play.

2. One person chooses, by any means he likes, a feeling which he wishes to express.

3. He says the word and expresses the feeling by his tone. Each person takes a turn expressing the same feeling by word and tone.

4. A new person chooses a feeling and the process is repeated.

5. When everyone has had a turn, discuss how you felt during the process.

GAME 2

The same as Game 1, with the following modifications:

1. After the feeling is chosen, each one takes a pose expressing his concept of the feeling. The pose should be held for two or more minutes.

2. There is discussion concerning the poses after each round.

GAME 3

The same as Game 2, with the following modifications:

1. Break into groups of between four and seven members.

2. After the feeling is chosen and announced, everyone attempts to express it by movement, gesture, expression.

3. Music may be used if desired. Alternative form: The group imitates the expressive movement of the person who chose the feeling. (See Dance Focus, page 196.)

GAME 4

The same as previous games with this modification:

1. The feeling chosen is to be expressed by sound without true words. Use tone intonation, volume, rhythm, etc.

GAME 5

Combine Games 3 and 4.

GAME 6

1. Each person takes a turn expressing a feeling, using gesture, movement, rhythm, and words. The other members of the group may give feedback during the process by imitating gestures or movement. (See Dance Focus.)

2. The process is critiqued after each round.

Series II: Role Playing to Learn about Oneself and Others

GAME 1—ROLE EXCHANGE

To be played in a group of up to thirteen players.

1. Two players volunteer to pretend to act like each other. Try to get voice quality, posture, gestures, pattern of movement, and style of thinking and responding.

2. After the role play, both players and observers critique the process. Emphasis should be placed on the feelings of participants.

3. Two more players volunteer to exchange roles and steps 1 to 3 are repeated until everyone has had a turn.

GAME 2—GUESS WHO

Optimum size of group: between four and thirteen players.

1. Every player writes his name on a slip of paper. These slips are put into a container. Each player chooses a name.

2. Role-play the name you chose.

3. All the players observe each other and attempt to identify the person that each player is acting out.

4. After fifteen minutes time is called. Each player tells whom he was playing and his guess as to the identity of each of the other players.

5. The process is then discussed with each of the players telling what he learned about himself.

6. A new round can then be played with steps 1 to 6 repeated.

GAME 3

Optimum size group: four to thirteen players.

1. One person volunteers to be first. He chooses a real situation from one of the following areas to role play: (1) family, (2) friendship or love, (3) work or school, (4) leisure, (5) politics, (6) religion, (7) self, (8) community.

2. He describes the situation, and the character of the other person or persons in the situation.

3. He chooses members of the group to role-play with him.

4. The process is discussed, with participants and observers telling what they saw and how they felt.

5. The situation is now role-played again, but this time the focus takes the part of the other, and one of the group pretends to be the focus person.

6. This process is again critiqued.

7. Steps 2 to 6 are repeated with another set of players.

Series III: Inventive Role Play

Objective: By consciously practicing satisfying and unsatisfying ways of expressing feelings, you may become better able to use your feelings constructively.

GAME 1—PATTERNS OF EXPRESSING FEELING

Optimum size: five to thirteen players.

1. Two players volunteer to play a round.

2. Each chooses one of the six ways of expressing feeling listed below. This may be a free choice, or it can be a chance choice using a single die.

WAYS OF EXPRESSING FEELING: CHOOSE ONE

1. Expressing only your own needs and feelings, and ignoring the other person's.

Suggestion: Talk without stopping, don't listen, ignore or misinterpret what the other person says.

2. Denying feeling: Talk about anything but yourself. Change the subject when feeling comes up.

3. Blaming or projecting.

Suggestion: Accuse the other person of feeling what you feel. Try to make the other person guilty. Deny responsibility for what you feel or think. A good way of doing this is to start every sentence with phrases like, "Don't you think that so and so . . ." or "What you mean is. . . ."

4. Manipulating.

Suggestion: Manipulate the other person into meeting your needs. Tell him what to do and why. Show that it will be a good thing for him. Seduce him with promises or expression of positive feelings you don't have. Use flattery, guilt, and threat to get him to do what you want.

5. Empathy.

Suggestion: *Focus only on the other person.* Forget about your own needs and feelings. Try only to meet the other person's needs. Listen, draw out, ask questions, show that you understand, offer help. Do not express your own opinions, needs, feelings, or thoughts.

6. *Intimacy.* Understand and be sensitive to the other person's needs, feelings, and ideas. Express your own as well. Look for common ground and common interests. Try to integrate or accept divergent interests.

PROCEDURE FOR GAME 1 (CONTINUED)

3. The two players engage in a dialogue, with each playing the part he has chosen.

4. After the round, the observers attempt to identify the role each participant chose to play. The participants describe how they felt in playing the role.

5. Steps 1 to 4 are repeated with two more players.

GAME 2

1. May be played with five to thirteen players.

2. One player volunteers to be focus. He selects a plot (six general plots are listed below), a set of roles, and invents a situation.

3. The focus person assigns parts.

4. Each player chooses a set of feelings to keep in mind and the pattern of expression he will attempt to use.

5. The group acts out the plot.

6. The process is critiqued.

7. A new focus volunteers and steps 1 to 7 are repeated.

1. Plots of conflict. Deciding who will get his way.

2. Plots of reaction. Faced with a particular situation, what will the characters do?

3. Plots of discovery. Things are not what they appear to be. Inner and outer reality are different. Through the events one discovers something of the inner, hidden portion of reality.

4. Plots of self-discovery. Faced with a decision or a problem, I discover what I really am by the way I think and act.

5. Plots of identity. Faced with a particular situation, problem, or conflict, I decide what I am through the choices I make.

6. Plots of transcendence. Through some experience or action, I transcend myself and achieve new powers and insights. (See the Transcendental games.)

THE OTHER SELF OR ALTER EGO GAMES

Whenever we say something, there are always things left unsaid—reservations, doubts, motives, feelings.

Whatever we think, there are always counterthoughts—affirmations, denials, facts, experiences, intentions that play against the thoughts we think.

Sometimes an inner conversation is started in which the various voices complete each other. But it happens that we don't listen, and only one of the voices is heard. In this game you will learn to listen to the inner voice of the other self.

Alter Ego Game 1

A group gets together to play. If it is a large group, break into smaller groups of between five and thirteen players.

1. One player volunteers to be focus or ego.

2. Another volunteers to be the other self, or alter ego.

3. Ego may sit, stand, or walk while thinking out loud.

4. Alter ego speaks as one of the inner voices of the ego. He says what the ego fails to say. He speaks the feelings, the thoughts, the wishes that are there but unexpressed.

5. The process is critiqued: Ego and alter ego say how they felt during the process. The rest of the group give their perceptions.

6. Steps 1 to 5 are repeated with new ego and alter ego.

Game 2: Four-part Dialogue

Same as Game 1 with these modifications:

1. Two persons are chosen as egos and two others are chosen as the alter egos of the first pair. Seating positions: Egos next to each other, with their respective alter egos on the outside, thus—

Alter ego–Ego — Ego–Alter ego

2. The two egos engage in a dialogue. This may be on a real issue or it may be a role play situation concerning a problem of one of the egos. It may be a conflict situation between the two egos.

3. The alter egos state what they perceive to be the real thoughts and feelings of their respective egos. They speak as *part* of their egos. Sometimes the alter egos bypass the egos and talk to each other directly.

4. The process is critiqued with the two egos, the two alter egos, and the observers describing what they thought and felt.

5. The process is repeated with two other egos and their two alter egos.

Game 3

A. ALTER EGO SOLITAIRE

1. On a sheet of paper, write down a series of thoughts that comes to you on a certain topic or issue.

2. Take another sheet of paper. Place it to the right of the first.

3. Next to every thought or feeling expressed, write the other thoughts or feelings that you had.

4. A third sheet of paper may be placed to the right of the second, and the process repeated.

B. ALTER EGO SOLITAIRE: DIALOGUE FORM

1. Write a dialogue using only the right-hand side of the page. This may be a dialogue that actually took place between yourself and somebody else. Choose a dialogue about a person or situation in which you feel you need more insight.

2. On the left-hand side of the page, write what you think the speakers really thought or felt. Place the real thoughts and feelings directly across from the spoken thoughts.

The Game of Inner Dialogue

Objectives

To explore in depth one's expectations, feelings, and ways of relating to some significant person in order to increase self-awareness as well as to free oneself from "ghosts of the past."

Group Needed

This game can be played in a group of up to twelve members. It should be a group in which a considerable amount of trust has developed.

Some Voting Questions

The facilitator may introduce the game with the following voting questions:

"Have you ever had the same conversation, argument, or interchange with somebody over and over again?

"Have you ever wanted to get out of the repeated pattern?

"Have you ever felt trapped by it?

"Have you ever found yourself slipping back into it against your will?

"Have you ever imagined talking to somebody that you know?

"Did you imagine their responses as well?

"Did you use your imagination to create a picture of what the exchange might be?

"Did you use the imaginary interchange to gain insight into your feelings and motives and patterns as well as those of the other person?

"In this game you will have an imaginary exchange with someone of your own choosing in which you play both parts. You will use this exchange to get insight into your motives and patterns as well as those of the other person. In this you will be helped by the other group members."

Procedure A, in which the focus person plays all the roles.

1. The game is introduced and the members agree to play. If the group is more than thirteen members, it is better to break into smaller groups of between four and thirteen members.

2. Think of significant situations and relationships concerning which you would like to get increased insight.

3. Select one of the situations to explore.

4. Some member of the group volunteers to be focus. The focus will role-play both himself and the other persons in the situation. If the focus concentrates on the situation and lets himself go, he will have less trouble doing this.

5. Others members watch the focus carefully, giving support only when it is necessary to encourage him to continue. In observing the focus, make particular note of posture, gestures, voice tone, changes in tempo or mood, or other verbal or nonverbal cues that might help one understand the focus's state of mind or feeling.

6. When the focus is finished, the group draws him out concerning his thinking and feeling during the focus period.

7. Using the rules of the discussion critique, the group discuss their perceptions of what happened with the focus.

8. The game continues with a new person taking the focus.

Procedure B: Role playing with the focus playing only himself.

1. All the procedures of game A are the same except rule 4.

2. Alternative to rule 4: A member of the group agrees to be focus. The focus describes the persons and situation that he wants to explore. He chooses members of the group to role-play the situation with him. If you are either the focus or one of the role-players, focus on the situation and let yourself go. You should find that you are really living the part.

NONVERBAL GAMES

Nonverbal Communication Games

The purpose of these games is to make us more relaxed and more accepting of ourselves as physical beings.

VOTING QUESTIONS

Did you ever get sick of words?

Did you ever feel that too many words sometimes got in the way of experiencing directly and intensely?

Have you ever experienced the warmth of silent understanding? In this series you will learn to experience and communicate without words.

INITIAL PROCEDURE

The game is introduced.

People break up into groups of between three and five members.

They sit in a circle with no table between them.

RULES: FOR ALL GAMES

1. Negative expression of feelings is not permissible during the game.

2. Laughing at, joking about, or ridiculing the behavior of others is curtailed unless seen as supportive by the group.

GAME 1

The group focuses on each member in turn. They tell him what is communicated by his posture, way of moving, expression, clothes, appearance, etc. In this, emphasis should be placed on positive feelings.

After the group completes a round, or after the focus on each person is completed, the focus person describes how he felt in being focused on, while the group members tell how they felt in focusing.

GAME 2

Same as Game 1, except that here the focus person moves expressively. The members tell the focus person the positive feelings they had toward his movement.

GAME 3

Same as Game 2, except that music is added and the focus person's movement approaches or becomes creative dancing. The group encourages this verbally and also nonverbally through expression and movement.

GAME 4

Three to five people get together to play the game. The focus person sits in the center of the circle.

The focus person communicates without speaking. He may use expression, movement, gesture, etc.

The other group members may speak. They may ask questions which the focus person answers nonverbally.

A series of questions and nonverbal answers may develop into a conversation.

After the focus indicates that he is finished, the group members talk about their feelings during the process.

Steps 1 to 5 are repeated with a new focus.

Nonverbal Dialogue

A group gets together to play the game.

Two individuals volunteer to conduct a nonverbal dialogue.

The two volunteers get into the middle of the group.

One expresses some feeling nonverbally—by facial expression, movement, or gesture. The other responds, and the nonverbal dialogue gets going.

PHYSICAL GAMES

The Dance Focus Game

This is one of the most popular games, and a source of great fun at parties, or most any time some spontaneous play is needed.

INTRODUCTION

Most of us would feel embarrassed to move freely and follow our impulses while dancing. We would be afraid of being laughed at or judged clumsy or inept. The problem is usually solved by dancing one or another conventional dance. This partially protects the dancer from judgment. Those who lack the time or the aptitude to learn the current conventional dances exclude themselves from dancing.

OBJECTIVES

The object of the game is to remove the inhibitions to creative dancing and movement, and to permit people to express themselves by creating personalized dances. This tends to involve everyone in dancing.

PROCEDURE

A group of between two and five people get together to play the game. If there are more people present, several groups may be formed.

One group member volunteers to be focus. (See suggestions for focus.)

The focus player dances as he chooses.

The other members try to move in such a way as to reflect the spirit and feel of the focus's movement. It is not necessary for their movements to be exactly like that of the focus. Any approximation is good, an exaggeration is even better.

WHAT IS THE POINT?

For some reason the focus's movements become freer, more expressive, and more graceful. Perhaps it is because it is fun to see two or three people doing what you are doing. The focus is drawn to experiment and do other things to see if others will continue to follow. Perhaps one doesn't feel foolish when others are doing what you are doing. Whatever the reason the game is tremendously exhilarating and freeing.

1. Start with simple movements. Repeat them with variations.
2. Watch the other players when they follow—you can go farther. If you are not being followed, go to something more simple and basic.

Other Communication Dances

GAME 1: FOCUS CONTRAST

The focus moves or gestures.
The group members move in contrast or opposition.

GAME 2: DANCE DIALOGUE FOR PAIRS

One partner moves, expressing a feeling or asking a question through movement.
The other partner answers through movement.
This is continued, making a dialogue.

GAME 3: DANCE ROLE-PLAY

Two or more players decide on a situation to role-play through dancing.
Players choose a feeling to express in dance.
Players choose a sequence of feelings to express.
The focus dancer names the feelings that the others are to express while the dance is going on.

Relaxation Game

This game may be played individually or in a group. If it is to be played in a group, one person volunteers to lead the game. He will ask the questions indicated below, and lead the exercises that follow. At later playings of the game, the leader may change the particular activities while sticking to the basic idea.

Voting Questions

Are you ever too stimulated?
Do ideas flow through your mind faster than you can get hold of them?
Are your muscles ever too tense to permit you to work?
Do you ever have trouble falling asleep?
Do you ever have trouble turning your mind off so you can relax or concentrate on one thing?

Have you ever felt so tense and high that you didn't want to make the effort to relax?

Do you think that the time to relax is when you're relaxed?

Do you think that the time to relax is when you're too tense?

Do you find a contradiction in your answers to the last few questions?

Would you like to learn some ways to relax?

Do you think you would use these ways when you're too tense?

Would you use them only when you have no reason to?

In this game we will learn to relax so that one may either engage in an activity with pleasure, or move into sleep.

Relaxing the Body

Muscles can best relax when they have been stretched or tensed to the fullest. In this exercise we will systematically stretch and tense all of our muscles so that we may relax them more completely.

1. Stretch neck and chest upward as much as you can. Hold it. . . . Hold it. . . . Relax. (Hold to the count of six for maximum benefit. Don't go beyond six or you'll get too tired.)

2. Push neck downward and strain it against chest as much as you can. Hold it . . . and relax.

3. Lean head to the right as much as you can. Move head backward as far as it will go. Now to the left. Rotate head around in a continuous motion in as large an arc as possible.

4. Close eyes as tight as possible. Clamp teeth as tight as possible. Grimace . . . and relax.

5. Extend arms and stretch out fingers and arms as much as possible. Hold it. Relax. Holding arms out, rotate wrist in a maximum arc, stretching fingers as much as you can in each direction. Relax.

6. Rotate arms in as large an arc as possible, stretching out as far as you can. Relax.

7. Bend arms, hands near shoulders, contracting muscles as hard as you can. Hold, and make fists as tight as you can. Relax.

8. Tighten chest muscles as hard as you can. Hold . . . relax.

9. Strain forward as far as you can, hands in direction toward floor. Return to erect posture and relax. Bend the torso to the right. Return to erect posture and relax. To the left, relax. Backward, relax. Now rotate the torso in a continuous arc. Relax.

10. Bend forward. Let out your breath and pull in your stomach as hard as you can. Relax.

11. With hand on a chair, extend right foot forward and hold it up for as long as you can. Relax. Extend right foot outward and again hold it. Relax. Backward, hold and relax. Repeat with left foot.

ALTERNATE OR ADDITIONAL EXERCISE

Tighten all muscles of the body as tight as you can. Relax slowly, first toes, ankles, calves, thighs, stomach, lower chest, chest, fingers, forearms, arms, shoulders, neck, jaw, eyes, forehead.

After the game has been played once, any member may suggest additional or alternate exercises to be used at the session. The group may vote to accept or reject the suggestion.

Breathing

Slow, deep breathing with complete exhalation makes for relaxation. Such breathing is known as yoga breathing.

Yoga breathing can serve a number of valuable functions in addition to relaxation:

1. It can be used to overcome fears or anxieties if one thinks about what is making one fearful or anxious while doing the yoga breathing.

2. It can be used as an aid in dieting. Doing yoga breathing while intensely hungry will reduce hunger and enable one to wait.

3. It can reduce the feeling of impatience if one does the breathing when one feels impatient.

4. It can be used to reduce various kinds of pain if one does the breathing while in pain.

Process: Empty your lungs as far as you can by forced exhalation through the nose. When you think they are completely empty, try to get more out by tightening your diaphragm. Breathe slowly through the nose and hold your breath when your lungs are full for as long as is comfortable. Breathe out, emptying lungs completely. Repeat process. Other breathing exercises may be suggested by group members on subsequent occasions.

Mental Relaxation

While breathing this way, close your eyes. As thoughts run through your mind, focus on those that are relaxing and pleasant. If this is done in a group, you may make some statement about the most relaxing and pleasant ones.

Ignore, *but do not attempt to inhibit,* unpleasant or anxiety-producing thoughts.

Other suggestions for mental relaxation may come from the group.

CHAPTER 8

The Transcendental Games

In the transcendent experience one steps beyond the limitations of the self and makes contact with a higher, broader, more enduring self. Yet our limited, practical, everyday selves remain. In the poem that follows, the limited and unlimited ways of being are contrasted. It is the feeling of the author that one should not give up either plane, but should attempt to exist on both.

I am changing my skin.
Like a snake I crawl into a dark corner.
The sun irritates me.
Noises pierce through me and make me tremble.
Do not be contemptuous of my incapacity.
Soon I shall glide out into the sun
And stretch my infinite length in its warmth.
And my scales like galaxies of stars shall move
    and glisten as I stretch.

Playfully I roll and twist in the infinite expanse
    of sand and sun.
I put my tail in my mouth and history repeats
    itself,
And this one moment has come and gone more times
    than times can count.
I coil and now a spiral pattern starts,
Like music growing from a simple melody.

Evolving life, and shapes that flower,
Uncoiling I spring through discontinuity,
Through rising stars,
Through wars, earthquakes,
Through new beginnings and cataclysmic ends.
Then I glide beneath the burning sun,
Like new creation and spontaneous joy.

Infinite thoughts that spin
Within the finite circle of this skull.
My tail eludes me, and the infinite reptile,
Whose coils pass through my stomach,
And the milky way and round each galaxy of stars,
Presents a gaping space to my human form.
The gap, the infinite gap of loneliness through
    which tears fall.
Oh Christ! I weep for you who tried to bridge the
    gap with love and death,
And you dear Buddha, who denied the human pole of
    this vast duality.

But I who should be fully human and divine,
I burn within the gap
Holding a human hand, and a burning star,
And the fire, and the fire.

With two bodies and two forms I rode through snow
    to visit.
And the snow dragon through my round pupils its
    slit eyes looked out.
"Will you have some coffee?" and I said, "no thanks."
"How are you?"
And I felt, my body twisting through the drifts of snow,
Coiled in clouds, and undulating in coils of whiteness
    on the barren fields,
"Somewhat disconnected," I answered.
"Isolated and alone."
She probed and the silences were overwhelming.
"Where is the milk?" she said.
Could I own the snake had drunk it?
"It's very bad to isolate yourself," she said.
My forked tongue was darting in and out,
    smelling the room.
She saw the obscure white shadow.
"If you have nothing to say,
Why don't you go."
Slowly, slowly I gathered myself
And drifted out into the snow.

*   *   *

I have left my skin
By the rocks near the river.
It glistens
Bleached transparent by the sun and the rain.
My new skin has hardened,
It sparkles like jewels
With my inner lights.
Once again I plunge into the waters.

*   *   *

Have you ever had a flash of insight or intuition?
Have you ever been struck by the beauty or wonder of something?
Have you ever identified yourself with people, places, principles?
These are all forms of self-transcendence.

The emotions of love, beauty, idealism, dedication, and religion are all transcendent feelings. They are the source of much that is meaningful in life. But transcendence has practical importance as well. Many of the problems we face cannot be solved without transcending a narrow, selfish point of view. As long as a manufacturer thinks primarily in terms of production and profits, problems of pollution, health, and safety cannot be solved. As long as nations consider their own point of view and self-interest, peace and disarmament remain visionary objectives. The very word "visionary" implies a transcendent function. In these games we will explore and expand our transcendent experiences so that they may become more fully part of the fabric of our lives, and available not only to make life meaningful, but to help us achieve the solution to problems or conflicts in a deeper, more satisfying way.

Kinds of Transcendence

There are four kinds of transcendence that we will consider here.

1. TRANSCENDING OUR PERCEPTION OF THINGS AND PEOPLE

Most of us have developed habits of seeing things. We use these habits and are blinded to things that do not fit them. In the section on transcending our perceptions, we will try to go beyond those habits of seeing.

2. TRANSCENDING OURSELVES

Most of us have developed ways of seeing ourselves and ways of acting. Some of these ways of seeing ourselves and of behaving limit us from reaching our full potential. In this section, we will explore ways of transcending these self-imposed, family-imposed, or group-imposed self-limitations.

3. TRANSCENDENCE IN PLANNING AND ACTION

In planning, if we consider only our own immediate objective, there are often secondary consequences that are undesirable. If we are working with others and consider only our own point of view and needs, conflicts arise which are either unresolvable or can only be resolved in an authoritarian, nondemocratic, exploitive way. In this exercise, we will learn to take the larger, transcendent view in decision-making.

4. TRANSCENDENCE OF SELF AS FINDING THE GOD WITHIN

While each person is a limited individual, he is also the product of the universal. He is thus finite in that he is a limited individual, but he also partakes of the infinite in that he is a product of the infinite. Religiously this is reflected in such notions as, "Man is made in the image of God," or "Christ, or Buddha, exists within you." Scientifically this is reflected in an understanding of how tremendous forces worked to shape us. Emotionally this is reflected in a feeling we sometimes have of oneness with others and with the world. In the games having to do with finding God within us, there will be an exploring of each player's experience of a feeling of oneness with others, with nature, with the universe, and with God, and an exploration of the meaning this has for the person.

Caution: These games invoke powerful and deep experiences.

Do them with people you know and trust.

Do them only after you have had considerable experience with the games.

The rule of discomfort applies to these games. Any player may stop the process if he feels discomfort, and his discomfort takes first priority. Only after his objections or difficulties have been met may the game continue.

TRANSCENDING OUR PERCEPTIONS OF THINGS AND PEOPLE

Game A. Becoming Aware of the Meaning Things and People Have for Us

Feelings get attached to everything we do or see: our house, our door, our street, our dishes, our clothes, our pictures, our shoes, each person we know, each corner of the room. These feelings permeate and penetrate the space these objects occupy. Some of these feelings and experiences that surround the people and the things we know are pleasant, some sad, some tense, some freeing, some confining.

We are usually unaware of this dense cloud of meaning that surrounds everything we touch or see. But it is nonetheless there and frequently prevents us from seeing the very things it surrounds.

OBJECTIVE

To become aware of the richness of meanings we attach to things and people in order to intensify these meanings; and also to be able to see things more directly, aside from the feelings we attach to them.

PROCEDURES

FORM 1

1. Three to five people convene to play the game. The game is best played in a setting familiar to all the players. This is not mandatory, but it is helpful.

2. Get into a relaxed state of mind by breathing deeply and slowly.

3. One player volunteers to be focus. He talks about the feelings, experiences, and qualities that are attached to the objects or people that he is with.

4. The other members of the group draw him out with a few unobtrusive questions to help keep him going.

5. After the focus person is through, others take a turn at being focus.

6. After each person has had a turn being focus, the group discusses the experience.

FORM 2

Form 2 is the same as Form 1, with the following differences:

a. Any player may say the meanings that objects or people have for him at any time.

b. If the statement of one player triggers an awareness of a feeling in another player, he may express it, allowing a few seconds of silence to elapse after the first speaker is finished.

c. There may be an occasional drawing out question or mini-focus, but most of the space should be filled not with questions, but with observations of the meanings which the objects and the people have for you.

Game B. Becoming Aware of Space

> The thirty spokes of a wheel unite in the one hub; but it is on the empty space through which the axle passes that the use of the wheel depends. Clay is fashioned into pots; but it is on their emptiness that their use depends. It is not the bricks and the walls, but the emptiness within that makes a house useful. What exists often gets its use from the emptiness it encloses.
>
> —*Lao Tzu*

Here Lao Tzu speaks about the usefulness of emptiness. In a deeper sense, Lao Tzu speaks of the unity of emptiness and fullness. When we focus on only one of these, the unity is broken, and our perceptions become one-sided, distorted, and unreal.

We are in the habit of looking at things. But often we do not see them. Instead we see our concept of them and our feelings about them, and the meanings they have for us. The thing itself is masked by our ideas. But when we look at the spaces around and between things, a strange thing happens. The things themselves become rounder, more real, more individual. For some, the healing of the unity between positive (filled) space and negative (empty) space gives a new sense of self, or reality, of the intimately near and the far, of the now and of eternity.

In this game we will explore the experience of concentrating on negative space and see how it affects us.

PROCEDURES

1. A group of between three and eight people convene to play the game.

2. The players get into comfortable positions and spend about five minutes in relaxing and clearing their minds. In relaxing, breathe deeply and slowly, holding the breath for a comfortable interval in intake. In clearing your mind, do not pursue or respond actively to the thoughts that enter consciousness. This will lead your thoughts to subside gradually.

3. After five minutes have elapsed, concentrate on the spaces around and between things. Observe your thoughts and feelings. You may find that you are perceiving more of the internal space within objects (the *insides* of things) as well as the external space. Do this for about five minutes in silence.

4. Continue the experience and share it. Let persons fill the silence by some description of what they see or feel. Let each statement be surrounded by an emptiness, becoming aware of the emptiness in sound as well as space. You may ask an occasional question, but focus mainly on pursuing your own experiences, and sharing your perceptions when moved to. This may be continued for an indefinite period of time, with a minimum of ten minutes.

5. Explore in depth your experience, using the focus technique or the Ongoing T-Group Game. (In using the latter, continue the experience in the here-and-now, or talk about how it continues to affect you in the here-and-now.)

6. Critique the total experience, using any one of the critiques, p. 60.

Game C. The Present Reality Game

Past ideas and perceptions often insulate us from what is; for we see our past ideas instead of what is before us. We say, "that is a tree," "that is a chair," "that is a person." Once we have named something, all we see is our idea of the name. The reality of the object or person is lost. Its color, shape, style, personality, weight, position slip from awareness, and we only see the purposes and conceptions we have in our own heads. In the Present Reality Game, we focus on what is.

PROCEDURES

1. A group of between three and ten people get together to play the game.

2. The members think about what they see and feel—their body sensations, the actual shape of things, the air and space between things, how group members look or move, the meanings that things have for one, textures, shapes, smells, sounds.

3. When a person's feeling or perception becomes very intense, he may share it with the group.

4. It is important not to interrupt anyone—so whenever there is a silence, a group member may say what he feels or perceives. The meanings we become aware of are inherent in objects or people. While a person speaks, others should listen to his mood, his tone of voice. They should be aware of the sound spreading through the room, aware of how it strikes them and others. Only when the reverberations of his words have ended and silence returns, may another speak, or gesture, or move, to express his perception of what is.

TRANSCENDING OURSELVES

Game A. Contacting One's Unconscious

Have you ever had flashes, insights, intuitions, or hunches that were accurate and helpful?

Have you ever had apprehensions for no obvious reason, which later proved accurate?

Intuitions, hunches, sudden insights, and premonitions are ways in which we are contacted by our unconscious. These often call our attention to facts, observations, needs, clues, and implications that we are consciously neglecting. If we are in communication with our unconscious, life tends to be more whole, more humane, more meaningful, better balanced, and more intense.

In the games that follow, we will find ways of getting into contact with our unconscious so as to make life richer and more meaningful, and to help meet the problems and issues that life presents.

PROCEDURES

FORM 1

1. Two to five people convene to play the game. They will use either the Reflection Game, the Game for Widening Communication in Pairs, or the basic Focus Game.

2. The focus person relaxes and closes his eyes. If he wishes to, he may ask himself a question concerning some issue or problem he faces, before closing his eyes; but this is not necessary.

3. He notes and tries to remember all he hears, sees, and feels when his eyes are closed.

4. He is drawn out concerning all of his associations and feelings about each thing he saw, felt, or heard in his mind while his eyes were closed.

5. When the focus has explored the meaning of his experience, he explores how his experience relates to his total life; or if he had earlier asked himself a question concerning some problem or issue, how the experience relates to the issue or problem.

Caution: The unconscious cannot solve any problems. Problems are best solved rationally on the basis of all relevant knowledge and feeling. What the unconscious can do is to point to facts, feelings, and possibilities that we have neglected to consider in our decision. If, in asking "Shall I marry Jane?" one sees a great flame when one closes one's eyes, it is probable that there are elements of great intensity in the relationship which one should consider before coming to a decision.

Sometimes our unconscious throws up fears and apprehensions experienced in the past, but inappropriate to the present. Such fears do not provide guidance or insight. Instead they are a hindrance which needs to be overcome.

FORM 2

Do the same as in Form 1, but use a dream as the subject of exploration.

FORM 3

Same as Form 1 or 2, but use ink blots, shapes in tea leaves, texture in a stone or bark, or grain of wood. Look at the object noting all shapes, images, thoughts, and feelings that come to mind.

FORM 4

Same as before, with this difference: Look through a magazine and pick out a picture that strikes a responsive chord in you. Make up a story concerning the picture. Note all the thoughts, feelings, and images you saw connected with the picture and the story.

Game B. Sharing Our Unconscious

When people sense not only the surface, but the depths which are taking place in each other, there is a greater sense of being understood, of warmth, of richness, and perhaps of love. Fantasy and imagination participate not only in the conscious levels of the self, but in the deeper levels as well. In this game, we will use shared fantasy and imagination to move to a deeper level of interpersonal communication.

OBJECTIVES

To facilitate communication on an unconscious as well as a conscious level among the members of a group; and thus to deepen, widen, and intensify the level of communication and the bond between the members.

PROCEDURES

1. A group of between two and ten people convene to play the game.
2. About five minutes is spent in relaxing. Breathe deeply and slowly, holding the breath for a comfortable period on the intake.
3. Close your eyes and note the shapes or images that flash before them, as well as the sounds and sensations that spontaneously arise.
4. Say what you feel or see, when so moved.
5. Each statement should be surrounded by a space of silence.
6. On occasion you may ask a question, but concentrate on your own visions, sensations, and feelings. Share them with the group when so moved. Note: Your fantasy may be influenced or triggered by another person's. This is all right; allow it to happen.

7. After an indefinite period of time (possibly ten minutes to a half hour) a stop is called.

8. The group now uses the Focus Game, or the Ongoing T-Group Game, to explore the experience.

Later, talk about the effect of tne experience in the here-and-now, or about how one feels about it in the here-and-now.

If the sharing was only between two people, the Reflection Game or Game for Widening Communication between Pairs may be used.

Game C. The Revealing Triangle

Who can see into the seeds of time
And say which seed will grow and which will not.

—*Sophocles*

SEEING THE CONSEQUENCES OF OUR WAYS

Suppose we try to meet fear with sensitivity and gentleness. What will be the outcome of this attempt? Will it be success or disaster? It is hard to guess the outcome by the use of unaided intuition. In the Revealing Triangle Game, we aid the intuition by systematically combining these qualities.

BACKGROUND OF THEORY

The game is based upon the fact that if we take any two human qualities and think about them for a while, some third quality will come to mind. When I try to combine the concepts of feeling and thought, the concept of wisdom comes to my mind. What comes to your mind when you try making the following mental combinations?

1. Love and hate.
2. Insight and determination.
3. Knowledge and skill.
4. Wisdom and skill.

The combinations the author thought of are as follows: 1. ambivalence, 2. planning, 3. power, 4. creation. The readers might combine the pairs in other ways. The important thing is, some third quality comes to mind when we think of any two qualities. Combining two qualities in a third is an interesting exercise, but it has no predictive power. If we add a third element, a complex process of interaction becomes possible that mirrors the actual interaction of these qualities in life.

1. Consider the following three qualities: color, rhythm, balance. Arrange these at the corners of the triangle. See below.

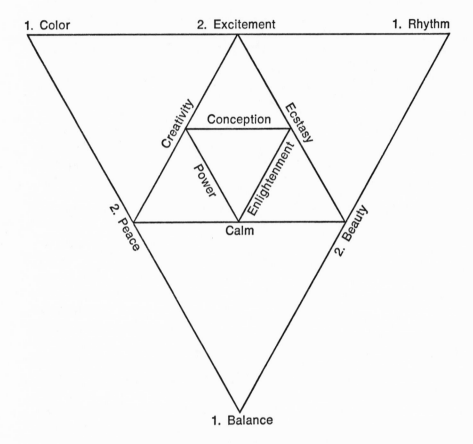

A "1" is placed next to each to show that they were the words we started with.

According to the author's associations:

Color and balance combine to form peace. . . . Write "peace" on the line between "color" and "balance."

Color and rhythm combine to create excitement. . . . Write "excitement" on the line between "color" and "rhythm."

Rhythm and balance make for beauty. . . . Write "beauty" on the line between "rhythm" and "balance."

The words "beauty," "excitement," and "peace" now make up the sides of the triangle. I placed a little "2" next to them to show that they were derived from our first words.

2. Divide each side of the triangle in half and connect the points, making an inner triangle. Each line on the inner triangle touches two lines of the outer triangle, on each of which is written a word. We use the words that the inner triangle lines connect to help us decide what to write on the inner triangle lines.

Excitement and peace give rise to creativity. . . . Write "creativity" on the line joining "peace" and "excitement."

Excitement and beauty give rise to ecstasy. . . . Write "ecstasy" on the line connecting "excitement" and "beauty."

Peace and beauty give rise to calm. . . . Write "calm" on the line connecting "excitement" and "beauty."

3. The process is repeated. Again we divide each side of the previous triangle in half, and connect the halves. This results in another inner triangle. We use the two words that each line connects to find a new word with which to name the line. The result is shown in the diagram. The process may be repeated infinitely, or until the patterns begin to repeat themselves.

Once we know how to use the triangle to illustrate the continued interaction of three qualities, we can use this knowledge to explore alternative ways of handling situations and feelings.

A person picks three traits. In the illustration below, two are felt to be positive and one is negative. The interaction may then be predictive of how these three traits actually interact. In the example below, fear, gentleness, and sensitivity were picked. These resulted in the following triangle, by the person's own choices.

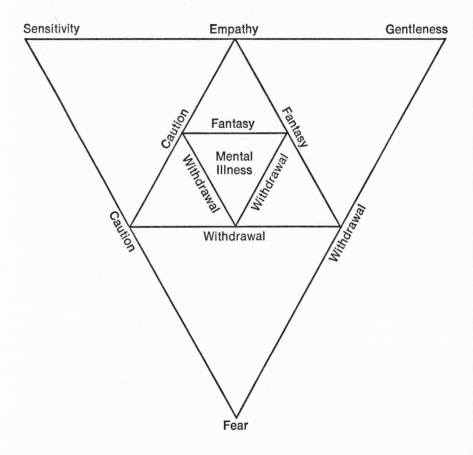

Handling fear with sensitivity and gentleness was seen to be disastrous, if indeed the triangle form of interaction followed reality. The person playing the triangle game had had a mental breakdown once using precisely this way of handling fear. We then used the triangle game to try two alternative approaches to handling fear.

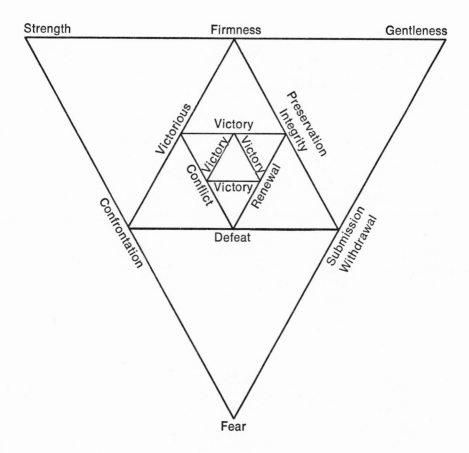

The person then tried using the triangle with the three positive qualities she chose: strength, sensitivity, and gentleness.

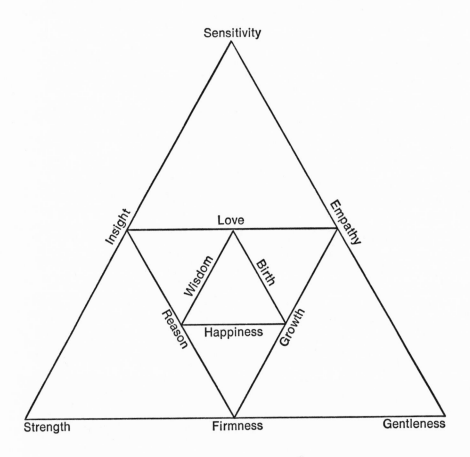

Using sensitivity, strength and fear, the person came up with the following triangle.

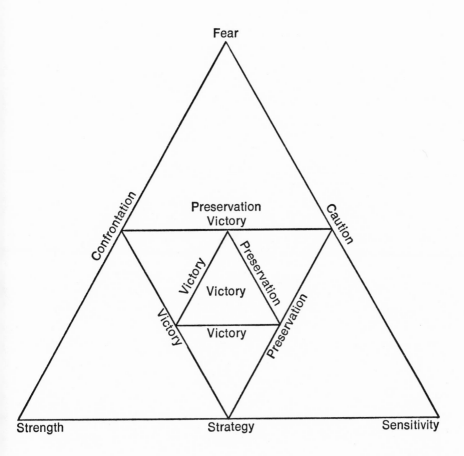

The use of strength with sensitivity to combat fear seems superior to the use of strength with gentleness to combat fear.

This hour-glass set of triangles illustrates alternative ways of handling prejudice.

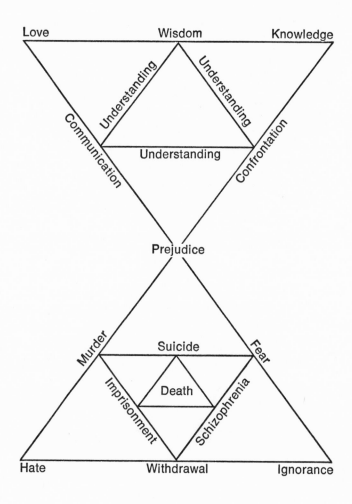

The art triangle may be used as an integration exercise with painting. By permitting the interaction of color, rhythm, and balance, the rest of the interactions indicated may emerge as they do in great art.

Below is a triangle showing the interaction of knowledge, feeling, and skill. This triangle has been used to form the game in which feelings, knowledge, and skills are integrated, page 180.

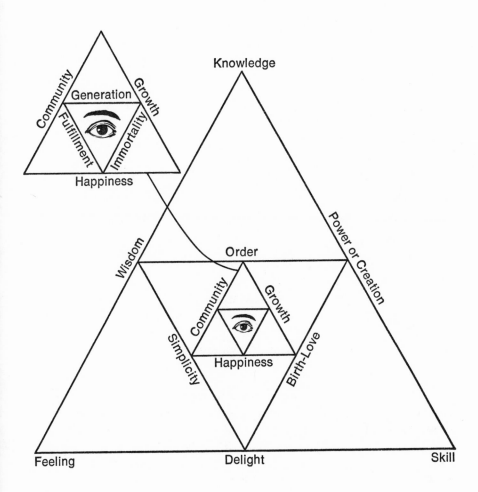

The Triangle Game may be played in a group with the focus person making several triangles to explore himself and alternative ways of handling self and the world. The group lends support by an accepting, calm attitude.

Game D. Magic Theater Games

We all have an image of what we are. This self-image controls what we are, what we can do, and what we cannot do. It controls whether we are graceful or clumsy, witty or dull, loving or selfish, open or conniving. It determines our interests, our capacities, our styles, our blindness, and our vision. It is a mask of the soul, tragic, comic. It is the script that we and others have written for us. Too often we dare not or cannot depart from it, no matter how tired or bored we are with our parts.

In the Magic Theater Game, masks are removable and scripts may be unwritten. We make ourselves and our fate.

THE FIRST MAGIC THEATER GAME: THE UNBURYING OF PAST SELVES

PROCEDURES

1. A group of between five and ten people who are committed to each other and trust each other get together to play the game.

2. All the members cast an eye over their lives. They select a period of time when they were the kind of self they wanted to be.

3. One volunteers to be the focus and begins to act it out.

4. The other group members support his revival of the self by acting appropriately.

5. After the round is completed, the focus person talks about his experience. He then discusses how he may integrate the revived self in his present life.

6. Steps 1 to 5 are then repeated with other focus people. It is possible for the game to continue until the players have brought to awareness many buried selves.

Note: The unearthing of a buried self makes for some temporary disunity. Given time, however, these buried selves become integrated into our total self, making for more real and complete unity.

SECOND MAGIC THEATER GAME: CHANGING OF THE EXTERNAL SELF

We all have a certain style that we think we are bound to. But that is an illusion. One can change one's style as easily as he can change a coat; but others place pressure to keep us consistent, and this pressure becomes a fear of change. When we change our style, they say we are not being ourselves. But here styles of being are like hats in a hat shop. Try on a new way of behaving. Do you want to be more loving, more aggressive, more intelligent, more witty, or more committed? Choose yourself. You can do so in this game, for the social pressure to be consistent is removed and replaced by support for the new style.

PROCEDURES

FORM 1

1. A group of from five to ten people who can trust each other get together.
2. The focus person describes his new self—and then proceeds to act it out.
3. The other members of the group support the reality of this self by what they say or do.
4. After a focus is completed, the group discusses the transformations that have been made.
5. This continues until each person has been the focus.

FORM 2

Form 2 is the same as Form 1, except that all the group members state their new selves at the same time, at the start. They all support each other in acting them out.

TRANSCENDENCE IN PLANNING AND CONFLICT RESOLUTION

The transcendent point of view is relevant in a practical way to planning and to conflict resolution.

The Transcendent Point of View and Planning

We can see the relevance of the transcendent point of view in planning if we consider the problem of production. When we act from the needs and objectives of the moment, it often happens that the solution of one problem creates one or more unforeseen new problems. Thus, in concentrating on the problem of production, we have seriously polluted our environment. Only if we try to solve the problem of production from the point of view of the total environment can we have production without the world becoming polluted, ugly, and unhealthy.

The Transcendent Point of View and Conflict Resolution

In confronting conflict on the lowest level, each person sees only his own point of view and needs. In general, the other is often perceived as stupid, cruel, evil, etc. He is not understood. The result is an intensification of conflict.

On a higher level, both parties to the conflict try to understand each other's point of view and needs. This often results in some compromise or in a lessening of the intensity of the conflict, but it usually does not lead to a solution that is fully satisfactory to anybody.

On the highest level, after exploring each individual's needs and point of view, the individuals take the point of view of the totality (the point of view of a humane God). This means that they think in terms that include everybody's point of view and needs. Solutions arrived at in this way are often more satisfactory to each person than he thought possible at the beginning.

Objectives

To learn to take the point of view of the totality so as to solve problems or conflicts in more humane, more real, more total, and more lasting ways.

Game A. Task-oriented T-Group:

To practice planning, conflict resolution, and action from a transcendent point of view.

1. A group of between five and fifteen people convene to play the game.

2. They have the task of agreeing on a task and accomplishing it in such a way that the needs of all group members are adequately met.

3. Each states his own needs and suggests a group task that would meet them. Use the focus technique for initial statement and the Ongoing T-Group Game to explore.

4. After there has been adequate exploration so that the individual needs and points of view are understood, the process is stopped either on the basis of consensus or near consensus; or when an agreed amount of time has elapsed (say, an hour or two).

5. There is a ten-minute period of silence while each person tries to form a more inclusive point of view in his head, one which includes the points of view and the needs of all the individuals.

6. When the time is up, the discussion continues, using the T-Group Game, with each player taking the point of view of the totality. This continues until consensus is reached on a task that the group can carry out.

7. The task is carried out.

8. The experience is critiqued, using any of the methods given in the critiquing section, pages 60–66.

Game B. Transcendent Conflict Resolution

1. Two people who are in conflict agree to play the game. They may invite a third person as referee.

2. First one person states his point of view, which is then explored using the Reflection or Widening Communication Game. The process is then reversed with the first person stating his point of view, and the second reflecting or drawing out. This may be done several times until both parties feel that they understand the needs and point of view of the other.

3. There is then a period of silence which may last up to an hour during which each member of the conflict attempts to construct a solution that will integrate both the needs and the points of view of both.

4. One states the new point of view while the other uses the Widening Communication or Reflection Game. This is then reversed, until both higher-level points of view are understood.

5. If both points of view are close enough, the solution can be compromised. If not, there should be another period of silence in which both try to integrate these higher-level points of view into a single solution that meets the needs of both. The process is repeated until a solution is reached.

TRANSCENDENCE OF SELF AS FINDING THE GOD WITHIN: THE UNIVERSE, OR GOD, IDENTITY GAME

Ideally man should exist and act on all levels. He is universal and infinite, because he is a product or expression of the infinite. Yet he is a finite biological organism. His will is a sign of universal purpose, yet there are definite narrow purposes which he must fulfill to live. The full person is a joining of the finite with the infinite, the particular with the universal, the all with the one. Each person is everything and everywhere, he is all persons and all times. Yet he is one person at one time with particular desires, a particular history, and particular needs. His vision is individual and unique. His perceptions, his mind, his mode of approach, are his own.

In the feeling of love and the perception of beauty, we exist on the universal and infinite levels. Through hunger, desire, sexuality, strife, conflict, and creation, are we linked to the particular. The contemplative mood of peace, universality, and beauty is broken into and disturbed by the clamoring needs of the moment. The existence of these two levels joined in one body, in one person, creates potential conflict.

In this game we will try to become aware of the infinite and universal extensions of ourselves. Man in his finiteness is a focal point through which all that was and is acts. We tend to separate and oppose ourselves to the forces that participate in our being, because of our particular needs. However, we sometimes identify ourselves with everything which has created us. When this happens, we experience our God or universal identity.

Below are two quotations describing this experience, one in poetry and one a prose rationalization of the experience. Read these and think about them before starting to play the game

O earth and sky,
O universe as one vast entity,
The blades of grass I squeeze between my toes
The buttercups the thistles
The straight flying yellow bees
The air which holds them up and which I breathe
The space around each blade of grass
Their branching seed heads
The bugs the caterpillars the ants which crawl about them,
The waving heads of grass
The wind I breathe
The little butternut tree, with its delicately hung bird's nest
Let the line between us fall away
And let me merge into you;
Let me become the Universe conscious of itself.

I am you sky mirror reflecting sun
I am the stars you hide
I am the air you push from under wing
O flying cow!
And I am the wing.
I am you and you are I
And we are one.
And as you,
What must I do
To obey your will.

He rose and the Universe spoke through his lips.

I am the blade of grass
I am the oak
And as the oak
Throwing its branches to the sun
I council you thus:
Let your body become my body.

Gather me in arms of light
And bring me to your fingertips
To learn my nature.
When you have become me
Merge others into me.
And if your fingers
Fired by the stars and men
Withdraw in pain,
Remember I have others at my bidding.

Objects are defined by planes, which are an invention of the mind, to which reality does not correspond. Matter crosses the imaginary boundaries with which we attempt to imprison it. A tree may be incorrectly thought a separate entity, but it is not separate from the sun, the rain, and the years of evolution which made it possible.

The rigidity of thought, which results from breaking up the universe into many diverse objects, is nowhere as pernicious as when applied to the self. When this pernicious and false mode of thought is applied to ourselves, the ego comes into existence. Man, thinking that he is limited, begins to act in accord with that false concept. His thought and action, which creatively belong to the entire universe, is narrowed down, and he becomes the objectified fiction of his thought. When man rejects the ego, however, he becomes in thought what he is in matter, the consciousness of the entire universe.

This concept caused him to see relationships, which is the beginning of intelligence; everything he was to learn, was a new discovery.*

The God Game: Form A

PROCEDURES

1. A group of between three and five players convene to play the game.

2. They spend five minutes in silence, thinking of experiences in which they have felt as one with a larger totality.

3. Each takes a turn as focus, relating his experience. The others act to draw him out.

4. When everyone has had a turn at being focus, the group discusses the process and how they felt about it.

The God Game: Form B

PROCEDURES: SAME AS FORM A WITH THIS ADDITION:

After everyone has had a turn relating his experience of oneness with a higher totality, a second round of focusing takes place. In this round

---

* From an unpublished work by the author.

the focus person tries to regain his experience of oneness with God. The other group members support this attempt by their questions and behavior.

The God Game: Form C, Group Mode

PROCEDURES

1. A group of between three and five players meet together to play the game.

2. Each person is to talk and act from the point of view of his universal or god identity. The god identity is the totality and the infinite as it is reflected in the individual person.

3. Support the god identity of the other players. Do not assert your own god identity by tearing down or trying to dominate other players.

4. Do not confuse your personal power or self with your god identity.

5. When a person says or does something that illustrates his limited personal identity, others should indicate this by something that they say or do. They should do something that comes to mind instantly. Its appropriateness cannot be debated, but felt.

6. We express the infinite aspect of ourselves when what we say or do is completely spontaneous, balanced, and definite. It must not express our preconceptions of our role or self-image, but our totality.

7. It should be remembered that the totality includes the part. Any denial of the part, to affirm the totality, denies a part of the totality. This denial should be pointed out.

8. Concentrate on the instantaneous, the flowing, what's being born, the spontaneous, and deny all limitations, preconceptions, formulas, boundaries, including this one.

9. Stick to the real, concrete, immediate, individual; avoid the abstract and conceptual, except when they are real, concrete, and individual.

PART THREE

COMMUNITY GAMES: SEEDS OF A NEW ECOLOGY

CHAPTER 9

The Helping Professions

This section is designed to meet some special group communication needs, with particular emphasis on the needs of persons in the helping professions. Contained herein are games, structures, and strategies to aid the following groups in becoming more human, more direct, and more effective:

Teachers, principals, superintendents, doctors, nurses, psychologists, social workers, lawyers, ministers, policemen, researchers, businessmen.

This chapter is divided into three basic areas of communication:

1. *Exploring and Sharing.*

2. *Conflict Resolution,* with special attention to breaking down barriers that exist in the following relationships:

a. Parallel and related professional groups (*territorial block*). For example, the insights of social worker, psychologist, and teacher haven't been fully shared; thus the totality of efforts of these groups is less efficient.

b. Relationships within *hierarchical ranks* of a group.

c. Relationships with the "client" population. This requires breaking down carriers between teacher and student, doctor and patient, social worker and client, police and public, and minister and congregation, etc.

3. *Teaching and Training; Creativity.*

＊　＊　＊　＊　＊

The basic professional situations and problems for which the games are useful are presented in a general way so that they are applicable to a wide variety of groups. In addition, there are examples that give suggestions for specific professions and groups.

The chart on pages 230–231 summarizes and gives a frame of reference for the content of the chapter. The text follows the chart, clarifying its meaning and providing specific examples of application to the helping professions. The majority of the applications are in areas where we've had the most experience, notably with educators and with the medical profession. However, since we feel that the same concepts are transferable to other professions, we have included some suggestions beyond our present experience.

Situational Applicability

The chart is applicable to the following relationships (it should be applied to these relationships in terms of group size and situational needs):

1. With colleagues in the same profession.

2. With members of one's own staff: those of equal status, and those of differential status.

3. With members of other professions, particularly closely related professions.

4. With those whom one serves or helps: clients, students, patients, community groups, etc.

5. With the community: as a representative of one's profession, an "expert"; as a representative or arbiter of the interests of one's "client" group; as teacher to the client group in helping them relate more effectively to the community at large; as teacher of the general public at open forum, lecture, or community workshop.

6. Finally, as a teacher who can teach the clients to relate to each other for mutual self-help and increasing independence. This kind of teaching could fill a great need at a time when professional assistance is scarce, and professionals are often troubled by a desire to do more than their time permits.

EXPLORING AND SHARING

In many organizations, individuals are either isolated from each other, or form small cliques with each guarding his own territory. This not only makes for unpleasant working conditions, but the skill, energy, and potential enthusiasm of the members remains unutilized. In this section, suggestions are given to improve sharing among individuals, small groups, and large groups.

Many of the examples given in this chapter have been successfully tried in workships for the teaching profession and the medical profession. We have thus used the teaching and medical professions most heavily in the following examples. However, we feel that almost any other profession can be substituted for the indicated medical and educational personnel.

Pairs

(Note: this section on pairs is also valid for larger groups which break into pairs.)

The paired interaction and focus games create an atmosphere of free communication and openness which tends to pervade the whole organization.

Widening Communication and Reflection Games

General use: In the course of teaching and using the games in a wide variety of situations, we have found that some of the basic game techniques tend to become a habitual part of one's normal functioning in communication. For example, the focus technique became a part of the communication patterns of many people who participated in the Nextep Program for Experienced Teachers at Southern Illinois University, where the authors were staff members. Nextep people would naturally fall into the focusing technique when it seemed desirable to give concentrated attention to understanding a particular individual's thoughts and feelings. This would happen frequently in informal situations as well as in formally structured situations; that is, it might take place in any personal, social, or professional situation, either at home, at work, or wherever the focus technique seemed useful.

The Game for Widening Communication and the Reflection Game, which are subgames of the Focus Game, are also useful in almost any communication situation between two persons.

WHERE ONLY ONE PERSON IN THE PAIR KNOWS THE GAME

An advantage of these games is that they can be used where only one person of the pair knows the games. Thus the area of discourse between two persons can be expanded in many informal situations not specifically set up for use of game patterns. An example of this usefulness was discovered at a workshop for a group from the Center for Educational Development, University of Illinois Medical Center of Chicago. One of the doctors who participated described the almost universal problem in the education of residents and interns in which the teaching staff is made

GROUP SIZE AND FUNCTION CHART

	EXPLORATION AND SHARING	RESOLVING CONFLICTS AND OVERCOMING BARRIERS	TEACHING-TRAINING; CREATIVITY
Pairs	1. Game for Widening Communication 2. Reflection Game 3. Role play	1. Challenge Game 2. Reflection Game for Resolving Conflict 3. Position Statement and Understanding Response 4. Prejudice Game 5. Problem Conflict Resolution Game	1. Student teaching student 2. Group Learning Game (2–6 people) 3. Sharing perceptions in learning (Widening Communication and Reflection games) 4. Challenge Game
3–5 members	1. Focus games 2. Free interchange	Same as above plus Focus Game	1. Focus and Discussion games for sharing 2. Positive Focus for (literature—any content) 3. Creativity Unit

6–12	1. Ongoing T-Group games 2. Focus Game in large group	1. Ongoing T-Group games 2. Core and Cross groups to work out resolutions 3. Community Meeting	1. Assembly model with members giving input. Then break into smaller groups (6–30 persons). 2. Cross groups
12–40	1. Core and Cross groups 2. Community Meeting 3. Feelings assembly 4. Voting questions and mini-focus	1. Core and Cross groups 2. Community Meeting 3. Breaking into small groups with one member of each polarity in each group. Challenge Game	1. Teacher Focus Game 2. Expert focus (4–40 people) 3. Assembly structure, and break into smaller groups for assimilation and competency

40–1,000	1. Large Group Participant Meeting
	  a. voting questions
	  b. mini-focus
	  c. open forum
	  d. breaking into small groups
		1. Large group participant meeting followed by breaking into pairs with polarities represented in each pair. Challenge Game and Reflection Game for Conflict
		2. Public Challenge Games
			1. Large group participant meeting
			2. Brief demonstration followed by breakdown into small groups for sharing and assimilation

up of practicing physicians working part-time and having only minor interest in the teaching aspect of their work. He stated that such physicians tend to be brief and incomplete in their explanations, and the resident physicians and interns are left to get what they can. In this situation it seemed difficult to help these physician-teachers improve their teaching skills, yet they were the only source of the necessary knowledge and experience. During the conference we hit upon the notion of getting the most out of their time by having the resident doctors and interns use the Game for Widening Communication to get needed information and other help from the teaching staff, then sharing what they got with each other.

This method is applicable to many other situations where only one member of the pair knows the game. Some suggested possibilities: in relating to client, patient, or student, as a means of drawing-out the other person concerning his thoughts, fears, desires, needs; for social worker, lawyer, minister and many others, as well as doctor and teacher.

It is also possible to start at the other end, by teaching the communication skills to clients, patients, and students, so that they can better relate to doctor, lawyer, teacher. This was in fact done very effectively at a high school that we worked with.

The Reflection Game is especially useful when one wishes to communicate a sense of understanding and support.

The best way of improving person-to-person communication within an organization is to take one day in which the Reflection Game and Widening Communication for Pairs is introduced to the entire organization. The skills can then be reinforced by practice on appropriate occasions. See chart on pages 230–231.

Role Play

See Role Play games, Chapter 7.

3–5 Members

FOCUS GAME (SEE CHAPTER 1)

The focus technique improves small group sharing. It will improve the work of any committee, any team, any small decision-making body, or small learning group.

Where a larger group is involved, break it down into smaller groups of three to five each.

One example of our use of this game was a job training workshop in East St. Louis. Participants in the workshop were preparing themselves to help hard-core unemployed to become employable. The workshop provided experience in the Focus Game; the content discussed in the game was (1) the job facing the participants in working with hard-core unemployed, and (2) their own feelings about their situation and about themselves. The participants felt favorably toward the kind of sharing and mutual support they experienced; and anticipated the training and support-giving value which the game would have for their "clients."

The Focus Game was used at a workshop for medical educators in order to gain insight into some of the personal tensions that interfere with medical effectiveness. Examples of some of the questions we used as focus topics with the doctors are given below. Similar questions can be constructed for other professions or groups.

1. Make a list of all the principles, formal and informal, that govern the relationships between doctor and doctor, and between doctor and patient. List all the possible consequences of each principle, and use the lists in a Focus Game.

2. Make a list of circumstances in which you're most uncomfortable with:

> medical students
> patients
> doctors, etc.

Explore in a focus.

3. The medical educators saw the focus game as useful in helping a doctor or medical student explore a problem or case in depth. The focus game would permit him to bring out all his thoughts and feelings in respect to a patient with whom he was concerned. The group would help him clarify his thinking, and afterward give whatever additional help was required.

These content areas could be more fully explored using techniques of empathy and role play, and worked through in such games as the Prejudice Game, Challenge Game, etc.

The Focus Game can be used in any professional group to explore areas of tension and as an aid in problem solving. It should be introduced and used in the small functional units of an organization.

6–12 Members

ONGOING T-GROUP GAMES

The Ongoing T-Group Game (see Chapter 2) makes for group cohesiveness by stimulating honesty, openness, sharing, as well as the facing and working out of differences. It is good for identifying and overcoming sources of tension within an organization or a social group. We believe that a group that uses it becomes more flexible, more resilient, and more productive.

One example of the use of this game for exploration and sharing is the social group. We worked weekly over a period of months with such a group made up of young adults who were mostly graduate students in sociology and psychology. The members had been friends prior to the start of the T-Group, but wanted the T-Group experience to grow personally and deepen their relationships. Not only did they achieve this objective, but some of them are now using the game professionally.

T-Grouping is becoming widespread in churches and schools, and the T-Group games could be useful in these situations, as well, since the games make the professional trainer less necessary.

We have recently tried the game with delinquent boys living in a half-way house. Other possibilities for use in an institutional setting might be prisons, homes for unwed mothers, youth centers. We feel the T-Group Games are generally applicable for sharing in any social or professional group.

12–40 Members

CORE AND CROSS GROUPS (SEE CHAPTER 10)

The concepts of the core group and the cross group are most fully dealt with in the next chapter, on large group structures. (The concepts of Community Meeting and Assembly, dealt with below, are fully developed in that same chapter.)

The Core Group. The community is broken down into small stable groups of four. These stable groups use the communication skills developed in the Focus Game and paired interaction games to facilitate their communication. In addition, the members of a core group lend support to each other in respect to the total group. The core group often undertakes projects together and functions as a team.

The Cross Group. The total membership is divided into a number of cross groups, each one of which is composed of one member from each core group. The cross group functions to keep cliques based on Core groups from fracturing the totality. In the cross group, there is a sharing of what goes on in the individual core groups. A cross group can also function as an action committee affecting the total organization. It can function in this way because it is representative of all the core groups and hence is in a position to involve them in an activity. The composition of this cross group may be fixed, or it may change at the discretion of the core group, which determines which of their members will represent them, and for how long.

The cross group is very useful for sharing and for overcoming barriers along cross-professional and cross-hierarchical lines. In workshops one may assume that the members of any homogeneous group, such as surgeons, or dietitians, or internists, represent a core group. The total population is then crossed by dividing it into small groups with one representative from each of the homogeneous professional groups in each.

At the workshop for the University of Illinois Medical Center, cross groups were composed of educators from the Nextep program at Southern Illinois University and medical educators from University of Illinois. Among the physicians there was further crossing between surgeons, dietitians, public health personnel, one psychiatrist, and one professor of anatomy. The medical participants were still further crossed in that they came from areas such as India, South Africa, and Thailand, as well as the United States. The sharing of such diverse perspectives was felt by all to be an unusually rich and profitable experience.

Wherever there is a polarization, cross-grouping can be used to heal the breach. We have cross-grouped police and juveniles. In doing so, the police were considered one homogeneous population, and the juveniles another; they were crossed by breaking up the total population into pairs, with one policeman and one juvenile in each pair. We have cross-grouped individuals for and against the Vietnam war, using the same principle for pairing.

In these cases, real communication is opened up along the cleavage lines of the polarization. All the members of the group are involved in this kind of confrontation, rather than a few leaders or representatives. The technique therefore opens the possibility of reintegrating groups and factions that have split off from each other—political, social, economic, professional, sexual, and racial groups.

The Core-Cross group structure was also used as part of the basic functioning structure of Nextep program for experienced teachers. We feel that it is transferable to other institutional settings besides the educational setting. The structures would be useful in situations where "clients" help other "clients" as well as those where professionals help other professionals, for example, schools, homes for the elderly, orphanages, homes for unwed mothers.

Community Meeting

A Community Meeting is a meeting in which all of the members of the community can get together and discuss matters of mutual concern and share experiences with every one present. (See pp. 248–261 for a complete description.) This structure is important for achieving a sense of togetherness as well as for sharing information that is of importance to everyone.

FEELINGS ASSEMBLY

This is a time when feelings are shared and explored by the total body. See pages 33–34.

40–1,000 *Members*

Voting questions and mini-focus. See page 172 for a description. These are valuable techniques for opening the assembly or meeting, for they give a shared experience to the total group in which each person can express his position. Through the expression of diverse views, the individual feels less isolated, and more a part of the group. If the group facilitator is flexible, he can use the expression of feeling and opinion to guide the progress of the meeting. This enables the audience to have the unique experience of guiding their fate in concert with the several hundred or thousand other people present, as contrasted with the situation in which they have no choice but to listen or leave.

LARGE GROUP INPUT FOLLOWED BY SMALL GROUP SHARING

At the March, 1970, national conference of curriculum directors in San Francisco (ASCD), a group of 600 participants broke into focus groups to share experiences, to exchange differences in views, and to resolve conflicts concerning issues raised by the speakers and by participants from the floor. The conference was held in a large hall with movable chairs. There was no difficulty in breaking into small groups. Focus games and paired interaction games were utilized to facilitate the small group interaction. Participants felt it was a constructive and creative experience, incomparably better than the lecture method usually used with that size group.

This method would be valuable for open community workshops, as well as professional meetings.

See "Large Group Participant Meeting."

RESOLVING CONFLICTS AND OVERCOMING BARRIERS

(See earlier material on Cross groups, under "Exploration," page 234.)

Pairs

CHALLENGE GAME, PAGE 75

To date this game has been used in the classroom: in the study of poetry, college level; and in the study of educational practice, and the theory of child development.

It has also been used in the midst of campus demonstrations, to permit a rational confrontation of opposed points of view.

PROBLEM CONFLICT RESOLUTION GAME, PAGE 87

This can be used wherever the Challenge Game can be used. It is a more powerful means of resolving conflict, but takes more time and practice to learn.

PREJUDICE GAME, PAGE 77

Played by a prejudiced pair, such as doctor and patient. One gives his idea or assumptions about the other, for example, the patient gives his idea of the doctor. He is drawn out by the doctor. The doctor then gives his idea of himself as doctor, and of his profession generally. Then reverse. (Any "prejudiced" pair can be substituted where we have indicated doctor and patient.)

3–5 Members

REFLECTION GAME FOR RESOLVING CONFLICT, SEE PAGE 78

This method proved very valuable in gaining understanding at a deep level within the setting of a core group at the Nextep program for experienced teachers. The game made it possible for two members of a core, who were in deep conflict, to hear each other. Other members of the core participated as facilitators.

THE FOCUS GAME (SEE CHAPTER 1)

Gives each person a chance to fully express his position so that there is greater understanding, and hence a greater chance to resolve the conflict.

6–12 Members

ONGOING T-GROUP GAME

Was used in a session involving police, who were primarily white, and militant black youth leaders. Before the encounter, each group had a dehumanized picture of the other. In the course of the experience, they moved toward an attitude of mutual respect.

This example suggests the use of this game in other situations involving polar groups. Some of these might be groups antagonistic in terms of:

race

sex

ethnic origin
religion
social orientation
political viewpoint
professional standpoint

As part of such a grouping, the polar positions may be crossed in pairs. (See earlier, pages 51–56, for details.)

6–12 or 12–40 Members

CORE AND CROSS GROUPS (SEE CHAPTER 10)

Often, in a group of forty, there are nearly as many views as there are individuals, and there seems to be no way in which a common, acceptable solution can be worked out. At such a time, the group can be broken into core groups, with each core developing a solution to the problem. The groups can then be crossed, with each cross group developing a compromise solution among all the cores. At this point, most of the compromise solutions by the various cross groups are very similar. A decision can be made as to which solution is to be used by a simple vote, with little ill-feeling generated.

COMMUNITY MEETING, SEE PAGE 249 FOR PROCESS

40–1,000 Members

Use voting questions to define the parameters of the conflict. Pair people on opposite sides of the conflict. Use the Challenge Game or Conflict Resolution Game.

See earlier, page 236, the San Francisco conference for curriculum directors, for techniques in resolving conflict in the large group.

TEACHING AND TRAINING: CREATIVITY

Pairs

STUDENT TEACHING STUDENT: THE GROUP LEARNING GAME, PAGE 118

The Group Learning Game can be used when both students are at about the same level.

CHALLENGE GAME

Can be used to gain an understanding of an opposite point of view. It has been used for this purpose in classes in child development and education. Also, in a clash of opinions in poetry classes on the college level. The game has potential also for learning between cross-groups: interprofessional and interhierarchical, for example.

3–5 Members

FOCUS GAME

a. For discussing subject matter of a course. This has been extensively used in college courses in literature and in education. (See Positive Focus for Literature, an example of use of focus for subject matter, page 115.) It has also been used in elementary and high schools for discussions on history, mathematics, science, German, and English, as well as for discussion on problems of a personal nature. The Focus Game can be used for discussions in most subject-matter areas.

The Focus Game has been used to teach classes for disturbed children, in a hospital setting as well as in a regular school setting. It has also been used for slow learners, and educable mentally handicapped learners.

b. To create an atmosphere of trust and acceptance in the classroom. The game has been used for this purpose on the elementary, high school, and college levels. Additionally, the Focus Game was used for this purpose in the Job Corps, where there had previously existed an atmosphere of conflict and mutual tearing down in the classroom. The Group Learning Game was also used by the Job Corps.

6–12 Members

CORE AND CROSS GROUPS, SEE PAGES 244–248

12–40 Members

TEACHER FOCUS GAME, PAGE 107

Can be used with cross-professional groups, as well as within homogeneous groups. Additionally, the forty can be broken up into smaller groups, using some of the previously defined methods.

EXPERT FOCUS, PAGE 114, USABLE WITH 4–40 PEOPLE

40–1,000 Members

The total group can be broken up into pairs or focus-size groups of four or five persons to deal with issues or problems brought up by speakers or raised by participants from the floor.

In Thornton, Illinois, the focus game was demonstrated to 1,500 teachers. They then broke into small groups and experienced the game. Approximately 60 percent of them have reported using it successfully in the classroom.

1. *Dealing with Various Modes of Behavior.* This program is helpful in increasing sensitivity and skill in dealing with various emotional and personality states.

2. *Task-Oriented Games.* Wherever there is a need to get people to work together, the task-oriented game may be helpful.

3. *Structures for Groups and Organizations.* These are useful in reorganizing the interactions of the staff and for organizing one's target population to be more effective.

CHAPTER 10

Structures for Groups
and Organizations

TYPES OF GROUPS THAT CAN USE THESE STRUCTURES

The games and game skills may be used within an organization to bring about a new effectiveness. In this chapter we will show how the games, with some additional group structures, can be used toward this purpose.

The structures outlined in this section are designed for and have been used by groups characterized by or desiring the following qualities and purposes:

1. Care for the personal growth and effectiveness of each individual member.

2. Enhanced creativity and productivity of individual members, and thus for the group as a whole.

3. Openness.

4. Sharing of the teaching-learning role.

5. Rationality in resolving conflicts.

6. Sharing generally of benefits and rewards gained by the group.

7. Mutual supportiveness, respect, trust, and creative stimulation.

Our assumption is that individuals will grow personally and interpersonally and be most productive within a group when their needs are met through the group, and when there are few pressing, competitive needs that can only be met outside.

When an organization or group doesn't permit members to meet their needs, but frustrates them, persons within the organization begin to feel angry or hopeless. They may have the feeling of being left out or tied up. They may feel that the tasks are alien, and that they are unable to make their values correspond with their acts. They may feel fear of speaking their minds, fear of being criticized, fear of being ignored. They may feel hopeless about confronting or resolving interpersonal hangups.

The structures in this chapter are designed to meet group relevant needs, and to facilitate and stimulate maximum participation and freedom of individual members. There is thus a strong trend toward democratic design; however, guidelines are also provided for hierarchical structure of a rational nature. The removal of irrational authority will help in reducing jealousies and antagonisms, and will improve morale and the level of creativity.

It is anticipated that groups using the structures will tend toward either of two basic purposes or axes:

1. *Person orientation.* Chief emphasis on personal development. Example: schools.

2. *Product orientation.* Chief purposes are creativity and created "products." Products can be either material or nonmaterial in nature. Examples: nonmaterial—ideas; material—kitchen sinks.

The structures and games discussed in this section are thus basically of two sorts, in keeping with these two orientations:

1. Means for promoting personal growth through improved self-understanding, self-development, and interpersonal communication.

2. Means for enhancing and increasing individual and group creativity and productivity. The means provided here are chiefly in the nature of creative atmosphere, with room to solve problems openly and to utilize the skills and ideas of all members which an open system fosters.

Any groups having or desiring to adopt the purposes outlined here could utilize the structures in this chapter.

IMPLEMENTATION FOR MEETING OF NEEDS AND PURPOSES OF GROUPS

The chapter is so organized that a particular group can select what is useful to its unique needs and ignore the rest; however, the basic group structures outlined do form a coherent, organic whole, with functional interrelationships. The basic structures are three:

1. Core group.
2. Cross group.
3. Community Meeting.

Structures

1. The Core Group: The basic unit is the Core Group, which is a stable group of four or five members. The key function of the Core is to meet the individual's needs for inclusion and support. Functioning of the Core is improved through use of the following game skills:

Focus game, Reflection game, Widening Communication for Pairs, Challenge Game, Production Focus Game, Ongoing T-Group games, and Creativity games.

Use of these games will create higher motivation within the group, deeper involvement, commitment, and creativity.

The Core Group is the basic building block of the organization. Four or five Cores form a community group. Two other structures are needed in order to unify the larger organization and prevent these building blocks from being simply autonomous units:

2. Cross Groups: Each Cross Group is made up of one member from each Core. Cross Groups meet together to discuss common problems and common policies.

3. The Community Group: This group is made up of four or five Core Groups, containing up to twenty-four members. The Community Meeting is a meeting of all the members.

In case of larger organizations, the community might be organized into larger units on the same principles by which the Core Groups were organized into a community group.

Within the broad scope of purpose and function outlined in this introduction, some groups and organizations which could use the structures are:

schools (interstudent, student-faculty, interfaculty)
hospitals
professional groups
work teams
higher levels of business organizations
research groups
community groups
groups of shared interest, such as recreational and study groups
groups of creative orientation
social or political groups

(See Chapter 9 on the Helping Professions for further possibilities of use of these structures in specific groups. Note the heavy reference to the use of Core groups, Cross groups, and Community Meeting in the chart for the Helping Professions. Much detailed description of the uses of these structures is presented in that earlier chapter.)

THE BASIC STRUCTURES

I. Core Group

In the Core Group we play down the principle of free choice to maximize security. A Core consists of four members, and is comparable to a nuclear family, in that it provides a stable base. It remains stable despite the often shifting feelings of attraction and repulsion among its members. As in a family, one stays even when one is angry or temporarily dislikes another member. One must face one's social problems within this group, because one cannot escape them. That is perhaps the price one pays for security.

The Core Group has two basic functions:

a. Giving security and personal support, and furthering the growth of the total community.

b. Working together to get some external task accomplished.

These two objectives often reinforce each other. However, at times they are in conflict, and it is necessary to emphasize one more than the other. It is important not to lose sight of the supportive, personal growth function of the Core. Part of the burden of decision-making can be accomplished through the sharing and coordinating of the Cross Groups.

SELECTION OF CORE MEMBERS

There are various methods for choosing the members:

1. Random selection.

2. Selection to maximize either diversity or compatibility. If the Core Groups are to be potential teams, one would want a diversity of skills within the group.

3. Temporary Core Groups may be randomly assigned while members are learning relevant skills. Later, when the skills have been learned and people know each other better, Core Groups can be formed on the basis of free choice.

FUNCTIONS OF THE CORE GROUP

1. Obligation of Core members to each other.

a. Support. Core members are obligated to support each other and help each other relate to the total group, and not to tear each other down in front of noncore members.

b. Limitation and Self-limitation. The obligation of support implies an obligation on the part of a Core Group member to refrain from doing things which go strongly counter to the feelings, needs, or perceptions of other core members. A member must check out and win the approval or permission of his core group before pushing things with the total organization, so that his core may in turn support his action. Conversely, the Core Group has the obligation to confront its members concerning behavior which they feel to be inappropriate.

c. Communication. Core Group members have the obligation to try to listen to and understand each other's feelings. They have the obligation to try to work through and cope with conflict and negative feelings without withdrawing. In doing this, they should avail themselves of all of the game skills and of neutral facilitators, should they be needed.

2. Learning of Skills.

The Core Group is a place where one learns and practices interaction skills. The Core uses the focus techniques primarily; but Paired Interaction games, T-Group games, Conflict Resolution games, Task-Oriented games and values techniques should also be known and practiced where appropriate.

In the early stages of Core interaction, there is a freeing of communication in depth, and people get to know each other well. On the basis of this deeper knowledge, personality differences and differences of value come into focus, as in a marriage after the honeymoon. At this point, paired interaction skills for facilitating the understanding of differences in depth, and for trying to resolve them or accommodate to them in a constructive fashion, becomes desirable if the Core Group is to become a fully functioning group. At these times, it is desirable for a third person, not in the Core Group, to facilitate and referee the paired interaction processes. A third person may be necessary because the members are so involved with their feelings and thoughts, that they are sometimes unable to stick to the rules making for constructive communication and confrontation.

3. Integration, Expansion, Problem Solving.

The Core Group is a place where each person integrates and expands his knowledge, his feeling, and his experience within the larger organization.

Periodically (about once a week,) evaluations can be made and discussed within the Core Group. Between times, there can be discussion of a member's significant experience in the organization, both gratifying and frustrating.

A key use of the group is for sharing one's problems and successes in creative or productive activity, and for getting help in working out the difficulties in these areas.

4. The Core as a Work Team.

The Core Group can function to create and maintain a working team. (See "Selection of Core members" for the concept of team balance in a work situation.)

The purpose of the core team is to improve group efficiency. Core groups may become teams by an agreement of the members to the following principles:

a. Members will share their knowledge and skills with each other. They will cooperate rather than compete, helping each other and supporting each other.

b. They will discuss and try to resolve their differences rather than complaining to others outside the group.

Caution: Where there is a Cross-Group structure, this principle should not prevent members from getting help in the Cross Group as long as they do not go into personalities.

c. There should be no attempt to form alliances within the group. Differences between individuals should be openly discussed and worked out without resort to criticism behind somebody's back.

d. Core Group members will support each other in relation to outsiders.

5. The Core Group may have the administrative function of allotting each individual's commitments and working relationship to the total organization; or of distributing the functions delegated to it among the core members. For example, if a person wishes to modify the contractual relations he has entered into with the total group, he may work out the changes with his Core Group first.

6. The Core Group is analogous to a staff in that it can have evaluative and change functions both for the individual and for the organization as a whole. The Core Group should cooperatively get a sense of where the organization as a whole is going, and what its strengths and weaknesses are. This knowledge should help the individual members not only to relate themselves better to the organization as a whole, but also to work out constructive, practical ways of improving the organization in terms of a sense of the totality of problems.

Not only should the group work out what should be done in the total group, but they should also work out constructive, nonmanipulative ways of trying to implement their views. This function gives core members some of the knowledge and skills involved in being on the managerial staff of an organization.

See as supplement: Introducing Democratic Forms into an Organization, page 266.

II. Cross Group

With or without the games, small groups have a way of running down. A Core Group structure, or any formation of small group alliances within a larger group, has these disadvantages:

1. Factions tend to develop, each one with a separate and partial view, leading to fracturing of the entire group.

2. An inbred atmosphere develops in the small groups, and narrowness, distortion, and errors accumulate and grow. Inner conflicts of the small group are magnified for lack of an objective or corrective outside view.

This process may be delayed by use of the games, but a special structure is still needed to counteract these advantages.

DEFINITION OF THE CROSS GROUP

Within a large group, the meeting together of one member from each core, or small group, forms a Cross Group. This may be done by having each member of a particular Core Group assigned a number, in sequence: 1, 2, 3, 4, etc. Then, all 1's, 2's, 3's, and 4's constitute the Cross groups. (Cross groups need not necessarily always be the same four or five people. The groups can be rejuggled, so that each person gains more contacts within the larger group.)

Core and Cross groups can each maintain a level of confidentiality. This is related to freedom of a core member to discuss with his Cross Group *issues* raised in the core, but not *personalities*. The same holds true for discussion within the core of issues raised in the Cross Group.

OBJECTIVES AND FUNCTIONS OF THE CROSS GROUP

1. Each member has the opportunity to get an impression of views and feelings of the entire group.

2. The drift toward distortion or error, arising in a Core Group, can be checked. To insure this, Cross groups, as well as Core groups, should meet at regular intervals.

3. Executive and legislative functions may be undertaken by a Cross Group, with each member representing his Core Group in the decision-making process. Notice that this permits several legislative groups or committees to function simultaneously, and to divide up the work so that each Cross Group has a different task; and yet each Cross Group represents the entire organization.

Properly organized, a cross committee has the advantage of being able to reflect the feelings of the whole organization through its representative character (one member from each Core Group). Also, it is an ideal structure for gaining support and commitment to the decisions made, with each member working to involve his Core Group. (See further the Planning-Executive Committee.)

Additional Principles and Guidelines for Core and Cross Groups

1. The time scheduled should be open-ended, as the cores frequently like to keep going for a long period.

2. Before Core and Cross Group meetings, a Community Meeting may be held in which issues, strong feelings, and questions as to the direction of the total group may be raised; with individuals expressing their own feelings on these issues without discussion of or reference to what others have said. The restriction on discussion (not to discuss the opinions of others) is made in order to permit a maximum number of issues to be raised in a minimum amount of time; discussion is to be saved for core or cross meetings which follow.

3. Core Group uses focus primarily. In addition, it may use Paired Interaction games, T-Group games, Conflict Resolution games, Task-Oriented games, and Values techniques.

The Cross Group uses the Ongoing T-Group Game primarily, though it may also use Focus games, Paired Interaction, Conflict Resolution, and Task-Oriented games at times.

4. Composition of groups: In a school, for example, Core groups might be within grade levels or departments; Cross groups could cut across grade levels or departments. This same principle of the inner group and the Cross Group can be applied to many other types of organization or institution. (See Chapter 9 on the Helping Professions for further detail on the uses of these two types of groups, pages 225–240.)

BASIC FORMS OF COMMUNITY MEETING

A community consists of all relations of the individuals with each other, their common feelings, experiences, and values, as well as the range of differences the organization can constructively assimilate, utilize, or tolerate. It consists of the image that individual members have of the group and that outsiders have of the group; and it consists of the way each member bears the group image toward outsiders, as well as the group characteristics which outsiders attribute to each member. Each individual identifies to some extent with this community through his group membership. It is therefore proper to maximize the opportunities of all group members to participate in creating the community.

Some organizations have one way of meeting all community relevant needs. The way generally chosen favors some of the community needs while neglecting others. The neglected needs then express themselves indirectly and covertly in ways that disrupt or inhibit group functioning. We propose to provide channels through which all the large group or community needs we know about can be met. When we discover other needs or better ways of meeting those we know about, these structures may be changed or new ones added.

Following are five basic types of Community Meeting to fill five different functions:

1. General Community Meeting.
2. Information Sharing Community Meeting.
3. Free Form Community Meeting.
4. Large Group Expression Meeting.
5. Community Meeting for Teaching: the Assembly.

1. General Community Meeting

This meeting functions to make general decisions and to integrate common group action. Once a general decision is made, the detailed working out should be left to a committee or individual. Where the decisions are complex and involve the total membership, a Cross Group committee should be used. Overall plans made by the planning committee sometimes gain support by ratification at the Community Meeting. (See "Planning-Executive Committee," page 262.)

PROCEDURES FOR COMMUNITY MEETING

1. An open agenda is established by using a chalk board. To place an item on the agenda, a group member simply writes an abbreviated statement of intent on the chalk board. He also writes how much time his item needs. If no agenda items appear on the chalk board, the meeting is not held.

2. After all agenda items have been established, the group decides upon the amount of time needed for conducting the meeting. The meeting is adjourned at the end of the time specified, after which evaluation may take place.

3. While a particular item is on the floor, the group member who placed the item on the agenda is chairman. The agenda is worked in a sequential fashion, with members taking turns in being chairman during the meeting.

4. A rotating time-keeper reminds the person in charge when his time is up, and smooths transition to the next item.

5. Upon the close of the agenda part of the meeting, or at the close of each item on the agenda, the process may be evaluated, with members identifying what and who was helpful or not helpful.

RULES

1. *Membership:* Each individual, no matter what his status in the organization, has equal influence in making decisions. No one member is appointed leader or chairman. Any individual may speak on any agenda item. He can call attention to himself by raising his hand, so that the person chairing the item can recognize his desire to speak.

2. *Keeping an open agenda:* Any individual has the right to put up an item on the agenda; however, the item should be of general concern to the members of the group. A lack of an open agenda often allows several persons to dominate the group interaction and prevents the full expression of others' feelings.

The focus person raising the agenda item is to state his issue, problem, or concern, and his expectation, in as concise a manner as possible. The group is then to ask him questions and attempt to help him clarify his thinking and feelings before stating their feelings or solutions prematurely.

3. *Decision-making:* The Community Meeting is not a place for technical decisions or for friendly chats. It is a place for decisions by consensus concerning vital policy issues or votes of confidence. The community should then delegate technical implementation of the policies to individuals or committees. Core groups or Cross groups make good functional committees. (See "Planning-Executive Committee.")

4. *Sharing feelings:* A key element is the expression of feelings on each agenda item. Each person must state his own feelings directly and clearly. This may be done at length or by agreeing or disagreeing with others who state feelings. The group member who raised the agenda item is responsible for assessing feelings. This process can be facilitated by the use of:

a. Voting.

b. Rank order questions.

c. Whips ("whipping" around the group, with each person briefly stating his feelings).

d. Public or group interviews (see chapter on Values games for the above).

For meetings whose primary purpose is the airing of feelings, see "Free Form Community Meeting," or "Large Group Expression Meeting."

5. *Challenging or confronting:* An individual may ask to challenge an issue or point. The group grants or withholds permission by vote of

confidence. If granted, the challenger proceeds according to the rules of the Challenge Game.

6. *Use of Consensus:* Only policies that vitally affect the organization, the group, or individual group members are appropriate agenda items. Therefore it is important, if the policies are to be carried out, that most or all members should be willing to support them. This may mean compromise and/or some delay in implementing decisions if consensus is difficult to reach; but the additional time spent gathering support by use of consensus will in the long run pay off. Majority vote is therefore to be avoided, unless used as a last resort for pressing decisions.

7. *Evaluation of process:* If the group is operating from a concerned and caring point of view, consensus on vital policy issues will be reached without great difficulty although the process may still be somewhat time-consuming. If the group is operating from a base of distrust, it will seem impossible to reach decisions through the use of consensus. In this type of group, evaluation and dealing with the process may be of more importance than spending time trying to reach consensus. However, the evaluation must deal with specifics: Who is blocking interaction and feeling? And for what reasons? The use of such terms as "they," "we," and "some people," is prohibited. Names must be substituted.

8. *Process Observer:* Periodically, a noncommunity member with experience in other communities is invited in to observe the process, critique it, and suggest alternative behaviors and norms. It is important for any community to accept and deal with this challenge. This suggests that the community members reveal as far as possible what they think is going on in the organization in terms of issues, problems, successes, failures, plans, and prospects. The outsider tries to understand, clarify, support, and challenge the community. The interaction should be a mutual process of learning.

2. Information-sharing Community Meeting

This meeting functions to inform the total organization of what individuals or subgroups are doing.

It has an open agenda. Individuals on the agenda may announce plans, involve new people in activities, and briefly describe some of the things they have done or plan to do.

This type of meeting is usually brief. It may be held independently, or as part of another meeting.

3. Free-Form Community Meeting

The Free-Form Community Meeting permits exploration and confrontation of complex issues and feelings in depth.

It is appropriate in a group trying to find its identity, exploring common objectives, confronting a crisis, charting a course, uncovering and dealing with hidden conflict and discontent that involves the group generally.

There is no set agenda. Anybody says what is on his mind.

PROCEDURES

1. Two people act as facilitators. They sit on opposite sides of the group so that between them they see the entire body.

2. When an unresolved conflict arises between two or more members where feelings threaten to be hurt, the facilitators legitimize both points of view by reflecting and accepting both sides of the conflict.

3. They watch the group and draw in the silent members.

4. If a person withdraws in hurt because of something that is said, the facilitators draw him back in by exploring his feelings and accepting their legitimacy.

4. Large-Group Expression Meeting

NEED FOR EXPRESSION MEETING

Every organization needs a place where general feelings, values, issues, and differences may be brought into the open. Where this is not done, strong feelings become attached to almost anything. They come out in interpersonal friction, or they are indirectly expressed in endless discussion about trivial issues, or they may be stifled, resulting in inner turmoil and external withdrawal.

PROBLEMS

The major problem in expressing feelings in a large group (of over thirteen members) is time.

1. There is not enough time for everyone to express himself fully without others feeling bored, left out, or tied up.

2. There is not enough time to resolve the issues expressed.

CRITERIA FOR A LARGE-GROUP EXPRESSION MEETING

The expression meeting must therefore be designed to permit important feelings and issues to be brought up without tying everybody up with the impossible task of resolving them.

PURPOSES OF AN EXPRESSION MEETING

To develop group unity and solidarity, to clarify common purposes, to establish a public identity, to raise issues and alternatives, to identify and expose feelings and differences, and to vent problems.

USES

The meeting can be used as follows:

1. As an opening experience.
2. As part of an assessment.
3. As a periodic ongoing activity to provide for expression of feelings and issues relevant to the entire group.
4. As part of a culminative activity including other evaluative meetings and devices, other forms of group interaction such as Games, T-Grouping, and parties of various sorts.

DEFINITION

The Large-group Expression Meeting itself is not T-Grouping or a place for unrestricted argument and confrontation, but a place where feelings can be expressed under conditions of safety in a large group. It includes such items as:

Public Interview, Values Questions, Feeling Statements, Whips, Challenge Game, Feeling Clarification Game, reports of individuals on meaningful happenings, time-limited discussion designed to further mutual understanding of feelings—not to resolve issues.

Presentation of poems, singing of songs, presentation of pictures, skits, role playing, etc.

Where strong feelings or conflict arise, use Challenge Game, Feeling Clarification Game, or break into groups to discuss (focus-size or T-Group–size groups) and report back at agreed time.

PROCEDURES

1. A large group meets together for the purpose of having an Expression Meeting.
2. Someone experienced in Expression Meetings acts as facilitator. At later meetings, someone volunteers to be the group facilitator. He functions nonjudgmentally, accepting the feelings expressed, and planning the order of presentation. Note: Several facilitators may have charge of different portions of the meeting.

3. Where members have planned to do something, they tell the facilitator in advance, to help him plan the meeting. The plan may have room for both planned and spontaneous expression of feelings.

4. After the individual or group expressions of feelings are completed, the group critiques the process, including comment on ways in which the facilitator was most or least helpful.

5. At each subsequent meeting a new facilitator is chosen. After a time, the facilitator's role may be dispensed with, if and when the group feels comfortable in doing so.

OTHER FORMS OF EXPRESSION MEETINGS

An Expression Meeting may be limited to only one or two of the suggested modes. What is important is that three elements of the meeting go together. Here are some possible ways that an Expression Meeting may be organized:

1. A sequence of several elements.

a. Voting questions which raise issues and feelings. This would be done with everyone free to ask his voting question.

b. Statements of feelings. The voting questions would undoubtedly give rise to feelings. This would permit these feelings to be expressed.

c. A feelings clarification, Challenge Game, or T-Group Game to confront the issue of values or feelings conflicts would be a good third activity. This would permit the conflicts concerning the expressed feelings to be confronted. (For T-Groups, break into groups of eight to thirteen members.)

d. A critiquing of the whole process would help bring the group together through the process of evaluating what happened.

2. A simpler form of expression assembly might consist of individuals expressing their feelings independently of each other.

Here the role of the facilitator might be to accept the feelings expressed—and to enforce the rule of minimizing interaction between individual statements.

3. A discussion meeting where the facilitator functions to draw out the expression of feelings about an issue as well as accepting the legitimacy of opposed feelings.

5. Community Meeting for Teaching: The Assembly

PURPOSE

To permit members of the group to share their knowledge, ideas, and feelings with the entire group. At this meeting, styles of large group instruction that permit group members to participate as thinking, feeling people are to be encouraged.

1. People take turns presenting something to the group. The turn is time-limited, fifteen minutes being a good limit except in special circumstances.

2. At the end of each session, there is a brief evaluation, with each person filling out a card, saying how he felt at the meeting.

3. Rules for the teacher:

a. Try to make your presentation meaningful and involving to the audience.

b. Be aware of both their verbal and nonverbal responses, and take account of them in modifying the presentation of your materials.

c. Your lessons may include breaking into groups for small group discussions, as well as large group discussions.

4. Rules for audience:

a. Give your complete attention to the person who is presenting his material.

b. Follow along with the presentation, withholding criticisms or arguments unless called for, until the period for evaluation.

5. A rotating facilitator will help the teaching assembly work better. His function is to make sure that there are members ready to present to the group, to survey needs of the group, and to schedule presentations.

Game for Assimilation of New Members

The assimilation of a new member involves mutual exchange and learning. In most groups the attempt is made to assimilate a new member to what is going on; but little attempt is made to utilize his unique point of view as an outsider, or to take advantage of his insight, observations, criticisms, knowledge, and skills. This game attempts to assimilate a member by having him share his insights, thoughts, and feelings about the group or organization, while learning about the group and adapting to it. His unique contribution arises from the fact that he starts as an outsider. This permits him to get an "objective" view of the organization. He may then serve as a catalyst to help people within the group or organization to define its objectives, problems, aspirations, and procedures, as they attempt to explain them to him.

1. Members in the group or organization attempt to explain the goals, purposes, objectives, aspirations, problems, issues, and contributions in the group or organization. They should be open about their feelings, conflict that is taking place, and differences between stated and actual ways of operating in the case of both the group and individuals.

2. The new member attempts to draw out and clarify the member's perceptions and to understand conflicts, hidden agenda, tensions, and problems within.

3. Using his position as an outsider, he attempts to open up channels of communication previously closed, bring up problems which people are ignoring, and assess individuals' perceptions of the goals, purposes, objectives, aspirations, etc., of the group.

1. The basic principle is for the group to learn from the new member, and the new member to learn from the group, each operating from his unique position.

2. Since assimilation is a long and continuous process, new members should not be admitted frequently.

3. If new members are admitted as a group, they should meet together to share perceptions and insights, and generally help one another to accomplish the objectives of the group.

Large Group Participant Meeting
(Group Size: 20–1,000 persons)

Large group meetings·are usually authoritarian in their structure: One person speaks and the rest listen. The members of the audience have no way to express themselves except to applaud, to hiss, or to remain silent. There is no way that a person can express his individuality in a large group.

Large groups do give participants a sense of power through identification with feelings aroused by the speaker. Unfortunately, this sense of power often goes with a loss of one's sense of oneself. Many people resist the feelings of submergence under the influence of group emotion. Some give way for the duration of a meeting, but later feel resentful and withdrawn. Those that succumb frequently become irrational and dangerous.

In the Large Group Participant Meeting, the individual is not asked to be passive and accepting. Instead of being asked to surrender himself to group feeling, he is encouraged to express himself actively in a realistic relationship with the other group members.

The Large Group Participant Meeting has two sets of objectives:

1. The ordinary objectives of large meetings:

a. To give information.
b. To listen to a speaker.
c. To get a sense of group participation and power.

2. Additional objectives:

a. To achieve active participation of the members of the audience without loss of individuality.
b. To help convey a sense of group belonging without loss of individuality.
c. To create an accepting, open, encouraging, active, and humanistic atmosphere.
d. To give each individual within the group the opportunity to express his thoughts and feelings, and a sense that these thoughts and feelings are respected and accepted.
e. To give each member of the group a sense of how other members of the group think and feel about certain issues.
f. To give time and space for individuals to explore and to clarify their relationship to the issues involved.
g. To give a sense of personal strength by providing a group with which individuals can identify without loss of self.
h. To give time and space so that like-minded groups may get together and actively plan and carry out activities in keeping with their convictions.

WHERE USED

1. In large organizations for meetings involving many people (20–1,000).
2. For temporary communities—at conventions, professional meetings, workshops.
3. At mass meetings of like-interest groups, workers, students, citizens, groups having various sorts of ties.

TECHNIQUES USED

There are four techniques that are helpful in carrying out these objectives: voting questions, mini-focus, open forum, and breaking into small groups.

I. Voting Questions

Voting Question Defined: The voting question is a way of surveying the feelings of a group.

Objectives

1. Voting questions give the members of a group a chance to express how they feel within a group.

2. Voting questions legitimatize a diversity of views within a group.

3. Voting questions give the total group as active, shared experience in which differences are accepted.

4. Voting questions help overcome feelings of isolation or rejection. This is particularly true for those who raise their hands in disagreement with a majority. The expression and acceptance of their dissent makes them feel more a part of the group.

5. If the group leader is sensitive in his questions and uses them to guide the meeting, the group members will have more of a sense of the control of their own destinies, a sense of confidence, and a sense of power.

Introducing Voting Questions: Voting questions are very simply introduced. You can start like this: "I am going to ask you some questions. They aren't meant to decide an issue but simply to show how you feel. If you feel strongly favorable to what is asked, raise your hand very high. If you feel less favorable, raise your hand less high. If you feel strongly negative, lower your hand as far down as possible."

Criteria of Good Voting Questions

1. Voting questions should be capable of a "yes" or "no" answer.
2. Voting questions should get at feelings as well as thoughts.
3. Ask enough questions so that all the positions may be expressed, e.g.:
How many feel that doing something about X is futile?
How many think it's futile, but would like to do something anyhow?
How many think it's not futile?
4. Ask an occasional question not directly related to the issue, in order to break the tension:
How many came here by plane? How many drove?
How many had eggs for breakfast?
Who feels that the air is getting stuffy?
5. Check out issues raised from the floor or podium by means of voting questions.

How many agree that the issue raised by this gentleman is an important one?

6. Show interest and acceptance of the response to the voting questions.

II. THE MINI-FOCUS

The Mini-Focus Defined: In the mini-focus, members of the audience are given a chance to speak.

The facilitator draws them out with a few questions to help them round out their thoughts and to convey interest and acceptance.

OBJECTIVES

1. The mini-focus gives a chance for people in the audience to express how they think and feel about an issue.

2. It helps create a warm, nonthreatening atmosphere in which people feel safer in speaking and more attentive in listening. It does this by creating a contagion of warm, interested, and safe feelings.

3. It sets a pattern for small group interaction, should that be part of the program.

INTRODUCING THE MINI-FOCUS

1. Use of the microphone.

In a large group, it is helpful to have several microphones in the audience to facilitate the use of the mini-focus.

2. Use of voting questions.

The mini-focus can begin with a voting question. After the hands have been raised, the facilitator asks if anyone would like to explain his vote.

The facilitator accepts a volunteer and may ask several drawing-out questions after the volunteer has finished.

This may be followed by several more voting questions on the issues the volunteer has raised.

The facilitator has the option of drawing several people out on both sides of an issue raised by a voting question.

3. Use of involving questions.

The facilitator asks all the members of the audience to answer a feeling and action question silently or on paper. He then calls for several volunteers to give their answers. Each person is drawn out by several questions.

Example: "A number of speakers have talked about problems of integration in their school districts. Think of two or three things you might do in your district to help solve the problem. Take about two minutes."

"Would anyone volunteer to share his answer with us?" A volunteer is drawn out for several minutes. Then a new volunteer may be chosen.

CRITERIA FOR A GOOD MINI-FOCUS

1. The issues chosen for focus should be involving and central.
2. The focus should be brief, usually not more than three minutes.
3. The facilitator should ask questions that help the focus clarify or expand the position in his own way. Leading questions are prohibited.
4. The facilitator should be accepting and nonjudgmental.
5. Where possible, someone representing each point of view expressed should take a turn as focus.

III. THE OPEN FORUM

The Open Forum Defined: The open forum is a less structured form of mini-focus. Here members of the audience are permitted to come up and state their positions.

A time limit of about three minutes is desirable with this technique.

When used: The open forum is best used when issues have been defined and the members of the audience have begun to express themselves using other, more structured forms.

OBJECTIVES

1. The open forum permits members of the audience to express their views without restraint or structure imposed by the facilitator.
2. It helps involvement and group identification by permitting individuals to express their strongest feelings or convictions to the group.

Introducing the Open Forum: Have one or two microphones in the audience. You might start like this:

"This part of the program is devoted to what you have to say. Try to keep it brief. . . ."

ROLE OF THE FACILITATOR

1. To remind speakers of time limits.
2. To say a few words after each speaker is finished, showing a respect for and understanding of his point of view. Failure to accept and legitimatize opposing points of view leads to group polarization and makes a resolution of differences more difficult.

IV. Breaking into Small Groups

Objectives

The total audience can be broken into small groups of between two to eight members for a variety of activities: 1. Brainstorming 2. Exploring one's relation to an issue 3. Confronting conflict between members, etc.

Procedure

Appropriate game forms may be distributed to facilitate the interaction process.

After the audience has interacted in small groups, the facilitator should reunify the group with voting questions, mini-focus, and open forum techniques.

Do's and Don't's of Breaking into Small Groups

1. Do not break into small groups until a participant, accepting atmosphere has been established through voting questions and mini-focus.

2. Play a demonstration game in front of the group as an aid to the interaction process.

3. Procedures for breaking into groups should be clear and the appropriate game forms distributed.

4. Choose issues with which the audience is already involved for use in the small groups.

5. Do not distribute various tasks to various groups until the central issues have first been explored in the small groups.

6. Use voting questions, mini-focus, open forum, and cross grouping as ways of reintegrating the totality.

Leadership of the Total Group

Rational and Irrational Authority

Authority is often based on irrational features, such as those transferred from early experience with parents. For those in the subordinate position, irrational authority mobilizes feelings of dependence and anger, rebellion and helplessness. For those exercising irrational authority, the possession of authority is seen as a defense against irrational feelings of dependence and helplessness as well as being a magical assertion of adequacy. When these irrational elements of the authority figures are challenged, this often reactivates within the authority figures the fear of dependence, helplessness, and the loss of the magical symbols of authority. In response to these reactivated feelings, the authority figure will begin to use prodding, and creation of anxiety through promotions, or withholding of promotions; smiles and frowns; pats on the head, and other manipulative devices to reestablish his authority. Where these fail, he will act patronizing, insulting, and superior to excuse his loss of real authority. This will turn people off and prevent them from producing. What people want is trust in their good intentions and awareness of their abilities.

Rational authority is based upon knowledge, experience, and status attributable to creators or founders. Within a rational organization, everyone has authority commensurate with his skills, knowledge, and experience. The only extra authority some members have is based upon their position as the original founders and organizers of the community. This authority will diminish as the organization becomes more mature and more independent in its functioning.

Role of the Founding Members of a Group

Initially, the individuals who bring the group together would be outside its structure. The power of this staff to influence the totality may be initially based on knowledge, wisdom, charisma, ability to organize, to give support, to give a sense of security, to plan.

Additionally, their power may be of a more formal nature, arising from the power to hire and fire, to promote, to control the budget and everything else associated with formal authority.

Using this authority, they would then set up Core and Cross groups and Community Meeting, and they would teach the group members the communication skills necessary to operate them. (See "Introducing Democratic Forms into an Organization," page 266.)

Shift of Power to the Total Group

Once the organization is set up, the founding group begins to operate increasingly within the structures. The Core Group, Cross Group, and Community Meeting structures permit a great deal of flexible organization and carrying through without staff intervention. At this time, founders exercise their power increasingly as do the other members of the institution: through the various structures as well as through personal relations with group members.

The Planning-Executive Committee

At this point, the overall control of the organization is largely in the hands of the Community Meeting and the Planning-Executive Committee.* The Planning-Executive Committee consists of a Cross Group, with each member representing a Core Group. The Core Group appoints the representative, and can change him at any time.

One staff member is a member of this Planning-Executive Committee. It is through this committee, as well as through the Community Meeting, that the staff, or founders, share collaborative control of the overall direction of the institution with the rest of the membership. Decisions tend to be collaborative and democratic. Of course, the weight of the staff member on the committee may be greater because of one or more of the following factors: charisma, skills and knowledge, habit of other group members of looking toward him for leadership, continued control over funds and all that that implies.

The Planning-Executive Committee tries to act from the point of view of institutional needs and objectives. It is concerned with plotting the long- and short-range goals and activities of the institution. It assesses the needs, problems, strengths, and weaknesses of the institution and its operation. It lends support to individuals and subgroups. It confronts individuals and the institution as a whole with errors, weaknesses, problems, responsibilities. Not only does it assess the feelings and needs of the members, but it explains and gains support for the solutions it proposes. Wherever it can, it involves the rest of the community in a consultative, collaborative, planning relationship.

Although the Planning Committee represents, coordinates, and facilitates the operations of the totality, it is different and in some aspects opposed to the totality. It is out of the tension and challenge of this difference that stimulation, growth, creativity, and commitment emerge.

THE PLANNING-EXECUTIVE COMMITTEE AND ITS RELATIONSHIP TO THE COMMUNITY MEETING

The Planning-Executive Committee may be a Cross Group with rotating membership. For the sake of the stability of this leader group, it is best that only one, or a small portion, of its membership change at any one time.

The Planning-Executive Committee has power delegated to it by the Core groups or the Community Meeting. Insofar as the power is delegated by the Core groups, the committee forms an alternative to the Community Meeting as a way of making decisions.

When both Community Meeting and Planning-Executive Committee share the planning functions, the Community Meeting is better used to define general policies and directions. The Planning-Executive Committee is better used for coordination and technical implementation of the operations of the group.

* See further, "Interrelationship of Planning-Executive and Community Meeting," page 264.

The Planning-Executive Committee may call a Community Meeting for guidance and support in planning. However, where there is strong and united feeling, the Community Meeting may make decisions that bypass or overrule the decisions of the Planning-Executive Committee.

The Planning Committee also has the function of making long-range plans in cooperation with the Core groups. These plans are then discussed, validated, or modified through cooperation and interaction with the Community Meeting.

Maintenance of Human Control Over the Structures

The various structures and modes of doing things outlined in this chapter must be subordinate to human intelligence and rationality. The structures should not become more powerful than the people involved.

In a democratic organization, decision-making, coordination, innovation, and growth can be maintained and actualized through the principle of rotating leadership as well as group decision-making involving the total membership. If there is time pressure for coming to a decision or implementing plans, authority is sometimes better placed in a rotating small group of Cross Group structure, than in the total group or Community Meeting. This is because there is more time to explore the thinking of the members in detail and to arrive at rational principles. The totality sometimes feels constrained to act on the basis of the lowest common denominator of its members, especially if there is pressure of limited time.

An important function of the Planning-Executive Cross Group is the maintenance or modification of the basic structures to meet individual and organizational objectives. This prevents the structures from being eroded with time, or becoming rigid and outmoded.

Interrelation between Core Group, Cross Group, Community Meeting, and Special.Interest Groups

The Core Group, Cross Group, Community Meeting, and Planning-Executive Committee form one organic whole.

Needs, ideas, and values in the Core groups get filtered and refined in the Cross groups. Sometimes, to save time, only one Cross Group meets— the Planning-Executive Committee. When the needs, ideas, and values reach the Community Meeting, a sufficient preparation should have been made to implement action, if necessary, and to convey the ideas in coherent form.

Once a need has been crystallized and identified in this process, it is shared by everybody and constitutes input for the Core and Cross groups.

Where an idea or need requires elaboration and exploration, it is shunted to a special interest group from which new learning, planning, and projects can arise.

Thus, through the Core Group, Cross Group, and Community Meeting, a forward-moving, spiral kind of process is generated.

Where needs or ideas are of particular concern or interest to a segment of the community, a subspiral or special interest group develops which may create projects. These projects then nourish the ongoing spiral process generated by the Core-Cross-Community Meeting movement.

Additional Strategies for Meeting Group Relevant Needs

In addition to the three basic structures, we have found in practice that the following principles and practices are helpful in meeting group relevant needs:

1. CONTROL OVER FEEDBACK

People are often insecure about the kind of feedback they may get. This insecurity may lead to a paralysis of expression and action. In order to create security concerning feedback, the following procedures are suggested.

When a person wants feedback, he may choose the person or persons he wants it from, or a group that have made themselves available for this function; and he may specify the kind of feedback he wants. No one is obligated to hear feedback except when he agrees to hear it. At certain points, he may want suggestions and encouragement; at other points, general criticism; at others, technical criticism.

2. FREEDOM AND CONTROL IN WORK

Persons are free to work alone or in a group. If one develops something individually, he has primary control over it. If it is developed in a group, the group members having primary responsibility have control. An individual who develops something and presents it to a group continues to act as group leader for a time, at least, until others have caught up. The person having developed the idea should not be tied up by the need of the group to control him or to get consensus; similarly, the group members should be free to develop the initial ideas without being tied up by the originator.

3. THE CONTRACT SYSTEM

It is difficult to engage in activities involving more than one person when there is no security concerning the commitment of others to the group venture. The contract is a way of insuring group commitment in activities requiring a group to carry out. Before a person agrees to teach or offer something to a group, he may require commitment to stay the course or time needed from each individual joining him. Before a person enters into a joint venture or project, he may require commitment from those with whom he joins, to stay the time needed. This is in contrast to group activities not requiring commitment, where one may go in and out as one chooses.

The General Community Meeting and the Teaching Assembly can be easily introduced once the Core and Cross group structures have been established.

To change an organization when you are administrative head or founder:

a. Form a Core Group of staff members.

b. Introduce the additional rules necessary for team formation. Note: You cannot have a team if you play one subordinate against another, or establish lines of privileged information within your core team.

c. Use your staff Core Group to introduce the team structure to the next lower level of your organization on a voluntary basis.

d. When it has proved itself, apply it generally.

In a hierarchical organization, always introduce the new democratic structures to those at the level below you, before you introduce it to peers; and introduce it to peers before you introduce it to supervisors.

Introducing Democratic Forms into an Organization through the New Group Structures

In general there are three steps in changing an organization through the new group structures whether you are an administrator or a group member.

1. Introduce the new structures informally on a voluntary basis.
2. Prove their effectiveness; expand and validate their informal use.
3. Introduce them formally to replace the old structural forms.

Changing an organization when you are a member (rather than an administrator).

a. Get together with a group of three or four people with whom you work. Introduce the Focus Game and the Ongoing T-Group games.

b. Introduce and try to get agreement on the additional rules that make the group a team. (See "Functions of the Core Group," item 4.)

Once the team rules have been introduced, the group will probably be more efficient and productive than any other four individuals within the organization. This fact permits one to undertake the subsequent changes.

c. Explain team formation to your colleagues and help them to form teams.

d. Summarize the achievements of your team and present a plan for re-organization to your administrator.

e. Link up the various teams that have formed into a Cross Group structure. This may be done formally if one has had one's plan approved, or informally if the plan has not yet been approved.

The reason for this is that it's best to start where you have the most direct control, and gradually expand from there.

Thus, if you are a teacher, introduce the core-cross structure to your students before introducing it to fellow teachers. Introduce it to fellow teachers before going to your principal.

Similarly, if you are in business as a sales supervisor, introduce it to your salesmen before introducing it to your fellow sales supervisors, etc.

Move step by step, downward and upward from your position in the hierarchy.

In making a change across levels of hierarchical structure, it is helpful to call in facilitators who are outside the organization and hence able to facilitate communication between and across organizational levels.

See also: Structures for Groups and Organizations.

1. *Obedience Game.* The Obedience Game is helpful in getting an understanding of the problems of leading and following. It is also helpful for getting at feelings concerning authority, dependence, and responsibility.

2. *Creativity Games.* The Creativity games are helpful in keeping a group alive and innovative.

3. *Task-Oriented Game.* Helpful in getting superior group planning, involvement and participation.

4. *The Helping Professions.* This chapter has suggestions involving inter- and intragroup relations and problems. The content of this chapter is closely interwoven with the chapter on Structures.